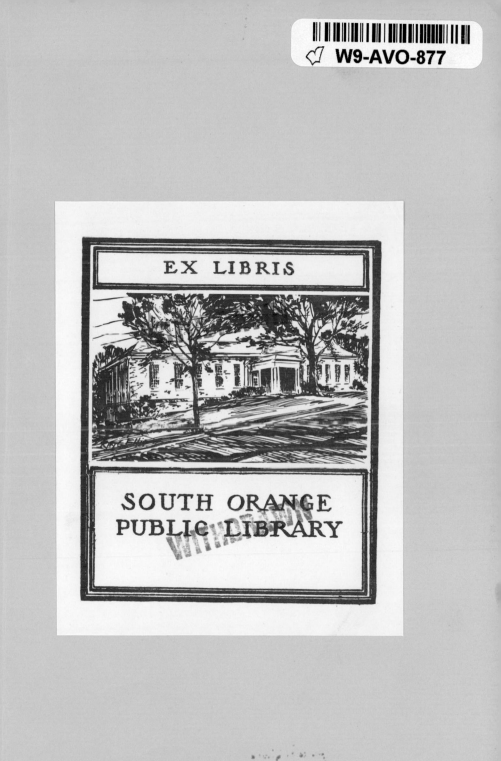

The Roots of Fundamentalism

THE ROOTS OF FUNDAMENTALISM

British and American Millenarianism 1800–1930

Ernest R. Sandeen

The University of Chicago Press
Chicago and London

International Standard Book Number: 0-226-73467-6
Library of Congress Catalog Card Number: 79-112739
The University of Chicago Press, Chicago 60637
The University of Chicago Press, Ltd., London

 Contents

Acknowledgments

THE ORIGINAL stimulus for this study came to me from Sidney E. Mead while I was still a graduate student at the University of Chicago. I owe much to him, most of all the fact that he offered questions instead of answers.

Librarians and archivists become the patron saints of all historians when, as so often happens, they serve far beyond the limits of simple competence. I wish to thank the librarians of Moody Bible Institute, the Speer Library of Princeton Theological Seminary and the Reverend Edward Starr of the American Baptist Historical Society. To Mrs. Jean Archibald, Reference and Interlibrary Loan Librarian of the Weyerhaeuser Library, Macalester College, I owe a special debt of gratitude.

Mrs. Wiladene Stickel typed the manuscript with great competence and a personal interest that extended beyond what I had any right to expect.

My colleagues at Macalester College have helped me much, as has the administration, from whom I have received many grants for research and travel.

Portions of chapter 5 are reprinted from my article "The Princeton Theology," which appeared in *Church History*, volume 31, September 1962; portions of chapter 8 were previously published in my article "The Fundamentals: The Last Flowering of the Millenarian-Conservative Alliance," which appeared in the *Journal of Presbyterian History*, volume 47, March 1969.

Introduction
Fundamentalism in the
Context of
The Millenarian Tradition

THIS BOOK is not the obituary of Fundamentalism. Ever since its rise to notoriety in the 1920s, scholars have predicted the imminent demise of the movement. The Fundamentalists, to return the favor, have predicted the speedy end of the world. Neither prophecy has so far been fulfilled. Instead, especially since 1950, the Fundamentalist movement, now calling itself Evangelicalism and rallying behind national leaders such as Billy Graham, has manifested an unexpected vitality and appeal. No doubt one reason for this surprising revival is that Fundamentalist predictions for the end of the world now seem uncomfortably close to the mark. However, no such change in fortunes seems likely to rescue the traditional attempts to explain and dismiss Fundamentalism. We need a new definition.

During the 1920s American Protestantism was seized by a paroxysm of contention over the sources of authority in Christianity and the validity of the theory of evolution and the techniques of biblical criticism. Harry Emerson Fosdick preached a famous sermon, "Shall the Fundamentalists Win?" and John T. Scopes was put on trial in Dayton, Tennessee, for violating the state statute forbidding the teaching of evolution. The Presbyterians and Baptists eventually suffered schism in their denominations and others were severely shaken. But although the events of this decade are hardly obscure, the history of the Fundamentalist-Modernist controversy has done little to explain the nature of Fundamentalism. Histories of the controversy have concentrated almost entirely upon the events of the twenties, thus reinforcing the episodic character of the events. To contemporaries the controversy of the twenties apparently came as a great surprise. They were shocked by the violence of the polemic and disconcerted to find such a high level of alienation among American Protestants. Possibly because the controversy seemed to erupt without preparation, historians of Fundamentalism virtually never made any effort to seek an understanding of the Fundamentalist by analyzing the background of the controversy. The assumption was made that he was no different from other conservative Protestants. W. E. Garrison expressed this traditional point of view when he argued, "In Fundamentalism considered merely as a reaction against the liberalizing tendencies of modern thought, there was nothing new except that it was a reaction against something new. The content of its teaching was identical with that of classical Protestant orthodoxy."[1]

This description of the Fundamentalist of the 1920s had the effect of removing theological and religious variables from the analysis of controversy. The attempt to explain Fundamentalist behavior was directed toward other aspects of life during the twenties, apparently, because Fundamentalists did not seem to hold any characteristic religious views. Explanations of the Fundamentalist-Modernist controversy often refer instead to the challenge of biblical criticism and the threat of evolutionary science. No student of this period would be so rash as to dispute the importance of these factors in American intellectual history. But how do they help us understand the nature of Fundamentalism or the twenties? The question to be answered in the study of the Fundamen-

---

1. "Fundamentalism," Encyclopaedia Britannica, vol. 9, 1960 ed. See the following for similar kinds of remarks: Robert T. Handy, "Fundamentalism and Modernism in Perspective," Religion in Life 24 (Summer 1955) : 390; J. M. Mecklin, Survival Value of Christianity (New York, 1926), p. 5; Norman Furniss, The Fundamentalist Controversy (New Haven, 1954), p. 14.

talist controversy is not the extent to which these factors affected the churches, but, in view of the acknowledged impact of these forces, why a minority of Christians responded in one fashion while the majority reacted in another.

Tension between rural and urban mind-sets plays an especially significant role in the study of Fundamentalism and deserves separate comment. No stereotype of the Fundamentalist dies harder than the picture provided by the Scopes trial. H. Richard Niebuhr expressed this picture more abstractly.

> In the social sources from which it drew its strength fundamentalism was closely related to the conflict between rural and urban cultures in America. Its popular leader was the agrarian W. J. Bryan; its rise coincided with the depression of agricultural values after the World War; it achieved little strength in the urban and industrial sections of the country but was active in many rural states. The opposing religious movement, modernism, was identified on the other hand with bourgeois culture, having its strength in the cities and in the churches supported by the urban middle classes. Furthermore, fundamentalism in its aggressive forms was most prevalent in those isolated communities in which the traditions of pioneer society had been most effectively preserved and which were least subject to the influence of modern science and industrial civilization.[2]

That this form of argument should have become prevalent is not surprising, for it represents virtually the only conceptual scheme with any explanatory power ever applied to Fundamentalism in the 1920s. Unfortunately, its application in this case is invalid. It might be possible to demonstrate that the campaign against evolution during the twenties was dominated by rural, southern interests, but this step leads nowhere. No historian of the controversy has ever maintained that Fundamentalism was only another name for the antievolutionary forces. Within the denominations, for ex-

2. "Fundamentalism," *Encyclo-*   vol. 5, 1944 ed.
paedia of the Social Sciences,

ample, the northern Presbyterians and Baptists faced controversy during this period and not the southern, more agrarian
branches of those churches. Oddly enough, no one has until
recently attempted to check whether demographic distribution of Fundamentalists within the northern Presbyterian or
Baptist denominations might possibly have confirmed the
hypothesis, but such an analysis, as seen in chapters 6–10 of
this study, shows that Fundamentalist leaders bore no re-
semblance to the stereotype presented by scholars such as
H. R. Niebuhr. Their base of support was indistinguishable
from that of the Modernists — what Niebuhr called "bour-
geois culture, having its strength in the cities and in the
churches supported by the urban middle classes."

Furthermore, none of the factors usually offered as an
explanation for the controversy of the twenties originated
during that decade, nor were they given any heightened
emphasis that could explain the unusually severe reaction
produced in the threatened communities. Urban growth, biblical criticism, and evolutionary theory had all existed for
at least two generations before the explosion of the 1920s.
The problem of the twenties, in fact, can be reduced to
seeking the explanation for the unexpected and disproportionate reaction of the twenties to forces that had been present in American life since the 1870s. Concentration upon the
religious history of the 1920s may have obscured the fact
that the Fundamentalist controversy represented only a part
of a general American intellectual crisis which probably
stemmed in large part from the exaggerated and artificially
sustained optimism of the First World War and the frustration, depression, and paranoia produced by the collapse of
those dreams and the widespread social turmoil of the post-
war era. In that context the Billy Mitchell trial might prove
as apt an illustration of the age as the Scopes trial.

There is, then, considerable evidence and reason for ques-
tioning the adequacy of traditional interpretations of the
Fundamentalist controversy. But, in spite of the difficulties
associated with this approach, the historiography of Fundamentalism has remained firmly chained to the decade of the

twenties, and students of Fundamentalism have consistently referred back to that decade as the touchstone of all explanation. But to those raised in Fundamentalist churches during the 1930s and 1940s this historiography seemed largely irrelevant. Many Fundamentalists after the decade of controversy continued to live as religious communities without direct reference to the events of the twenties. If Fundamentalism was only the name of a party in a controversy, why did that party exist after the controversy had ended? If Fundamentalism was only the name of a role played by otherwise indistinguishable conservative Christians, then, when the need for that role had disappeared, Fundamentalism ought to have disappeared as well. That it did not demonstrates the weakness of traditional explanations.

In this book these traditional explanations are challenged and an attempt is made to support a new approach to Fundamentalism. The primary function of this study has been to provide historical evidence for the argument that Fundamentalism existed as a religious movement before, during, and after the controversy of the twenties. This involves, in the first place, the separation of the Fundamentalist *movement* and the Fundamentalist *controversy*, and the assertion, substantiated in the following pages, that the movement existed independently of the controversy. The Fundamentalist movement passed through the controversy, of course, and was greatly affected by it; but its identity and existence were in no sense predicated upon the events of that decade. The argument also involves, in the second place, a demonstration of the fact that the Fundamentalist movement was a self-conscious, structured, long-lived, dynamic entity with recognized leadership, periodicals, and meetings. In contrast to, say, Americans of Swedish ancestry or the patrons of Sears-Roebuck, who might be made the subject of scholarly analysis but could never be accurately described as a movement, the Fundamentalist movement possessed a self-conscious identity and structure similar to the Republican party, the Knights of Columbus, or (probably the closest parallel) the Puritans. Assuming for the moment that there was both a Fundamentalist movement and a Fundamentalist controversy, it immediately becomes clear that the relationship between the two will require analysis. As a secondary function of this study, some attention has been devoted to this problem in chapter 10, though the presentation is suggestive rather than comprehensive.

Before summarizing the history of the movement (and the argument of this book), however, we must persist further in the critique of traditional Fundamentalist historiography. Whenever Fundamentalist beliefs have been discussed in the past, a prominent place has inevitably been given to what are called the five points of Fundamentalism — a list of doctrines which all Fundamentalists were supposed to accept as the irreducible quintessence of their faith. As is often true of the most durable fallacies, there was just enough evidence for belief in the five points to perpetuate the mistake and prevent scholars from probing for adequate answers. It is true that Fundamentalists were quite partial to a dogma-oriented definition of their Christianity and to creed building, but they showed no particular preference for five rather than fourteen, nine, or seven articles. The one five-point declaration which did influence the Fundamentalist movement was adopted by the General Assembly of the Presbyterian church in 1910 and reaffirmed in 1916 and 1923. By that action the following doctrines were declared to be essential: the inerrancy of Scripture, the virgin birth of Christ, the atonement of Christ, the resurrection of Christ, and the miracle-working power of Christ.

Confusion over the five points was probably magnified considerably when Stewart G. Cole, the early and ordinarily careful historian of the Fundamentalist controversy, erroneously stated that the five points of Fundamentalism were first published in 1895 by the men associated with the Niagara Bible Conference.[3] That Niagara creed, one of the most significant documents in the history of the Fundamentalist movement, was first written in 1878 and contained fourteen

3. *History of Fundamentalism* (New York, 1931), p. 34.

[xiv]

articles (see Appendix A). Building upon this confusion and ignoring the fact that the five points of the Presbyterian General Assembly did not duplicate those attributed to the Niagara Conference by Cole, students have learned to define the Fundamentalist as one who believed in the five points. This approach has had the effect of reinforcing the conviction that Fundamentalists were merely old-fashioned believers who defended the time-honored, broadly taught doctrines common to most evangelical Protestant churches in the nineteenth century. This thesis cannot even be defended for the statement of the Presbyterian General Assembly, as is argued in chapter 5. The crucial distinction, however, lies in the fact that the Niagara creed was millenarian and the Presbyterian declaration was not. For it is millenarianism which gave life and shape to the Fundamentalist movement.

During the last half of the nineteenth century there existed a millenarian movement within the United States which, though it gave itself no particular name and attempted to function as a corrective to denominationalism, possessed a distinct identity and all of the characteristics of a new sect. Like eighteenth-century Methodism, the millenarian movement developed as a church within the church. Its leadership was drawn largely from Episcopal, Presbyterian, and Baptist ministers of good standing and considerable abilities. Many of these men, such as James H. Brookes, Adoniram J. Gordon, Arthur T. Pierson, William J. Erdman, Nathaniel West, and William R. Nicholson, had won the respect of their denominations for their zeal, piety, and knowledge of the Scriptures. These millenarians gathered their followers together in the summer at annual conferences such as the Niagara meetings and in the winter at occasional conventions such as the Bible and Prophetic Conference held in New York City in 1878. Through periodicals such as *Truth* and *Watchword*, they shepherded and taught those who were separated from any congregation in which they might have heard the millenarian message. Although they began with a single-issue focus, the imminent second coming of Christ, the millenarians broadened the compass of their beliefs as they increased the size of their following. By the end of the century their theology, though built in the style of and upon many of the same presuppositions as other evangelical denominations, differed in ways that were crucial to the millenarians and their opponents and are clearly perceptible to the historian.

Millenarianism, like other vital movements, passed through a series of developments during this period in response both to the dynamics of its own intellectual life and to social change in the surrounding American society. Down to about 1890 the movement battled to convince the rest of American Protestantism that it was neither heretic, lunatic, nor unpatriotic. Millenarians argued that they correctly understood Bible teaching regarding the second coming of Christ and that their doctrines were taught by the apostles and believed by the church fathers. They sought to escape being associated with the traditions of William Miller's adventism and protested against being pictured as a band of fanatics ready to don ascension robes. In the face of American nationalism, they offered a sober and pessimistic view of the future of all human society, including the United States. Late in the nineteenth century, criticism of millenarianism considerably moderated, and the movement began to gain a measure of respectability. Its leaders were recognized as gifted teachers and its staunch advocacy of the authority of the Bible began to win honor from those who viewed the attacks of biblical critics with alarm. Most significantly, the mood of the Protestant evangelicals changed in response to the tensions of industrialization and immigration from one of cocky optimism to chastened uncertainty. The pessimistic millenarian world view, even in those conditions, failed to appeal to more than a minority of American evangelicals, but those who continued to reject it did so with far more charity and respect than had been the case in the seventies.

Since the second advent did not occur with the rapidity which millenarians predicted, it has been too easily assumed that the movement failed. This is quite unfair. Millenarian leaders did not believe that they could do anything to hasten, much less to bring about, the second advent of Christ. Their aim was to awaken the sleeping church to the imminence of judgment and to call sinners to repentance before the day of salvation passed away. Although apparently paradoxical, it is possible to show that the millenarians were at the same time convinced of the irreversible downgrade tendencies at work in human society and the utter futility of attempts to ameliorate the effects of sin, while working for the success of their own movement when that success was defined as awakening Christians to their peril.

When seen in this light, millenarian leaders did come close to success during the last decade of the nineteenth and the first decade of the twentieth century. In their campaign against Liberalism they felt that they had at least partially dammed the tide of infidelity. Within the newly revitalized foreign missions movement they worked as equals with other evangelical clergy, recruited and trained a great many of the new volunteers, and contributed a considerable amount to the new philosophy of missions. Conservative leaders, particularly within the Baptist and the Presbyterian denominations, showed marked favor to millenarians and began to cooperate with them in a new alliance which culminated in the conferences at Northfield, Massachusetts, organized by Dwight L. Moody, in the American Bible League, and in the publication of a series of pamphlets entitled *The Fundamentals.*

The foundations of this success were not soundly laid, however. The cooperation of the conservatives and the millenarians occurred in great part because they faced a common enemy and saw in Modernism a threat to the basic assumptions of their world view. The alliance was intended to oppose the teachings of the Liberals but also to maintain control of the denominations. Although the millenarian leaders for a time basked in the unaccustomed role of denominational statesmen, the old order was actually passing away. In the same generation in which agrarian politics was celebrating its last, most eloquent hour in the person of William Jennings Bryan and the entrepreneur achieving a late, magnificent success in the person of John D. Rockefeller, the theology of evangelicalism was rejoicing in its accomplishments, for example at the 1893 Columbian Exposition, while actually threatened with imminent collapse. In rallying the millenarians to the defense of this faltering establishment, the conservative leadership in Protestant evangelicalism accomplished little in sustaining their cosmology or prolonging their denominational control, but they did a good deal to create the difficulties of the twenties. The millenarian movement had developed in a climate of virtually unanimous hostility and was betrayed by its brief moments of success and approbation. When the millenarians' apparent triumph turned to ashes in the 1920s, when they found that Modernism could not be contained or excluded from the churches, they were led into activities and protests that were subversive to the very nature of the movement they were attempting to save.

Millenarian development may also be traced as a part of the history of ideas. In this study, however, that tradition has been traced only from 1800 because nineteenth-century millenarians reached their theological conclusions without the benefit of the influence of their most immediate millenarian predecessors. Although millenarianism in Western thought has a long history, it is a discontinuous one. The modern revival of millenarianism originated in the era of the French Revolution, and there has seemed no need to retreat further. The intellectual history of this movement was undertaken because it seemed necessary to an adequate understanding of the roots of Fundamentalism, but the resulting narrative may prove useful to readers whose primary concern is with millenarianism rather than Fundamentalism. It ought to be understood, however, that not every manifestation of nineteenth-century millenarianism receives equal treatment in the following pages, and that some millenarians, the Jehovah's Witnesses, for example, are not discussed at all.

In chapter 1 the revival of millenarianism in Britain is discussed, its theological shape analyzed, and some of the early controversies examined. Eventually, British millenarianism was brought to the United States, but it competed there with the native variety developed by William Miller. The complexities of that relationship are discussed in chapter 2. Miller's adventism subsided and, though remaining active in some localities, took a much less prominent place after 1845. Early British forms of millenarianism also faded, and by the middle of the century the type of millenarianism known as futurism and especially the form of futurism taught by John Nelson Darby and known since then as dispensationalism began to outdistance other varieties in both Britain and America. The millenarian movement was strongly marked by this British tradition, and much of the thought and attitudes of those who are known as Fundamentalists can be seen mirrored in the teachings of this man.

This study is intended, then, to lead the reader from the early nineteenth century to 1930, introducing him first to the thought of the millenarian revival and then to the organization of the American millenarian movement after 1870. The nature of that thought and that organization provide support for the hypothesis that Fundamentalism ought to be understood partly if not largely as one aspect of the history of millenarianism.

The Roots of
Fundamentalism

1

The Revival of
British Millenarianism
1800–1845

The testimony of Jesus is the spirit of prophecy
— Rev. 18:10

CHRISTIANITY has never disengaged itself from the testimony of Jesus, nor the historian of Christianity from a fascination with the diversity with which that testimony has been interpreted. John called down judgment upon the Roman Empire of the first century, predicting the reappearance of Jesus as a flame of fire, "bearing a name which no one knows but himself." But in a manner which he himself could not have prophesied, the visionary of Patmos has spoken for men in every age of Christian history. In Daniel, from which John evidently learned much and borrowed much, and in Revelation, Christendom has found its textbooks in the spirit of prophecy.

The world view so graphically and influentially portrayed in these two works is known as apocalypticism. As was true for both Daniel and Revelation, apocalypticism has flourished in periods of world crisis. Unable to resign himself to a passive acceptance of any lot that fate may bring him or to a mystical transcendence of worldly cares, the apocalypticist finds himself caught up in the affairs of this world, deeply troubled about the outcome of a struggle which he usually depicts in cosmic proportions and stark contrasts. He is, moreover, racked between despair at the prospects of his cause and a desperate desire to triumph despite the odds against him. The fuel for this hope is generated by the prophetic message, Hang on! What may seem like folly will be turned into victory by the coming of a savior who will

[3]

vindicate his faithful followers and scatter the hordes of the enemy. The specifically Christian form of apocalypticism, shaped by John's metaphors, has faced an almost two thousand year succession of crises, including imperial persecution of the church, war, invasion, plague, forced migration, enslavement, and, most recently, atomic annihilation. Against this burden of mankind, John's words have held out the hope of the imminent return of Christ, robed now in power and majesty, whose coming will signal the final and complete defeat of the enemy and inaugurate a peaceful kingdom that will last a thousand years. Christian apocalypticism, focused upon this millennium, is called millenarianism.[1]

Although the imminent bodily reappearance of Jesus on earth was fervently anticipated by many early Christians and has continued to form a part of some Christians' expectations in most ages, this same hope has not been shared by all believers. The theology of the post-Nicene fathers, especially Augustine, emphasized the allegoric rather than the literal fulfillment of prophecies and taught Christians to look to the ministry of grace in the church for the realization of their eschatological hopes. Dialogue — often warfare — between these two views about the end of the world has proved to be a persistent characteristic of church history. With millenarianism most frequently the expression of the sectarian, minority party and the "Augustinian" point of view supported by the established authorities, the disputes have usually been marked by claims on the part of the millenarians that they were restoring apostolic Christianity, whereas their antagonists have accused them of heresy and fanaticism. The most recent antecedents of the early nineteenth-century millenarians had been the Puritans, particularly that radical party known as the Fifth Monarchy Men. These followers of Thomas Venner had been only the most violent and notorious of the Puritan millenarians, but their excesses served to damn the whole movement.[2]

1. Harold H. Rowley, *The Relevance of Apocalyptic*, 2d rev. ed. (Naperville, Ill., 1961).
2. See the bibliography for a discussion of millenarian historiography. No adequate treatment of Puritan millenarianism exists.

The Revival of British Millenarianism

In reaction to the excesses of the Puritan revolution, millenarianism fell into disfavor in the eighteenth century, but churchmen did not return to the Augustinian position. In harmony with the Lockean tradition of rationalism and optimism, a new eschatology, most influentially stated by the Salisbury rector Daniel Whitby, emphasized the continued success of the church, the steady improvement of man and society, and the eventual culmination of Christian history in the coming of a literal millennium. Only at the end of that blessed age was Christ's second coming expected. These progressive millennialists refused to accept the pervasive allegorizing of the Augustinian school and anticipated that an age of worldly peace and harmony would dawn upon the earth; but they were confident, in opposition to the millenarians, that this era could be brought about without any supernatural intervention.[3]

THE FRENCH REVOLUTION was directly responsible for the revival of prophetic concern. To live through the decade of the 1790s in itself constituted an experience in apocalypticism for many of the British.[4] The violent uprooting of European political and social institutions forced many to the conclusion that the end of the world was near. And just at the time that an apocalyptic cosmology seemed the most

3. Ernest L. Tuveson, *Redeemer Nation: The Idea of America's Millennial Role* (Chicago, 1968), pp. 33–34 especially, where Tuveson suggests that those who accepted the Whitbyan position be called millennialists to distinguish them from the millenarians, who were pessimistic and believed that only the return of Christ (who was usually imminently expected) would remedy the earth's problems. In the nineteenth century the two terms were often used interchangeably. In later years the millennialists were often called postmillennialists and the millenarians referred to as premillennialists, the prefixes indicating whether the party expected Christ's second advent after or before the beginning of the millennium.

4. For examples see M. H. Abrams, "English Romanticism: The Spirit of the Age," in *Romanticism Reconsidered*, edited by Northrop Frye (New York, 1963). No one, perhaps, caught that spirit better than William Blake, and for that reason his drawing *The Ancient of Days*, taken from Daniel 7, has been selected as the jacket illustration for this book.

realistic outlook, one of the biblical prophecies appeared to have been exactly fulfilled. In a famous passage in Daniel 7 the prophet described a procession of four fanciful animals, each symbolizing an empire, the last of which possessed ten horns. In Daniel's vision a little horn grew up among these ten horns, rooting out three of them. In the interpretation of the prophecy (Dan. 7:15–28), the little horn was stated to be a king or ruler who would "wear out the saints of the Most High, and think to change times and laws: and they shall be given into his hand until a time and times and the dividing of time." In Revelation 13 a somewhat similar beast with ten horns was described as enduring for forty-two months, and the two visions were traditionally interpreted by Protestants as two descriptions of the same event — the tyrannical reign of the pope for 1,260 years.[5]

As the unbelievable events of the 1790s unfolded, students of this apocalyptic literature became convinced (in a rare display of unanimity) that they were witnessing the fulfillment of the prophecies of Daniel 7 and Revelation 13. The Revolution brought the cheering sight of the destruction of papal power in France, the confiscation of church property, and eventually the establishment of a religion of reason; the final act occurred in 1798 when French troops under Berthier marched on Rome, established a republic, and sent the pope into banishment. Commentators were quick to point out that this "deadly wound" received by the papacy had been ex-

---

5. The chronological estimate was based upon what was known as the year-day theory. The prophetic secrets of the Scripture could be unlocked, it was argued, by substituting "year" wherever "day" was mentioned in prophetic chronology. When weeks were described (as in Daniel 9), they were interpreted as periods of seven years, and when months were mentioned, as periods of thirty years. Using this mode of calculation, commentators arrived at the figure 1,260 years for the duration of papal hegemony. Forty-two months (Rev. 13:5) was quite easily figured out at 1,260 years (when the month was calculated to be worth thirty years), and only a little more ingenuity was necessary to correlate "time, times, and a half" (Dan. 12:7) with three and one-half years or forty-two months. The influential commentator Joseph Mede had come to that conclusion as early as 1631, and many others had followed him.

plicitly described and dated in Revelation 13. Although prophetic scholars had previously been unable to agree on what dates to assign to the rise and fall of papal power, it now became clear, after the fact, that the papacy had come to power in 538 A.D.[6]

> Is not the *Papal power*, at Rome, which was once so terrible, and so domineering, at an end?
> But let us pause a little, Was not *this* End, in other parts of the Holy Prophecies, foretold to be, *at the* END *of 1260 years?* — and was it not foretold by Daniel, to be at the END of *a time, times, and half a time?* which computation amounts to the same period. And now let us see; — hear; — and understand. THIS IS THE YEAR 1798. — And just 1260 years ago, in the very beginning of the year 538, *Belisarius* put an end to the Empire, and Dominion of the Goths, at Rome.[7]

Thus we sense the special significance of the French Revolution to the student of prophecy. That cataclysm undermined the progressive and rationalist cosmology of the eighteenth century, but its most important contribution to the millenarian revival was the spur it provided to further prophetic study. The identification of the events of the 1790s with those prophesied in Daniel 7 and Revelation 13 provided biblical commentators with a prophetic Rosetta stone. At last a key had been found with which to crack the code. There could now be general agreement upon one fixed point of correlation between prophecy and history. After 1799, in Egyptology as in prophecy, it seemed as though there were no limits to the possibility of discovery.[8]

6. This was only one of many dates, indicating many different phases in the evolution of papal government, which had in the past been seized upon as possessing prophetic significance.

7. Edward King, *Remarks on the Signs of the Times* (London, 1798), as quoted in L. E. Froom, *The Prophetic Faith of Our Fa-* *thers* (Washington, D.C., 1948), 2:767.

8. Thomas Carlyle, in a passage in *Sartor Resartus*, gave this variant interpretation to the prophetic mania of the day: "Great Men are the inspired (speaking and acting) Texts of that divine BOOK OF REVELATIONS, whereof a Chapter is completed from epoch

CHAPTER ONE

In the first place, then, the British millenarian revival was characterized by a new passion for the interpretation of the prophetic scriptures. The vast bibliography of prophetic studies published during the first half of the nineteenth century is as bizarre, to modern eyes, as the material interpreted.[9] In the periodicals, where a taste for anonymity seemed to prevail, authors frequently identified themselves by cabalistic pseudonyms such as Talib, Epsilon, or Crito. The Church of England supplied the greatest number of contributors, men such as the Reverend George Stanley Faber whose *Dissertation on the Prophecies, That Have Been Fulfilled, Are Now Fulfilling, or Will Hereafter Be Fulfilled, Relative to the Great Period of 1260 Years* was among the first evidences of the revival.[10] Many Scots Presbyterians also became involved in prophetic studies, the most widely known author being William Cuninghame of Lainshaw, an odd, cantankerous layman who never seems to have rested from a labor of vigorous attacks upon fellow millenarians whose opinions or motives he questioned. Cuninghame eventually built a small nondenominational chapel near his estate and became its minister, a pattern often repeated among millenarians.[11] The great lay interest in this movement was also represented in James Hatley Frere, whose *Combined View of the Prophecies of Daniel, Esdras, and S. John Shewing That All Prophetic Writings Are Formed upon One Plan . . . with Critical Remarks upon . . . Mr. Faber and Mr. Cuninghame* can be described as a paradigm

to epoch, and by some named HISTORY; to which inspired Texts your numerous talented men, and your innumerable untalented men, are the better or worse exegetic Commentaries, and wagonload of too-stupid, heretical or orthodox, weekly Sermons" (J. W. Bowyer, ed., *The Victorian Age* [New York, 1938], p. 163).

9. See, for example, the bibliography cited in Froom, *Prophetic Faith*, 2:757–89.

10. London, 1804. Faber also wrote *Eight Dissertations . . . on Prophetical Passages* (London, 1845) and *Remarks on the Effusion of the Fifth Apocalyptic Vial* (London, 1815) in which he attacked J. H. Frere.

11. His earliest work was *A Dissertation on the Seals and Trumpets of the Apocalypse* (London, 1813). In later works he attacked Frere, Faber, and Edward Irving.

of prophetic scholarship, combining as it does an interest in the construction of a perfect synthesis of all prophetic literature with attacks on Frere's benighted co-laborers.[12] Convinced that the prophecies of Daniel 11 referred to Napoleon, Frere went so far as to see the fulfillment of Dan. 11:30 in the battle of Aboukir Bay and to predict on the latter part of that passage that English spies had consulted with Napoleon immediately after that defeat.[13] Frere was immensely gratified in later years to learn from Las Cases's *Mémorial* that he had been right.[14]

The origin of the second aspect of the nineteenth-century millenarian revival, renewal of interest in the state of the Jews, can be traced most directly to the intriguing eccentricities of Lewis Way. Trained as a barrister, he was dramatically enriched in 1804 by the bequest of three hundred thousand pounds from a John Way who had been first attracted to Lewis Way by the accidental similarity of their names. "Released from the bondage of an irksome profession," as Way wrote, he purchased Stansted Park near Emsworth, Sussex, and set about fulfilling the role of the gentleman. Although he spent one hundred fifty thousand pounds on his estate and another twelve hundred pounds on deer alone, he professed an obligation to philanthropy and Christian service. "My mortgages will be turned into land, and my money invested in stocks," he wrote. "Whatever must be the produce, beyond what is necessary to the station I must henceforth hold in life, will be the portion of all those who want."[15]

His interest in the condition of the Jews of Europe was aroused when, in about 1811 while visiting in Devonshire,

12. London, 1815. He wrote at least five other books on prophetic subjects.
13. "For the ships of Chittim [i.e., Britain] shall come against him: therefore he shall be grieved, and return, and have indignation again the holy covenant: so shall he do; he shall even return, and have intelligence with them that forsake the holy covenant."
14. *Prophetic Herald* 1 (1846) : 376.
15. A. M. W. Stirling, *The Ways of Yesterday . . . Chronicles of the Way Family from 1307–1885* (London, 1930), esp. pp. 115–16.

he was told about a grove of trees which were not to be cut down until the restoration of the Jews to Palestine. The owner of the wood had left a will which contained the clause, "These oaks shall remain standing, and the hand of man shall not be raised against them till Israel returns and is restored to the Land of Promise."[16] Stimulated by this strange expression, Lewis Way began to investigate both the ancient prophecies relating to the restoration of the Jews and the contemporary agencies that were devoting their attention to this problem. He discovered the existence of a faltering group named the London Society for Promoting Christianity among the Jews, founded in 1809 and led by a converted Jew, Mr. Joseph S. C. F. Frey. When Way became concerned with it in 1815, the society was deeply in debt and troubled by rivalries between church and dissenting supporters. Way, who had by this time been ordained as an Anglican, settled the obligations of the society at a cost of over twelve thousand pounds, virtually buying out the dissenters and converting the society at the same time into an Anglican agency and a vehicle for his own ministry. Way turned the LSPCJ, previously concerned only with proselyting London Jews, into a missionary society devoted to the training and support of Jewish converts to Christianity, who were then sent into eastern Europe, Russia, and the Middle East. His own estate at Stansted was turned into a training college for these missionary converts. Way made a journey to Russia for the purpose of settling one of these men and, at the same time, obtaining a first-hand picture of the condition and beliefs of European Jews. The climax of this venture occurred when Way was introduced to Czar Alexander I and influenced him to submit a memorandum on the condition of the Jews to the European powers assembled at the Congress of Aix-la-Chapelle in 1818.[17]

The Jews Society, as it was referred to by its members,

16. Ibid., p. 127.
17. Ibid., and H. H. Norris, *The Origin, Progress and Existing Circumstances of the London* *Society for Promoting Christianity amongst the Jews* (London, 1825), which is critical of the LSPCJ.

millennialists in a radical critique of their own churches, which often resulted in complete disaffection if not schism. It has not been possible to determine which of these forces — the psychological state of the believer, the biblical prophecies of judgment and destruction, or the historical situation — was primary and which secondary, or to determine whether there were causal links between them. But the presence and mutually supportive role of all three factors both in the millenarian movement as a whole and in the individuals associated with it is clear.

IF EARLY nineteenth-century millenarianism had produced a hero, he would have been Edward Irving. Instead, Irving came to the end of his life in 1834 as an outcast among the millenarian party, his very name transformed into a term of reproach among evangelicals and decent citizens. In his meteoric career the whole scope of millenarianism is displayed and most of its weaknesses are magnified.[24] The young (he was born in 1792) Scottish preacher came down to London in 1822 to minister in the unpretentious Caledonian Chapel in Hatton Garden. It was his first parish, his only other experience having been gained as an assistant to the Reverend Thomas Chalmers in Glasgow. That he became an overnight sensation among London society probably laid the foundation for his destruction — at least his friend Thomas Carlyle thought so. Probably because of a chance remark dropped by Canning during a debate in the House of Commons, Irving's melodramatic sermons achieved a short notoriety, and the small chapel was crowded every Sunday with the highborn and influential. But it did not last. Carlyle gave this impression of the scene:

24. Oliphant, *Life of Edward Irving* is a typical Victorian life; Edward Miller, *The History and Doctrines of Irvingism*, 2 vols. (London, 1878) is hostile; Andrew L. Drummond, *Edward Irving and His Circle* (London, 1934) is sympathetic but derivative to the point of plagiarism, particularly in connection with Oliphant. Thomas Carlyle was a boyhood friend of Irving and followed his career quite closely in London. The manuscript sources quoted so freely by Oliphant have now apparently been destroyed.

achieved its greatest success as an advocate of Protestant Zionism. The efforts to evangelize the Jews had little success. The seminary at Stansted did not prosper; very few of Lewis Way's student-converts fulfilled his expectations, and some even robbed him. Only Joseph Wolff, a flamboyant Prussian Jew who became an Anglican after having previously become a convert to Catholicism, could play the role of the missionary hero; and he, it must be said, played it with such flair that one suspects he must have been half adventurer and impostor.[18] But the restoration of the Jews to Palestine — the return of the chosen people to the promised land — became firmly established as a plank in the millenarian creed. Through the monthly issues of the *Jewish Expositor*, the LSPCJ journal, and in dozens of other books, this question was discussed in never-wearying detail.[19] The Zionist cause won rather wide sympathy at this time; the Jews and the Greeks seem to have been classed together as heroic but downtrodden people. But millenarian interest in the restoration of the Jews stemmed explicitly from the interpretation of prophecy. The prophetic text which described the cataclysmic events apparently fulfilled in the French Revolution also predicted the second advent of Christ and the restoration of the Jews.[20] The prophetic timetable had joined these expectations inextricably. The millenarian accepted both events as the will of God, prayed for the coming of both, and, if he could not work for the accomplishment of the second advent, did what he could to aid the cause of Palestinian resettlement. Some of this interest appears lunatic in retrospect, such as the many reports of the discovery of the ten lost tribes among the American Indians or in Kashmir, but there can be no question that the millenarian

18. Joseph Wolff, *Missionary Journal and Memoir*, 2d ed. (London, 1827); Joseph Wolff, *Travels and Adventures of the Rev. Joseph Wolff* (London, 1861); H. P. Palmer, *Joseph Wolff* (Heath Cranton, 1935).
19. The *Jewish Expositor* 1–16 (1816–31) was published in London. Nonmillenarians often accepted the idea of a restoration of the Jews. One such was S. T. Coleridge (*Notes on English Divines* [London, 1853], 2:337).
20. See for example, Isa. 11:12 or Isa. 27:12–13.

movement played a significant role in preparing the British for political Zionism.[21]

By about 1825, Lewis Way had sold his Stansted estate, broken his connection with the LSPCJ, and settled in Paris as the minister of an English congregation. The chief cause of his break with the society was his adamant avowal of the doctrine of the premillennial advent of Christ. Apparently stimulated by contacts with some European rabbis and his own study of biblical prophecies, Way published a series of articles in the LSPCJ journal under the pseudonym Basilicus, in which he argued that Christians ought to expect the personal return of Christ before the beginning of the millennium.[22]

The doctrine of the premillennial advent, the third aspect of the millenarian revival, seemed novel, probably mistaken, possibly heretical to most Anglicans of the day. In keeping with the standard Whitbyan eschatology, Christians had not been taught to expect the second coming during their own lives. The second advent, they felt, would occur only after the millennium and, therefore, must be more than one thousand years away. Many of the clergy had never troubled themselves over this kind of bewildering eschatological question or were frankly skeptical of the divine import of the apocalyptic mysteries of Daniel and Revelation. The tracts of "Basilicus" seemed to catch fire, however, among many of the evangelical party. This series of letters was given credit, years later, by leaders of the millenarian movement for having first turned their attention to the doctrine of the premillennial advent.[23]

---

21. For their location in Kashmir see Margaret O. W. Oliphant, *The Life of Edward Irving* (London, 1862), 2:49; and for the United States, Barbara Ann Simon, *The Hope of Israel: Presumptive Evidence That the Aborigines of the Western Hemisphere Are Descended from the Ten Missing Tribes of Israel* (1829). Joseph Smith taught this doctrine to the Mormons.

22. "Thoughts on the Scriptural Expectations of the Christian Church," *Jewish Expositor* 5 (1820): 24–30, 59–68, 139–46; 6 (1821): 57–62, 102–12, 184–92; 7 (1822): 129–37, 199–209.
23. Henry Drummond, *Dialogues on Prophecy* (London, 1827–29), 1:206.

Renewed interest in the second coming of Christ was, of course, tied closely to prophetic study and concern with the condition of the Jews. The apparently complete and precise fulfillment of biblical prophecies during the French Revolution had a direct impact upon the biblical interpretation generally. It became a hallmark of the millenarian party that literal rather than figurative or spiritualized fulfillments should be sought for every biblical prophecy. When "kingdoms" were prophesied, for example, literal, historical events involving flesh-and-blood kings ought to be expected rather than the triumph of one or another virtue. Millenarians became convinced that allegorical and spiritualized interpretations of prophecy were a manifestation of unbelief and a denigration of the authority of Scripture. Thus when the study of prophecy, as in Lewis Way's case, revealed that the return of the Jews and the premillennial return of Christ were, in fact, quite literally prophesied, the millenarian felt obliged to believe the teaching and expect its fulfillment. There was combined with this literalism, moreover, a pronounced sense of disillusionment with contemporary society and a kind of failure of nerve. Wellington's triumph over Napoleon did not, at least among the millenarians, vindicate faith in the ultimate success of virtue and reason. The nineteenth-century converts to millenarianism looked upon the French Revolution as the frustration of hopes built on faith in man's abilities but the fulfillment of hopes built on God's promises.

Thus belief in the pre- rather than the postmillennial return of Christ involved much more than a question of the timing of the second advent. Converts to premillennialism abandoned confidence in man's ability to bring about significant and lasting social progress and in the church's ability to stem the tide of evil, convert mankind to Christianity, or even prevent its own corruption. The premillennial return of Christ presupposed a view of the world in which judgment and demolition were the only possible response from a just God. Christ's return would mean salvation and blessedness for a few but judgment for the world. And it involved most pre-

Irving's preaching at Hatton Garden, which I regularly attended while in his house, and occasionally afterwards, did not strike me as superior to his Scotch performances of past time, or, in private fact, inspire me with any complete or pleasant feeling. . . . The force and weight of what he urged was undeniable; the potent faculty at work, like that of a Samson heavily striding along with the gates of Gaza on his shoulder; but there was a want of spontaneity and simplicity, a something of strained and aggravated, of elaborately intentional, which kept gaining on the mind. One felt the bad element to be and to have been unwholesome to the honorable soul. The doors were crowded long before opening, and you got in by ticket; but the first sublime rush of what once seemed more than popularity, and had been nothing more — Lady Jersey "sitting on the pulpit steps," Canning, Brougham, Mackintosh, etc., rushing day after day — was now quite over, and there remained only a popularity, of "the people;" not of the *plebs* at all, but never higher than of the well-dressed *populus* henceforth, which was a sad change to the sanguine man.[25]

Irving was usually described as a handsome man — tall, large head, striking features crowned with a mass of black hair, but the total effect a little marred by a squint. His oratory was stilted, owing to the fact that he abhorred the stylists of the eighteenth century and consciously modeled his own rhetoric after the pre-Restoration divines. Eventually he forgot how to use colloquial English, addressing even friends in casual conversation "with an undeniable self-consciousness, and something which you could not but admit to be religious mannerism," as Carlyle put it.[26] This ability to assume a role so completely as to forget that he was wearing a mask made him seem like a poser to many — which he was not. It does, however, reflect the chief weakness of his character. He was a ship without a keel. Although he was earnest and serious in every pursuit, he swung around in each new breeze until at last he was blown over.

25. *Reminiscences* (New York, 1881), p. 117.   26. Ibid., p. 146.

The first influence was that of Samuel T. Coleridge, whom he greatly admired and visited regularly. Coleridge may seem like strange company for a minister of the Scottish kirk and an evangelical at that, but Irving relished the association. Whether he understood Coleridge completely may be doubted, but the Coleridge style he found only too easy to imitate. Coleridge, consciously or not, seems to have encouraged Irving's aversion to logical structures and rational analysis. Irving loved the mysterious — "loved to see an idea looming through the mist." [27] And once captured by such an idea, once seized by its mystery, he would become its slave, never asking what contradictions or complications might follow.

His 1824 anniversary sermon to the London Missionary Society illustrated those characteristics perfectly for our purposes and painfully for those who had to hear him. Pleased and honored by the invitation, Irving determined to give the society no ordinary discourse and lost himself in preparation. When he emerged, his sermon had become a book, and it was not one of Irving's habits to trim his orations to the stamina of the congregation. He preached for nearly three hours, reducing the society to a helpless frenzy. To make matters worse, the burden of this marathon discourse was a celebration of the virtues of apostolic poverty and self-help. During his days of study, he had been captured by a vision of Saint Paul's missionary labors as the model of all missionary work, and his sermon became virtually an attack (though he never understood that it was) on the very society he was attempting to help. [28]

Irving was next caught up in the ferment of prophetic studies, becoming a disciple of James Hatley Frere. Irving was conducting semipublic discussions every Wednesday afternoon with Mr. Frere during 1825 and appeared in the same year as the apologist for the millenarian cause when he delivered another anniversary sermon — this time before

---

27. Irving used the words himself (Drummond, *Edward Irving*, p. 67).

28. Oliphant, *Life of Edward Irving*, 1:193–208.

the Continental Society, a body dedicated originally to the spread of evangelical principles in France, Switzerland, and Germany, but very quickly dominated by millenarian concerns.[29] This characteristically long oration, published in 1826 as *Babylon and Infidelity Foredoomed,* was also, characteristically, misunderstood. Because of the identification of Babylon with the Church of Rome in Irving's sermon and because of the contemporary agitation over Catholic enfranchisement, many felt that Irving was alluding to Catholic emancipation — though whether he was attacking or supporting it they could not agree. Although fear of Catholicism and alarm over Catholic emancipation can scarcely be used to explain the rise of millenarianism, it is significant to note that this pairing of anti-Catholicism and millenarianism was more than casual. Millenarians without exception were stoutly anti-Catholic and viewed every agitation by English and Irish Catholics as confirmation of the increasing corruption of the world and thus of the increasing likelihood of the second advent.

Irving spent the whole of the summer of 1826 on leave from his parish duties, translating a millenarian treatise by a Chilean Jesuit, Manuel Lacunza. *The Coming of Messiah in Glory and Majesty* was a ponderous two-volume work, seldom cited by later British millenarians; in fact, many of Lacunza's positions were rejected by the British school and by Irving himself. Yet the aura of mystery and providential intervention surrounding the book drew Irving into the labor of translation and seems to have stimulated a short period of popularity for its name if not for its substance. Lacunza (1731–1801) was forced out of Chile in 1767 when the Society of Jesus was suppressed by the Spanish crown and lived the remainder of his life in Italy as a scholar-recluse. His treatise, completed about 1791, was not published during his lifetime for fear of condemnation by the authorities, but manuscript copies circulated and some printed editions ap-

29. Ibid., 1:220–27; and Ridley H. Herschell, *"Far above Rubies": Memoir of Helen S.*   *Herschell* (London, 1854), pp. 104–14.

peared in Spain and Latin America beginning about 1812. Shortly before Irving's translation appeared, the work was placed on the Index, which is not surprising since Lacunza had concluded that the Catholic hierarchy and priesthood were the Antichrist.[30]

Irving had not known any Spanish until a few months before he was sent a copy of Lacunza's book. That he had begun learning Spanish (while trying to assist some Spanish refugees) just at the moment that this startling work from the Catholic "underground" appeared at his door convinced him that he was being providentially prepared to present the work to the British public. Even though Lacunza's prophetic interpretations often varied from the customary British views, he did make a strong case for the premillennial advent of Christ, and this was the aspect of his work that Irving and the British millenarians emphasized. Lacunza might have been confused on some points (so the defense ran), but notice the manner in which testimony from this Roman Catholic scholar reinforces our heralding of the imminent return of Christ.

In January 1827, just before he sent off the manuscript of Lacunza's book to the printer, Irving added a short postscript to his very long introduction describing the first Albury prophetic conference. About twenty interested laymen and clergy were invited by the Honorable Henry Drummond to spend the first week of Advent, 1826, at his Albury Park estate in an extended discussion of prophetic truth. The same kind of meetings were repeated in 1827 and 1828. These conferences brought together almost every British millenarian scholar of note and created a context in which they could reinforce their central convictions and isolate and clarify the issues on which they disagreed. The Albury conferences, more than any other event, gave structure to the British millenarian revival, consolidating both the theology

---

30. Manuel Lacunza (alias Juan Ben-Ezra), *Venida del Mesias en Gloria y Magestad* (*The Coming of Messiah in Glory and Majesty*), trans. by Edward Irving, 2 vols. (London, 1827). See also Froom, *Prophetic Faith*, 2:303 ff.

and the group of men who were to defend it. Throughout the nineteenth century millenarianism followed a similar pattern, with conferences such as the Mildmay conference (in Britain) and the Niagara and Northfield conferences (in North America) providing structure and outreach for the movement.

The host at the Albury conferences, Henry Drummond, was the grandson of Henry Dundas, Viscount Melville, in whose house he had been raised. After pursuing a career in banking and in the House of Commons for almost a decade, he dramatically quit them both and planned a journey to the Holy Land, declaring himself "satiated with the empty frivolities of the fashionable world." [31] In the early 1820s he was prominently associated with both the Continental Society and the London Society for Promoting Christianity among the Jews, a friend of Lewis Way and the sponsor of Joseph Wolff's missionary activities. Also a friend of Irving's, Drummond eventually left the Anglican church and joined his congregation.

As might be expected, many of those attending the conference had been previously associated in the work of the Continental Society and the LSPCJ. In addition to Drummond and Irving, there were Lewis Way, Joseph Wolff, and Charles S. Hawtrey, editor of the *Jewish Expositor*; William Cuninghame of Lainshaw and James Hatley Frere, prophetic expositors; George Montagu, Lord Mandeville and later Duke of Manchester; and the Reverend William Marsh, at this time serving a parish in Colchester, later to move to Birmingham where he was known as Millennial Marsh. Others who seemed to play a prominent part were the Reverend Hugh McNeile, the rector of Albury; the Reverend Daniel Wilson, later to become Bishop of Calcutta; John James Strutt, later Baron Rayleigh; Spencer Perceval, son of the former prime minister; the Reverend Robert Story of Rosneath; the Reverend James Haldane Stewart, the Reverend James Stratton, and the Reverend Edward T. Vaughn,

31. "Henry Drummond," *DNB*.

all three Anglicans and early advocates of the millenarian cause; and two laymen, John Bayford and John Tudor, both millenarian authors.[32]

The conference was dominated by Anglican clergymen, with scarcely three or four participants not affiliated with either the English or Scottish national churches.[33] This profile of Drummond's guests is representative of millenarianism as a whole. The old dissenting groups and the Methodists provided very few converts to this cause, and participants in the movement — Irving for example — often expressed antagonism to dissenting principles. This is ironic considering that so many millenarians, including Irving, left the established churches to form sects which proved more hospitable to their millenarian doctrines.

In the conference sessions themselves, the program was about equally divided between the three chief concerns of the day — prophetic chronology, the second advent, and the restoration of the Jews.[34] No appeal to authority or argument

32. There was an agreement among participants at Albury not to publish accounts of the conferences, and so the yearly roster of participants has not survived; but there is sufficient scattered evidence from which to reconstruct a list of those who attended one or more of the sessions. Other than those already mentioned, the following attended at least one session: Rev. G. Beckett, Mr. T. Borthwick, Rev. W. Bryan, Rev. H. T. Burder, Mr. T. W. Chevalier, Rev. T. W. Cole, Rev. W. Dodsworth, Rev. Wm. Dow, Capt. G. Gambier, Mr. A. Haldane, Rev. J. Hawtrey, Mr. W. Leach, Rev. H. B. Maclean, Lieut. Malden, Rev. Dr. Okely, Rev. H. J. Owen, Rev. G. W. Phillips, Rev. Probyn, Rev. J. Simons, Mr. E. Simon, Mr. Staples, Mr. R. Sumner, Rev. J. White, Rev. R. Wolff, and Rev. R. Wolff, Jr. (James H. Bransby,

Evan's Sketch of the Various Denominations, 18th ed. [London, 1841], gives a complete list which seems based upon primary evidence, though not very accurate; see also Robert H. Story, *Memoir of the Life of the Rev. Robert Story* [Cambridge, 1862], pp. 102–4; Wolff, *Travels and Adventures*, p. 234; and Joshua W. Brooks, *A Dictionary of Writers on the Prophecies* [London, 1835], p. lxxi).

33. Miller, *History and Doctrines of Irvingism*, 1:40. Miller based his list of attendance upon Bransby, *Evan's Sketch*. He was confused about other aspects of the conferences.

34. Although publication of the Albury conference proceedings was withheld by common consent, Henry Drummond did publish three volumes entitled *Dialogues on Prophecy* which summarized, to some extent, the substance of

was allowed in these sessions except the authority of direct biblical quotation or an argument designed to reconcile scriptural references. As Irving described the proceedings, Drummond's guests rose early and assembled at 8:00 A.M. to hear an address on the topic appointed for the day. They breakfasted at 9:00 A.M. and then spent the time until 11:00 A.M. searching their Bibles for support or refutation of the views presented at 8:00 A.M. From 11:00 A.M. until 3:00 or 4:00 P.M. they all sat around a large table and argued out their differences. After dinner they spent another three or four hours attempting a synthesis. In all this process, as Irving noted, "No appeal was allowed but to the scriptures, of which the originals lay before us." [35]

In 1829 Drummond summarized the conclusions reached at the conferences into a table of six points on which all of the participants had been in substantial agreement.

1. This "dispensation" or age will not end "insensibly" but cataclysmically in judgment and destruction of the church in the same manner in which the Jewish dispensation ended.
2. The Jews will be restored to Palestine during the time of judgment.
3. The judgment to come will fall principally upon Christendom.
4. When the judgment is past, the millennium will begin.
5. The second advent of Christ will occur before the millennium.
6. The 1260 years of Daniel 7 and Revelation 13 ought to

those meetings. Since Drummond chose to present this material in the form of dialogues between personae identified only by pseudonyms and seems to have exercised considerable editorial freedom, it would be rash to treat these volumes as a kind of stenographic report of the conferences. The seven chapter headings of the 1827 volume of *Dialogues*, however, correspond exactly with the list of topics which Irving stated (in the preface to Lacunza, 1:clxxxviii–cxciv) to have been considered at the 1826 Albury conference. Thus there seems to be good warrant for using these volumes in general as a summary of the program of the conferences.

35. Irving, *Coming of Messiah*, 1: cxci.

be measured from the reign of Justinian to the French Revolution. The vials of wrath (Revelation 16) are now being poured out and the second advent is imminent.[36]

These six points clearly and concisely convey the platform of the millenarian revival. Basic to the whole statement was the assumption that an irreversible deterioration in religion and culture had now reached crisis proportions and that the final act in this era of world history had already begun. Some members of the Albury conference spoke confidently about the second advent happening in 1843 or 1847, but, whether they set dates or not, all the participants expected Christ's return within a few years.[37] Although a variant form of millenarianism later took shape in the United States, and although British millenarianism was split by controversy, the fundamental outlook and, to a large extent, the doctrinal formulation of this eschatology were established by 1830.

MILLENARIANISM had come of age in 1828. After almost two decades of inquiry and exploration by solitary scholars such as Frere and Cuninghame and after the formation of organizations designed to press one or another aspect of millenarianism, such as the Jews Society, the leadership and doctrines of the movement had been drawn together and consolidated at Albury. The next phase of the movement was marked by publicity and proselyting. The *Christian Observer*'s reaction to the millenarian revival illustrates this maturation process. This voice of the evangelical party in the

---

36. *Dialogues*, 1:ii–iii. These volumes were published serially and then bound together with a single preface which gives internal evidence of having been written after the third conference in 1828. The six points appear to be conclusions of the participants rather than prerequisites for participating.

37. Interest in the years

1843–47 was aroused by another prophecy, the vision of the desolation of the sanctuary for "two thousand and three hundred days" in Daniel 8. Encouraged by the fulfillment of the 1,260 days in Daniel 7, prophetic scholars became convinced that the next great event would be the fulfillment of the 2,300 days, which they dated to 1843–47.

Church of England first noticed the millenarian revival in July 1825; the journal reviewed ten books on millenarian issues, including works by Lewis Way, John Bayford, and James Haldane Stewart. The reviewer seemed very much like Alice in Wonderland — stumbling around in an unfamiliar landscape, rather astounded at what he was finding and often quite cross. Failing to see what an important place the restoration of the Jews played in the millenarian movement, for instance, he offhandedly rejected the arguments for this doctrine.[38] By 1827, however, the editors of the *Christian Observer* had become more knowledgeable about millenarianism and for two years devoted much space to the questions being raised by the movement. Although they professed to remain unmoved concerning the urgency or necessity of the great debate about the second coming or the interpretation of the Apocalypse, correspondents deluged them with articles and criticism, and they published them.[39] But by 1830 the flurry was over. The *Observer*'s editors, unmoved by the best arguments of the millenarians, turned their attention to problems then besetting the Bible Society and to the crisis over disestablishment. Having failed to capture this citadel of evangelicalism, the millenarians made their voices heard, nevertheless, in their own periodicals and in special prophetic societies.

All the millenarian periodicals of the thirties survived for only a few years at best, but they did illustrate the vitality of the movement. The *Morning Watch* (London, 1829–33) was associated most closely with the Albury group and contained much from Irving's pen. When the excitement over "speaking in tongues" began to dominate Irving's congregation, The *Morning Watch* also became preoccupied with that subject; and when the new Irvingite sect was established, the editor, John Tudor, broke off publication with the explanation that the burden of establishing the new church left no time for editorial work. The *Christian Herald*, published in

38. *Christian Observer* 24 (1825) : 427 ff., 489 ff.

39. Ibid., 27 (1827) : 667 ff., 713, and passim through 28 (July 1828).

Dublin from 1830 to 1835, offered an illustration of fading enthusiasm on the part of at least one millenarian. The editor, Edward N. Hoare, rector of Saint Lawrence, Limerick, began the periodical as a monthly, reduced it to a quarterly in 1832, and then abandoned his efforts altogether in disappointment over the controversies and schism which seemed to result from the preaching of prophetic truth. Although made of sterner stuff, Joshua W. Brooks found the editing of his periodical, The *Investigator* (London, 1831–36), too difficult to continue. He established the journal with a policy of welcoming any article regardless of its position if it was well written and gentlemanly in tone. The noble experiment failed; his contributors became enraged and his readers confused, Brooks found. He began a new series of volumes in 1836 on a more restrictive basis, but gave up the whole project after the first number.

The flourishing of prophetic societies served as a second indication of millenarian vitality. The Society for the Investigation of Prophecy was founded in London in 1826 before the first meeting of the Albury conference. J. H. Frere's comments on the founding of this society offer a quaint example of the precise correlations then being sought between prophecy and contemporary events. Frere had invited Edward Irving, Thomas White, and James Stratton to join him in establishing the society, but felt that he might be usurping divine prerogatives in going ahead with the event when he discovered a Scripture reference which he believed foretold the founding of just such a society at just that time. One can readily believe that he was highly gratified and his faith in the fulfillment of prophecy strengthened when, a few months later, Lewis Way arrived in London and proposed the formation of such a society.[40] This society failed to survive more than a few years, in spite of its place in prophecy, but another with almost the same name — the Prophecy Investiga-

40. John Tudor, Henry Drummond, Dr. Thompson, T. W. Chevalier, and Thomas White contributed to a volume entitled *Papers Read before the Society* *for the Investigation of Prophecy* (London, 1828). See also J. H. Frere, "A Minute Interpretation of the Apocalypse," *Prophetic Herald* 1 (1846) : 380.

tion Society — was founded in 1842. The Reverend W. R. Freemantle, rector of Claydon, Bucks, stated in the 1860s that the society then had about fifty members and met twice a year for conferences lasting three days, and that it had also been responsible for a series of Lenten lectures on millenarianism which were held in Saint George's Church, Bloomsbury, and Trinity Church, Marylebone. Over a dozen Anglican clergymen delivered addresses annually in this London series during the 1840s.[41]

Edward Bickersteth, one of the most respected evangelicals of the nineteenth century, became a millenarian later than most men of his generation. He became concerned with the question of the second advent during Advent, 1832. The published version of the sermons which he preached during that season brought him into contact with Cuninghame of Lainshaw, whom he began to entertain annually at his rectory. These yearly visits were made the occasion for local prophetic conferences.[42] A number of leading millenarians seem to have made a practice of using their parishes as a base for broader outreach. After 1829 William Marsh held such a conference annually in his parish, and there is evidence of other meetings in Oxford, Plymouth, and in Ireland.[43]

Apart from the publications and preaching of William Cuninghame, the first millenarian voice in the prophetic wilderness of Scotland was Edward Irving's. Irving preached on the second coming of Christ before dawn each morning of Assembly week, 1828, to crowded congregations in Saint Cuthbert's Church. Horatius Bonar, the leading millenarian of the second generation, recalled that series of sermons

41. James Grant, *The End of All Things*, 2d ed. (London, 1866), 2:91 ff. The lecturers in 1848 were C. J. Goodhart, A. R. C. Dallas, James H. Stewart, William Cadman, W. Wilson, W. R. Freemantle, W. W. Pym, Leland Noel, B. Philpot, Edward Bickersteth, T. R. Birks, and H. M. Villiers (Alexander R. C. Dallas, ed., *Lift Up Your Heads* [London, 1848]).

42. T. R. Birks, *Memoir of the Rev. Edward Bickersteth* (London, 1851), 2:42 ff.

43. Catharine M. Marsh, *The Life of the Rev. William Marsh* (London, 1867). The other conferences are discussed later in this chapter.

forty years later as one of the formative influences of his life. Although there was no Scottish prophetic journal during the thirties and early forties, the Edinburgh Association for Promoting the Study and Illustration of Prophetic Scripture was organized in 1841 with the intention of sponsoring a semiannual series of lectures, the first of which was delivered by Joshua W. Brooks.[44]

DURING OCTOBER 1831, much of London was excited and alarmed by an apparently sudden recovery of the apostolic gift of tongues in Edward Irving's church. Carlyle's attitude, though strongly antagonistic, reflects the varying reactions of Londoners.

> The "Gift of Tongues" had fairly broken out among the crazed and weakliest of his wholly rather dim and weakly flock. . . . Once or twice poor Eliza Miles [a servant] came running home from some evening sermon there was, all in a tremor of tears over these same "Tongues," and a riot from the *dissenting* majority opposing them. "All a tumult yonder, oh me!" . . . It was greatly talked of by some persons, with an inquiry, "Do you believe in it?" . . . One night in one of our walks we did make a call, and actually heard what they called the Tongues. It was in a neighboring room. . . . Mrs. Irving had retired thither with the devotees. Irving for our sake had stayed, . . . when there burst forth a shrieky hysterical "Lall lall lall!" . . . to which Irving, with singular calmness, said only, "There, hear you, there are the Tongues!"[45]

This outbreak of tongues in Irving's congregation neither dismayed nor surprised the leader of the "dim and weakly flock." Irving, along with many other evangelicals, had been praying and preaching for a restoration of the apostolic gifts — healing and tongues in particular. Many millenarians

44. Horatio Bonar, "Irvingism," *Quarterly Journal of Prophecy* 18 (1866) : 210. A prospectus for the society is bound with the British Museum copy of Joshua W. Brooks, *Lectures on Subjects Connected with Prophecy* (Edinburgh, 1841), the published edition of his lectures to the society.

45. Carlyle, *Reminiscences*, p. 158.

felt that the Scriptures predicted a restitution of Pentecostal charisma in the last days, and this hope for a revival of apostolic fervor found a more generalized expression in other parts of the church as well. The latitudinarian, Erastian, and skeptical stamp of contemporary church life was abhorred by the evangelical and the Tractarian alike. Of course, in the early nineteenth century zeal for restoration and an awakening interest in the emotive side of human life were hardly the exclusive preoccupation of millenarians or churchmen. The pursuit of the gift of tongues, when viewed in this context, seems less strange or inexplicable to us than it did to the many Englishmen who agreed with Carlyle's judgment: "Why was there not a bucket of cold water to fling on that *lah-lalling* hysterical madwoman?" [46]

When a number of apparently miraculous healings and utterances in tongues occurred in 1830 in western Scotland, Irving was not alone in believing that the expected outpouring of the Holy Spirit had begun. But although much interest was aroused, most of those who sought to discover whether this was indeed the anticipated renewal of the gifts of the Spirit went away disappointed, convinced that there was too much enthusiasm and too little adherence to strict scriptural principles for this little group of Scots to be considered the recipients of Pentecostal grace. Irving, however, was convinced and began to hold special meetings in which his small group of disciples prayed for the gift of tongues. When the utterances came, Irving — who, to his chagrin, never received the gift — found himself a captive in the hands of these charismatic prophets, though he did make a feeble effort to "try the spirits." Moreover, for several weeks he discouraged the utterances in his Sunday services until he was warned by one of the prophets not to quench the Spirit. Impressionable as ever and only too ready to believe that the Spirit of God spoke most forcefully and immediately through the mystical and incomprehensible, Irving agreed that God alone had a right to decide whether or not there

46. Ibid.

would be an outburst of tongues in the regular service.[47]
A London reporter described the scene.

> Immediately after the Rev. Mr. Irving had finished
> his "oration" he rose and informed his congregation
> that this Church was destined to be greater than
> the Church of Corinth; that he would yield up his
> Church to no one except a woman and a prophet-
> ess; . . . that she was now within these very walls,
> but that she never spoke but when the gift of
> prophecy was on her; and that if she prophesied on
> the present occasion he hoped that no one would be
> alarmed, but that every person should listen to her
> with the most profound attention.
>
> No sooner had the Rev. Divine concluded this ex-
> traordinary announcement than the ears of the con-
> gregation were assailed with the most discordant yells
> proceeding from the prophetess, who only wanted
> the hint to be inspired with the aforesaid gift, when
> she roared and bellowed in such a manner that the
> whole of the congregation were thrown into a state
> of the greatest confusion. Some rushed forward to
> have a nearer view of the frantic bedlamite, while
> not a few amused themselves amidst shouts of
> laughter by indulging in the coarsest of jokes. Here
> was to be seen ladies fainting — there ladies calling
> for help — while the more sober-minded part of the
> congregated assembly made for the outer door with
> all imaginable haste, anxious to escape the conta-
> gion of such a scene of sacrilege and profanation. In
> this state of chaos and alarm Parson Irving stood
> up in his pulpit, and with his eyes fixed towards
> Heaven, as if in a state of mental aberration, and
> seemingly unconscious of the scene which was acting
> around him, he looked, or pretended to look, as if
> he were in deep converse with his God.[48]

The notoriety of these events was detrimental to the cause
of millenarianism but was fatal to Irving himself. He was

47. The most influential account of the tongues was written
by a man who was at one time
a believer in and practitioner of
the gift, but became disillusioned
(Robert Baxter, *Narrative of
Facts Characterizing the Super-*

*natural Manifestations in
Members of Mr. Irving's Congregation*, 2d ed. [London, 1833]).
48. *John Bull*, 24 October 1831.
See also the London *Times*,
26 October 1831.

able to hold the allegiance of influential friends like Henry Drummond and willing workers like John Bayford and John Tudor, but most of the evangelicals and millenarians abandoned him. When he was tried for heresy, he found he could not count on friends even in Annan, his home presbytery. Defrocked by the Scottish church, rejected by most of his former friends, not even given much honor within the new Catholic Apostolic church which he helped to found, Irving gradually lost his strength, though not suffering from any disease that doctors of that day could identify. He died while on a preaching tour of Scotland in 1834, in disgrace with all but a few in the world.[49] Irvingism, however, was not dead; the "angels" of the Catholic Apostolic church were quite visible during the next decades. But even had there been no Catholic Apostolic church the opponents of millenarianism would have kept Irving's memory alive. In the fifty years after his death there were few opponents of millenarianism who were able to resist recounting the career of Edward Irving as proof infallible that these pernicious doctrines would lead to heresy and schism. There were few who echoed Carlyle's epitaph:

> It must be said Irving nobly expiates whatever errors he has fallen into. Like an antique evangelist he walks his stony course, the fixed thought of his heart at all times, "Though he slay me, yet will I trust in Him."[50]

EDWARD IRVING's impact upon the millenarian movement had been dramatic and brief. After his death the Catholic Apostolic church won some converts but, other than that, played an insignificant role among millenarians and evangelicals. By contrast, the Plymouth Brethren, who also withdrew from the established church in an effort to revive apostolic Chris-

---

49. He was convicted of heresy concerning the person of Christ. Irving might not have been overly cautious or precise in his doctrinal statements, but what he said was so nearly orthodox and the church generally so lax that one is forced to conclude that he was tried on that charge as a pretext and principally because his other activities had alarmed his ministerial colleagues.

50. Carlyle, *Reminiscences*, p. 165.

tianity, cooperated with other millenarians and eventually almost captured the movement. The early history of the Plymouth Brethren was dominated by rivalry and controversy between Benjamin Wills Newton and John Nelson Darby. This quarrel precipitated a schism among the schismatics — the first stage in the fragmentation of the sect — and has little significance for the history of the millenarian movement. But disagreement over the interpretation of prophecy formed the substance of the controversy, and the distinctive positions they elaborated were debated, adopted, refuted and castigated by millenarians for the next century.

Newton, who was born in Plymouth in 1807, passed through an evangelical conversion experience and developed his first interest in prophecy while a student and fellow of Exeter College, Oxford. During 1827 to 1830, the years of intense millenarian excitement, the Oxford evangelicals, like many others, speculated about the coming judgment and the coming Christ. Newton was especially influenced by Henry B. Bulteel, former fellow of Exeter and curate of Saint Ebbe's, whose influence played a part in his 1827 conversion, and by Francis W. Newman, with whom he was informally preparing for ordination and through whom he developed an interest in the study of prophecy. It was with F. W. Newman that Newton discussed one of the primary questions of the millenarian movement: "Is it possible that the world will be converted by the preaching of the gospel?" And it was F. W. Newman who brought John Nelson Darby to Oxford where Newton met him for the first time. This small group of fervent evangelicals sent one of their number, G. V. Wigram, to Scotland in 1830 to give them first-hand evidence of the outbreak of tongues and healing. Bulteel became convinced of the authenticity of the tongues and healing, later joined Irving's group for a short time, and cured three people before becoming disillusioned. But before he became involved with Irving, Bulteel had preached a university sermon, Sunday, 6 February 1831, which shocked Oxford by the vigor of its denunciations and, incidentally, persuaded Newton that the Church of England could not be purged of its secularity and laxness. He soon left Oxford for Plymouth and the Church of England for the Plymouth Brethren.[51]

John Nelson Darby deserves better treatment from historians than he has received either from those who have praised him or those who have reviled him. The assessment of his career has not been objectively written or the scope of his influence adequately appreciated. Some have called him a saint, but if he was he belongs to the hermit saints like Saint Anthony. In many ways he resembled John Wesley, though in his condemnation of the established church he stands in stark contrast. But like Wesley he was an itinerant man of few domestic pleasures, a man with magnetic, electric personal qualities combined with a tyrant's will to lead and intolerance of criticism. Perhaps he should be described as a petty tyrant, for he was most tyrannical about petty things. Unlike Wesley he often demonstrated as much zeal in destroying a work of his own building as he did in its first construction. The will of God seldom blurred before his vision. Also unlike Wesley and most unfortunately for his historical reputation, the clarity with which he perceived the will of God was never matched by his ability to write it down. He left a massive set of *Collected Writings* which are almost uniformly unintelligible.[52]

F. W. Newman met Darby, in Dublin in 1827. Darby had trained in law at Trinity College, Dublin, but had abandoned the profession as quickly as he had entered it. Taking orders, he had rushed into the work of a county Wicklow parish with his usual energy and abandon and had soon

51. J. S. Reynolds, *The Evangelicals at Oxford, 1735–1871* (Oxford, 1953), provides background. Some of Newton's letters are printed in George H. Fromow, ed., *B. W. Newton and Dr. S. P. Tregelles* (London, n.d.), including one dated 1827 describing his conversion. The best book on the subject is Harold H. Rowdon, *The Origins of the Brethren* (London, 1967), which is based upon some previously unused manuscript material.

52. William Kelly, ed., *The Collected Writings of J. N. Darby*, 2d ed., 34 vols. and index. (London, 1967). W. G. Turner, *John Nelson Darby: A Biography* (London, 1926), is not adequate. There are some Darby manuscripts in the possession of Mr. Henry Sibthorpe of Redruth, Cornwall, whose kindness I am happy to acknowledge.

acquired a reputation among the peasantry as a holy man. In later years Newman still vividly recalled the dominating force of the man he called only the "Irish clergyman."

> His "bodily presence" was indeed "weak!" A fallen cheek, a bloodshot eye, crippled limbs resting on crutches, a seldom shaven beard, a shabby suit of clothes and a generally neglected person, drew at first pity, with wonder to see such a figure in a drawing room. . . . He more and more made me ashamed of Political Economy and Moral Philosophy, and all Science; all of which ought to be "counted dross for the excellency of the knowledge of Christ Jesus our Lord." For the first time in my life I saw a man earnestly turning into reality the principles which others confessed with their lips only.[53]

At the time Newman and Darby met, Darby was staying with a brother-in-law, recuperating from an injury to his leg. He was also suffering from doubts about the wisdom and ethics of the Erastian policies of the archbishop of the Church of Ireland.[54] Twenty years later he described this physical and spiritual crisis in a letter to the Halle theologian Friedrich A. G. Tholuck which not only summarizes the early development of the Plymouth Brethren but also provides another example of the pervasiveness of dissatisfaction with the church, the interest in prophecy and the second advent, and the desire to break through apathy and tradition to the heart of the apostolic faith.

> It then became clear to me that the church of God, as He considers it, was composed only of those who were so united to Christ, whereas Christendom, as seen externally, was really the world, and could not be considered as "the church," save as regards the responsibility attaching to the position which it professed to occupy — a very important thing in its

53. F. W. Newman, *Phases of Faith* (London, 1850), pp. 27, 29.

54. J. G. Bellett, one of the early Brethren, stated that he brought news of the London prophetic revival to Darby at about this time and that the news had influenced Darby's views (*Interesting Reminiscences of the Early History of "Brethren"* [Weston-super-Mare, n.d.]).

place. At the same time, I saw that the Christian, having his place in Christ in heaven, has nothing to wait for save the coming of the Saviour, in order to be set, in fact, in the glory which is already his portion "in Christ."

The careful reading of the Acts afforded me a practical picture of the early church, which made me feel deeply the contrast with its actual present state, though still as ever, beloved by God. At that time I had to use crutches when moving about, so that I had no longer any opportunity for making known my convictions in public; moreover, as the state of my health did not allow me to attend worship, I was compelled to remain away. It seemed to me that the good hand of God had thus come to my help, hiding my spiritual weakness under physical incapacity. In the meanwhile, there grew up in my heart the conviction that what Christianity had accomplished in the world in no way answered to the needs of a soul burdened with the sense of what God's holy governmental dealing was intended to effect. In my retreat, the 32nd chapter of Isaiah taught me clearly, on God's behalf, that there was still an economy to come, of His ordering; a state of things in no way established as yet. The consciousness of my union with Christ had given me the present heavenly portion of the glory, whereas this chapter clearly sets forth the corresponding earthly part. I was not able to put these things in their respective places or arrange them in order, as I can now; but the truths themselves were then revealed of God, through the action of His Spirit, by reading His word. . . .

In effect, the cross of Christ and His return should characterise the church and each one of the members. What was to be done? Where was this unity, this "body"? Where was the power of the Spirit recognised? Where was the Lord really waited for? Nationalism was associated with the world; in its bosom some believers were merged in the very world from which Jesus had separated them; they were, besides, separated from one another, whilst Jesus had united them. The Lord's supper, symbol of the unity of the body, had become a symbol of the union of this latter with the world, that is to say, exactly the contrary of what Christ had established. Dissent had, no doubt, had the effect of making the true children of God more manifest, but here they were united on principles quite different from the unity of the body of Christ. If I joined myself to these, I separated myself from others everywhere. The disunion of the body of Christ was everywhere apparent rather than its unity. What was I to do? Such was the question which presented itself to me, without any other idea than that of satisfying my conscience, according to the light of the word of God. A word in Matthew xviii. furnished the solution of my trouble: "Where two or three are gathered together in my name, there am I in the midst of them." This was just what I wanted: the presence of Jesus was assured at such a worship; it is there He has recorded His name, as He had done of old in the temple at Jerusalem for those who were called to resort there.

Four persons who were pretty much in the same state of soul as myself, came together to my lodging; we spoke together about these things, and I proposed to them to break bread the following Sunday, which we did. Others then joined us. I left Dublin soon after, but the work immediately began at Limerick, a town in Ireland, and then in other places.[55]

Among the other places where these gatherings sprang up were London and a number of towns in the west of England, particularly Bristol, where George Müller preached, and Plymouth, which flourished under the pastoral care of B. W. Newton. But this success came years later; in the early 1830s these dissidents and reformers were groping about, seeking identity and direction. They sought it, and to a degree found it, in a series of conferences which paralleled those at Albury to a remarkable degree. The parallel was probably intended, for the hostess at the Irish conferences, Lady Theodosia Powerscourt — young, attractive, widowed, and very pious — had visited Henry Drummond at Albury and entertained Edward Irving when he visited Dublin on a preaching tour. Early autumn conferences were held beginning in 1831 at the county Wicklow home of Lady Powerscourt, presided over by the rector of Powerscourt, Robert Daly. Thirty-five clergymen, fifteen laymen and twenty ladies attended the

55. *The Letters of J. N. D.,*   2d ed. (London, n.d.), 3:298–301.

1831 conference, which was conducted in the same format as those at Albury.[56]

Excitement over tongues speaking in Irving's church proved to be a potentially divisive issue. Leaders of the conference had already condemned Irving's followers, but could not avoid further discussion of the issue. Although the subject was excluded from the agenda of the 1831 conference, an informal discussion of "gifts of the spirit" was held on the evening before the opening of the conference. When the subject popped up again in 1832 it was branded as error. The correspondent for the *Christian Herald* reported:

> There was but one individual who introduced anything which could have given pain to any on these subjects; and that was a reference to the reception of "the gifts" and the principles connected with it. Little, however, was said upon it; and while the principles were calmly inquired into by a few, it did not, I think, affect the meeting, otherwise than to direct the earnest desires and prayers of many, for the more abundant presence of that Holy Ghost, by which alone, error can be brought to light, and the believer guided into all truth.[57]

The topics discussed at the first two Powerscourt conferences do not, at first glance, appear to differ significantly from those usually debated among millenarians. In 1831 those gathered at Powerscourt discussed the interpretation of the 1,260 days, the corrupt state of contemporary Christendom, the imminent return of Christ, and clues by which the Antichrist might be identified. Topics for 1832 followed a similar pattern: "Should we expect a personal Antichrist?" "An inquiry into, and a connection between Daniel and the

56. Although several authors have claimed that Lady Powerscourt attended one of the Albury conferences and that Irving attended one of those held at Powerscourt, there seems to be no evidence to support more than visits between the parties. Only three Powerscourt conferences are here discussed, but there were more than three (Rowdon, *Origins of the Brethren*, p. 87).

57. The *Christian Herald* quoted in *Letters of J. N. D.*, 1:5. The correspondent was probably Darby.

Apocalypse." "What light does scripture throw on present events, and their moral character? What is next to be looked for and expected? Is there a prospect of a revival of Apostolic churches before the coming of Christ?"[58] Only in retrospect can the implications of some of these phrases be discerned. In the first place, the note of despair over the present condition of the churches, common enough among millenarians, had become, in the hands of Darby and his followers, a strong if not violent attack upon the established church. In closing the second conference, the Reverend Robert Daly, evidently deeply disturbed by what he had heard, delivered a plea for understanding, forgiveness, and unity, noting that "there have been great differences of opinion upon what appear to be fundamental points of doctrine. . . . I see before me the prospect of divisions in the church." Lady Powerscourt did leave the church, and the third Powerscourt conference was dominated entirely by the Plymouth Brethren.[59]

Secondly, Darby and almost all the Plymouth Brethren advocated a futurist rather than historicist interpretation of the book of Revelation. This issue would have been discussed at Powerscourt on 27 September 1832, when the topic announced was "An Inquiry into, and a connection between Daniel and the Apocalypse." Daniel and Revelation contain independent but related chronologies of future events — this point was assumed by all millenarians. But how much do the two prophecies overlap? This was a key problem, one intriguing enough and significant enough to wage war over. The historicist party, represented by almost all those millenarians discussed earlier in this chapter, judged that much of Daniel was recapitulated in the book of Revelation and that the two accounts could and should be used to interpret

58. Ibid., p. 7.
59. Mrs. Hamilton Madden, *Memoir of the Late Right Rev. Robert Daly* (London, 1875), p. 153. The editor of the *Christian Herald*, who had printed reports of the early Powerscourt conferences, refused to mention the 1832 conference and abandoned his publication in 1833 in disgust over the controversies being created by millenarian teaching.

each other. They believed that the events described in the Apocalypse were being fulfilled in European history (thus the name of the party).[60] Henry Drummond went so far as to state that all of the first fifteen chapters of Revelation had already been fulfilled and that in 1827 European history was hovering somewhere between the twelfth and seventeenth verses of Revelation 16.[61] The futurists believed that none of the events predicted in Revelation (following the first three introductory chapters) had yet occurred and that they would not occur until the end of this dispensation. Associated with this rejection of the historicists' harmonizing of Daniel and Revelation was the futurists' attack upon the year-day theory, so vital to the dating of the 1,260 years to 1798. At the first Powerscourt conference the announced topic for Wednesday was "proof if '1260 *days*' means days or years. . . ."

The futurist position did not originate with the Plymouth Brethren. Sixteenth-century Roman Catholic commentators had countered Protestant attacks upon the papacy as the Antichrist by insisting that none of the events relating to Antichrist had yet occurred.[62] Lacunza's *Coming of Messiah in Glory and Majesty* (1827), the work of the Spanish Jesuit whose testimony to the premillennial advent of Christ Edward Irving considered so valuable, belonged to that tradition. The earliest and strongest Protestant statement of futurism came from Samuel R. Maitland in his *Enquiry into the Grounds on Which the Prophetic Period of Daniel and St. John Has Been Supposed to Consist of 1260 Years* (1826). Maitland, however, was no millenarian or even a friend to the evangelical party. His futurism, described as a hawk in the historicist dovecote, represented an attack upon the millenarian party by an outsider with no means of perpetuating

---

60. In this study, this party will be referred to as historicist rather than, as some have preferred, historic premillennialists. This latter term has sometimes confused students of the subject because it seems to imply (erroneously) that the historicist party represented long or continuous tradition among millenarians in contrast to futurism.

61. Drummond, *Dialogues*, 1:296.

62. Froom, *Prophetic Faith*, 3: especially 489 ff.

his influence.[63] As has been true so frequently in the history of religious controversy, futurism did not become a real threat to the historicists and an attractive alternative prophetic position until accepted by believers. This occurred when Darby, Newton, and the Plymouth Brethren adopted futurism.[64]

Darby used the third Powerscourt conference in September 1833 to continue his attack upon the apostasy of the churches and to stress the need for all true believers to gather in the name of the Lord alone.[65] In a sense this was the first assembly of the new sect, but it was also the first occasion of disagreement between Darby and Newton. Darby introduced into discussion at Powerscourt the ideas of a secret rapture of the church and of a parenthesis in prophetic fulfillment between the sixty-ninth and seventieth weeks of Daniel. These two concepts constituted the basic tenets of the system of theology since referred to as dispensationalism, the thorough discussion of which must wait until chapter 3. Neither Darby nor Newton seems to have become estranged at this time. Darby held an open mind on both of these subjects as late as 1843. Newton remembered, years later, opposing both positions. Commenting upon Darby's interpretation of the seventy weeks of Daniel, Newton remarked, "The secret rapture was bad enough, but this was worse." [66]

---

63. Maitland was especially concerned to discredit the year-day theory. A good many of the Tractarians were also futurists whose support was not welcomed by the Brethren.

64. Graduates of Trinity College, Dublin, for reasons that are not clear, were among the earliest and most able defenders of futurism; for example, both William Burgh and James Henthorn Todd wrote futurist works.

65. J. B. Stoney recalled the setting of that meeting as follows: "Mr. John Synge was in the chair. He called on each to speak on a given subject. Mr. Darby spoke last, and for hours, touching on all that had been previously said. Mr. Wigram sat next to him. Captain Hall, Mr. George Curzon, Sir Alex. Campbell, Mr. Bellett, Mr. Thomas Mansell, Mr. Mahon, Mr. Edward Syne [sic] were there. There were clergymen present and Irvingites" (Interesting Reminiscences, pp. 20–21).

66. Letters of J. N. D., 1:58; and Rowdon, Origins of the Brethren, pp. 96–97.

The Revival of British Millenarianism

THE DIVERGENCE between the historicists and the futurists remained the only serious source of dissent among the millenarians during the first generation of the movement. Even this rift was sometimes overlooked, though the fact that futurism had originated with the Jesuits and won favor among the Tractarians alienated many historicists from any futurist, no matter how evangelical he might be in other aspects of the faith. However, the basic tenets of the millenarian creed, as has been stressed throughout this chapter, were held with a surprising degree of unanimity: the belief that acceptance of the divine authority of Scripture required that the believer expect a literal rather than a spiritual fulfillment of the prophecies; the belief that the gospel was not intended nor was it going to accomplish the salvation of the world, but that, instead, the world was growing increasingly corrupt and rushing toward imminent judgment; the belief that Christ would literally return to this earth and the Jews be restored to Palestine before the commencement of the millennial age; and the belief that this whole panorama of coming glory and judgment was explicitly foretold in the prophecies where one could, if taught by the Spirit, discover the truth and be ready for the coming of the bridegroom. Almost every British millenarian of the early nineteenth century would have given ready consent to these statements. The point must be emphasized, for the opponents of millenarianism continually used the stick of diversity to beat the millenarians. Diversity existed, of course, but in the elaboration of prophetic chronologies, not in the fundamentals summarized above. In the detailed commentaries and exegeses of the apocalyptic Scriptures, diversity grew luxuriantly. The millenarian seems to have found it difficult to distinguish between the essential and peripheral elements in his own prophetic synthesis, and paper wars were the rule, not the exception, in the prophetic journals. This kind of struggle became a scandal among the millenarians themselves, and it is this kind of disagreement that prompted the reproaches of their antagonists. The failure of the millenarians to produce a method of prophetic exegesis that could win widespread support must be considered the most serious weakness of the movement.

As we have seen, the millenarian movement grew by leaps and starts. Originating in the tracts and sermons of a few scattered pioneers, millenarianism won hundreds of converts in a sudden rush of notoriety during 1825–30. Whether owing to Irving's experiment with tongues or not, accessions to the movement appear to have slowed down during the 1830s, but those who had joined during the earlier years seldom deserted the movement. The size of millenarian forces can only be estimated, and even an estimate is hazardous. Among eighteenth-century dissenting groups only the Baptists seem to have been affected, whereas the Methodists remained virtually immune. Many who joined dissenter ranks during the early nineteenth century became or had already become converts to millenarianism, the obvious illustrations being the Irvingites and Plymouth Brethren. In Scotland the movement had only moderate success; most of those ministers of the Church of Scotland who adopted millenarian views joined the Free Church during the schism of 1843. In the Church of England almost all the millenarian converts were recruited from the evangelical party, although the Tractarians did show some interest in a form of futurism. A commentator in the *British and Foreign Evangelical Review* in 1855 estimated that more than half of the evangelicals in the church favored millenarian views, but that is little more than a straw of evidence. Another contemporary observer, the Reverend Thomas G. Bell of Lynmouth, noticed that ministers from the Church of England led the millenarian revival in the north of England and in Ireland, that a few Presbyterians spoke out in Scotland, and that "in the south and west of England they were ministers and Christians of various denominations, who have many of them since become known as 'the Brethren.' "[67] Unlike the tongues movement, millenarianism never became the possession of a single group, a doctrinal badge of allegiance or aversion —

67. *British and Foreign Evangelical Review* 4 (1855):697–710; and *Rainbow* 1 (1864):36.

an accident of history that greatly influenced the later spread of millenarian doctrine.

The millenarian has often been contemptuously dismissed as a fanatic and neurotic. Devout and respectable millenarians were dismayed and hurt by such charges, but it must be admitted in retrospect that the charges, when stripped of pejorative connotations, contain a good deal of truth. However, if one suspends judgment on millenarians long enough to analyze their fanaticism, he will find that it is based upon a kind of rationalization or justification which, if it does not completely vindicate their behavior on some occasions, does much to place it in a more comprehensible context. One would scarcely dispute the assertion that the millenarians often acted imprudently. They did so, however, not because of some personality deficiency but because they had convinced themselves that prudence was a vice, perhaps the most grievous evidence of the worldly character of their age. Christians, so Henry Drummond argued, are not supposed to be prudent, but to obey the commands of God.[68] Since the millenarian believed that the pages of Scripture contained the literal truth of God's prophetic plan, he was only behaving consistently when he set out to obey divine commands in an equally literal fashion. What F. W. Newman most admired in J. N. Darby was precisely this dedication to the literal sense of the gospel in place of prudence. It need hardly be mentioned that Irving's whole life was marked by this same sense of obedience and dedication which in turn delighted, astonished, and scandalized the world. One last ingredient ought to be added to this characterization. In contrast to the similarly imprudent millenarian of the seventeenth century, the nineteenth-century millenarian was a political reactionary. Since the course of history led straight to judgment, change could only produce a crescendo of corruption. Catholic emancipation, the Reform Bill, democracy, industrialization — the millenarian opposed them all, but with a sense of resignation born of the knowledge that the world must grow more evil day after day.

68. Drummond, *Dialogues*, 1:198.

2

The Millenarian Tradition in the United States 1800–1845

BY THE MIDDLE of the nineteenth century British millenarian theology had been imported into the United States and had become the most popular form of American millenarianism. But this triumph occurred only after the luxuriant flourishing of a native millenarian species that imposed special conditions and traditions upon every other American adaptation. The development of American millenarianism owes most of its character to its British heritage. However, William Miller began to teach a similar kind of eschatology at nearly the same time as the British millenarians were creating excitement by their second advent proclamations; the early success and ultimate collapse of his movement prejudiced the country against all millenarian doctrines and forced every later millenarian advocate to take a stand against "Millerism" as virtually the first sentence in every speech and the first paragraph in every treatise. William Miller, like Edward Irving in the British movement, became a theological leper whose ceremonial denunciation was a part of the litany of millenarianism for the next century.

America in the early nineteenth century was drunk on the millennium. Whether in support of optimism or pessimism, radicalism or conservatism, Americans seemed unable to avoid — seemed bound to utilize — the vocabulary of Christian eschatology. In those decades of American utopianism men spoke the language of the Apocalypse, which later generations have either ignored or freely translated into their own idiom. Some day, it may be hoped, a book with the scope and lucidity of Henry Nash Smith's *Virgin Land* will help us appreciate the significance and variety of this American preoccupation with the millennium. This chapter cannot hope to fill that gap, but is intended only to sketch the millennial context of United States history, to comment upon some aspects of William Miller's movement, and to explain why British millenarian teachings made no appreciable impact upon the American churches until after 1845.

The eschatology of United States Protestants, reflecting their brimming optimism and hope, was expressed most frequently as a blending of millennialism and American nationalism. Stemming from the Puritan conviction that the colonists were a chosen people and their commonwealth a "citty set vpon a hill," reinforced by the War for Independence and the potentialities of the West, Americans vied with each other in producing grander and more glorious prospects for the United States. As early as the eighteenth century the concept of America's destiny was influencing American theology, Jonathan Edwards himself leading the way as the first postmillennial theologian in United States history.[1] Systematic theology seldom proved congenial to early nineteenth-century tastes, but the optimism and confidence of postmillennial eschatology did. The leaders of the largest Protestant denominations, faced with the challenge of evangelizing the pagan West and reforming the moral life of the nation without the aid of the state, plunged into their work with optimism about their methods and confidence that God was blessing their efforts. And as this campaign began to succeed, their confidence and optimism found expression in no theme more common than millennialism. Samuel H. Cox, "new school" minister and moderator of the General Assembly of the Presbyterian church for 1846, expressed the idea

1. C. C. Goen, "Jonathan Edwards, A New Departure in Eschatology," *Church History* 28 (1959) : 25–40. See also David E. Smith, "Millenarian Scholarship in America," *American Quarterly* 17 (1965) : 535–49; and Perry Miller, "The End of the World," in *Errand into the Wilderness* (New York, 1964).

in a speech delivered in London in 1846 at the first meeting
of the Evangelical Alliance.

> Allow me to say, that, in America, the state of
> society is without parallel in universal history. With
> all our mixtures, there is a leaven of heaven; there
> is goodness there; there is excellent principle there.
> I really believe that God has got America within
> anchorage, and that upon that arena, He intends to
> display his prodigies for the millennium.[2]

The brashness and chauvinism of Cox's remarks were
often duplicated by other American clergymen whose attitudes were expressed so flamboyantly as to seem a parody of
British postmillennialism. It would be a mistake, however,
to turn from this postmillennial exuberance to a study of the
Millerite millenarians, expecting to find in their apocalypticism a similar exaggeration of the British attitudes and to
embrace within that contrast the entire scope of American
millennialism. The Millerites rank as the largest and most
influential early nineteenth-century American premillennial
group, and in their emphasis upon the exact year of the second advent they did give unusual prominence to one aspect
of millenarian expectations. But the commonly repeated tales
of their fanatical behavior — dressing in ascension robes and
gathering on hilltops to await the coming of Christ, consequent insanity, murder, and suicide — have been amply refuted.[3] Furthermore, when American millennialism is portrayed as a contrast between the ebullient postmillennialists
and fanatic Millerites, the thought of each group is too simply
polarized and the apocalyptic emphases in other groups are
entirely ignored. Six years before Samuel Cox's address to
the Evangelical Alliance, his son, Arthur Cleveland Coxe,
published these stanzas:

> *We are living, we are dwelling*
> *In a grand and awful time;*

2. Evangelical Alliance, *Report
of the Proceedings of the Conference Held in . . . London . . .
1846* (London, 1847), p. 413.

3. Francis D. Nichol, *The
Midnight Cry* (Washington, D.C.,
1944).

> *In an age on ages telling*
> *To be living is sublime.*
>
> *Hark the waking up of nations*
> *Gog and Magog to the fray;*
> *Hark! What soundeth? Is Creation*
> *Groaning for its latter day?*
>
> *Hark the onset! Will you fold your*
> *Faith-dead arms in lazy lock?*
> *Up, O, up! thou drowsy soldier —*
> *Worlds are charging to the shock!* [4]

That these lines, by a future Episcopal bishop, were sung with equal acceptability by both Episcopalians and Millerites ought to warn us against contrasting these groups too simplistically.[5] And when one turns to an examination of some of the other millennial groups of the period, the complexity and variety of the theme is further illustrated.

Alexander Campbell for three decades directed the expansion of the Disciples of Christ through his monthly journal, the *Millennial Harbinger*. The title accurately reflected Campbell's fascination with the millennium, but his views cannot easily be categorized. Intensely anti-Catholic, Campbell made frequent use of the apocalyptic symbolism of Daniel and Revelation to belabor the papacy. Biblicistic, he was intrigued by the chronological conundrums posed by the 1,260 and 2,300 years, accepted the year-day theory of interpretation, and speculated about the manner in which these prophecies ought to be interpreted. He devoted a great deal of space in the *Millennial Harbinger* to the writings of millenarians such as Samuel M. McCorkle, a Disciples' layman, and paid tribute to William Miller, though disagreeing with him about the date of the second advent.[6] For several years he sounded like

---

4. James D. Morrison, ed., *Masterpieces of Religious Verse* (New York, 1948), p. 356. A. C. Coxe changed the spelling of his family name to what he thought was an older and more authentic version.

5. The hymn was printed in the Millerite hymnal, *The Millennial*

Harp. Alice Felt Tyler, finding it there, quoted it as an example of Millerite extremism, not realizing that it had been written by the Episcopalian Coxe (*Freedom's Ferment* [Minneapolis, 1944], p. 73).

6. Samuel McCorkle wrote a column in the *Millennial Har-*

a millenarian convert. But, as Ernest Tuveson has shown, one need not have been a millenarian to find a place for cataclysm in his cosmology.[7] Campbell was only expressing his belief in progress through destruction when he wrote in 1831:

> Christendom is to be the theatre of the most tremendous calamities and sudden disasters, terminating in that unexampled earthquake, which is to destroy the monarchies, hierarchies, and all the bastard progeny of the Mother of Harlots . . . as preliminary to the commencement of the reign of a thousand years.[8]

Fifteen years later he reacted to an extensive journey into the West with a glowing apostrophe to the glories of America's future.

> The ultimate history of our country seems too vast for human conception. The experiment of millions of men living under a republican government, and left to the fruition of an unfettered body and free mind, joined together in advancing the interests of humanity, and accomplishing the highest perfection our nature is capable of, who can conceive the result?[9]

For Campbell, apparently, the cataclysmic vocabulary was the expression of his mood rather than an intrinsic part of his theology.[10]

---

binger during 1833 and 1834 which was called "Signs of the Times." One reference to Miller is found in *Millennial Harbinger*, January 1841, pp. 8–10.

7. *Redeemer Nation.*

8. *Millennial Harbinger*, April 1831, p. 167. Froom, *Prophetic Faith*, quotes this passage in part (4:261), and leaves the impression, no doubt unintentionally, that Campbell was ready to accept McCorkle's premillennialism. But in later comment in the same article, Campbell says, "But whether christendom can be converted to Jesus Christ, unless it be by the outpouring of all the vials of wrath . . . is a question of serious discussion . . . We constitutionally incline to look at the bright side of the picture, and to take the most cheering view of things; but in defiance of our bias, deepening gloom overspreads our ecclesiastical heavens" (Ibid.).

9. Ibid., June 1846, p. 356.

10. The Christadelphians, a small splinter sect from the Campbellites led by a British doctor named John Thomas,

The first decades of Mormon history likewise reflected intense interest in the latter days, as the official name of their denomination made obvious. Originating in upstate New York and winning early converts primarily from Yankee stock, it would have seemed anomalous indeed if the new sect from the burned-over district had not shared the common millennial preoccupations of that day. Joseph Smith taught an apocalyptic and premillennial eschatology; the Mormon's periodical was entitled the *Millennial Star*; and as they gathered for worship, the Latter-Day Saints could choose from dozens of hymns, like the following one, which focused their attention on the dawning glory and the imminent judgment.

> *Let Zion in her beauty rise;*
>   *Her light begins to shine:*
> *Ere long her King will rend the skies,*
>   *Majestic and divine.*
> *The Gospel's spreading through the land,*
>   *A people to prepare,*
> *To meet the Lord and Enoch's band,*
>   *Triumphant in the air.*
>
> *Ye heralds sound the Gospel trump,*
>   *To earth's remotest bound;*
> *Go, spread the news from pole to pole,*
>   *In all the nations round,*
> *That Jesus in the clouds above,*
>   *With hosts of angels too,*
> *Will soon appear, his Saints to save,*
>   *Her enemies subdue.*
>
> *Alas! the day will then arrive*
>   *When rebels to God's grace*
> *Will call for rocks to fall on them*
>   *And hide them from his face.*
> *Not so with those who keep his law,*
>   *They'll joy to meet their Lord,*
> *In clouds above, with those who slept*
>   *In Christ, their sure reward.*[11]

---

were particularly involved in prophetic interpretation. Thomas taught that the churches were apostate in a fashion that is reminiscent of J. N. Darby (Froom, *Prophetic Faith*, 4:286).

11. *Sacred Hymns and Spiritual Songs for the Church of Jesus Christ of Latter-Day Saints*, 12th ed. (Liverpool, 1863), hymn no. 180, stanzas 1, 2, and 5.

Early Mormon millenarianism was so intense, in fact, that Joseph Smith felt obliged to restrain his followers, particularly during the excitement caused by Miller's prediction of the advent in 1843. Like Alexander Campbell, Smith seemed to lose his earlier convictions concerning an imminent apocalypse. He told his followers in 1842 that he had, after praying earnestly about the time of the second advent, heard a voice saying "Joseph, my son, if thou livest until thou art eighty-five years old, thou shalt see the face of the Son of Man; therefore let this suffice, and trouble me no more on this matter." [12] As their headquarters moved from Ohio into Missouri and then Illinois, the Mormons began to concentrate more upon Zion as a place than upon 1843 or 1844 as a date. Like so many Americans, the Mormons found themselves much more concerned with space than time. [13] Their expectations about the future, however, remained curiously mixed. The triumph of the Mormon cause was anticipated through a cataclysmic judgment rather than the gradual conversion of the world; and since natural calamities had been predicted as one of the indications of the nearness of this judgment, reports of fires, wars, and railroad and steamship disasters were regularly reported in the *Millennial Star* under the heading "Signs of the Times" — the same title used for a column in Campbell's *Millennial Harbinger*. But while the Latter-Day Saints waited anxiously for the fulfillment of these signs of the times (including the restoration of the Jews to Palestine), they were also laboring mightily to build the New Jerusalem in Utah. [14]

The Shakers — officially named the Millennial Church of the United Society of Believers in Christ's Second Appearing — taught a millennial doctrine that surpassed even the literality of the Mormons. The second advent had already occurred, they believed, in the incarnation of God in Mother

12. Klaus J. Hansen, *Quest for Empire: The Political Kingdom of God and the Council of Fifty in Mormon History* (Lansing, 1967), p. 16.
13. Sidney E. Mead, "The American People: Their Space, Time, and Religion," in *The Lively Experiment* (New York, 1963).
14. Hansen, *Quest for Empire*, chap. 1, which is entitled "The Kingdom of God and the Millennial Tradition."

Ann Lee, the female and complementary form to the Christ of the first advent. The coming of Mother Ann had inaugurated the millennium, the Shakers taught, and life in their celibate and semimonastic communities represented their ideal of holiness and Christian perfection. They were established late in the eighteenth century near Albany, New York (after emigration from Britain), but did not begin to prosper until about 1820. Although their messiah had already returned, the Shakers during the 1830s experienced an outbreak of enthusiasm which included direct revelations, speaking in tongues, and visions of prophetic significance.[15]

The leader of the Oneida community, John Humphrey Noyes, also concluded that the second advent had already taken place — in 70 A.D. But during the exciting 1830s, in the days before he had formulated his distinctive theology, he recalled that "the Millennium was supposed to be very near. I fully entered into the enthusiasm of the time. . . . My heart was fixed on the Millennium, and I resolved to live or die for it." Like Alexander Campbell and Joseph Smith, he later tempered his zeal, remarking in explanation, "It is certain that in 1831, the whole orthodox church was in a state of ebullition in regard to the Millennium. A feeling of expectation on this point lay at the bottom of that triumphant march of revivals which shook the land for several years from that time. The Millerites have since met with unbounded ridicule; but it should be remembered that all that portion of the churches who were spiritual, who believed in revivals, and who were zealous and successful in laboring for them had a fit of expectation as enthusiastic and almost as fanatical as the Millerites." It was in such a climate of opinion that William Miller began to predict the end of the world.[16]

15. Edward Deming Andrews, *The People Called Shakers*, 2d ed. (New York, 1963). Jemimah Wilkinson, the Universal Friend, while not directly influenced by the Shakers, taught a similar doctrine.

16. J. H. Noyes, *Confession of Religious Experience* (Oneida Reserve, 1849), p. 2; and J. H. Noyes, "Signs of the Times," *Spiritual Magazine* 2, no. 13 (5 August 1848): 193. Noyes's views were more fully expressed in *The Berean* (Putney, Vermont, 1847), pp. 275–300.

CHAPTER TWO

THE MOST FAMOUS millenarian in American history, William
Miller, was far from being a fantatic. A self-educated farmer
from Low Hampton, New York, he showed no interest in
prophecy during his early years and was, in fact, something
of a skeptic until converted in 1816. During the next few
years, precisely at the time that British prophetic interest began to stir, Miller became fascinated with interpretation
of prophecy. Depending almost entirely upon his own exegesis of the Bible, Miller developed a system of prophetic interpretation that came remarkably close to duplicating that
being developed by the historicist premillennialists of Britain
discussed in chapter 1.[17] Untrained in public preaching and
naturally diffident, Miller for many years refrained from any
public discussion of his views. Gradually, however, he felt
compelled to speak up in the Baptist churches of his neighbor-
hood; by 1834, when his message had begun to arouse interest, Miller abandoned farming and devoted all his energies
to spreading his advent message in upper New York State
and New England. Miller's local success was transformed into
a national movement by the organizational and promotional
talents of the Reverend Joshua V. Himes, whom Miller had
won to the millenarian cause in 1839. Through centralized
organization, the publication of an enormous volume of periodical and occasional literature, and the use of camp meetings and a very large tent, the Millerite campaign mush-
roomed within five years into a movement with fifty thousand
adherents.[18]

William Miller taught a doctrine of the last times that
differed remarkably little from that proclaimed by the British

17. Nichol, *Midnight Cry,*
which is the source of most of the
following comment on Miller,
claims that no evidence exists
for Miller's dependence upon any
other sources than the Bible and
a concordance. He was known
to have read only two books on
prophetic interpretation, one by
G. S. Faber and one by Newton
(though whether Sir Isaac

Newton or Bishop Thomas Newton is not clear) (p. 150). W. S.
Hudson's attribution of Continental Society influence was based
upon the similarity of their
argument and not upon any direct
evidence (*Religion in America*
[New York, 1965], p. 194).
18. Froom, *Prophetic Faith,*
4:783.

nineteenth-century millenarians. The main thrust of Miller's teaching was that Christ would return, the wicked be judged, and the world cleansed by fire about 1843. His convictions were founded upon the same assumptions as were those of the historicist premillenarians of Britain — that the prophecies of the Bible were always literally fulfilled and that chronological sequences in the apocalyptic books should be interpreted according to the year-day theory. Miller described his convictions in these words:

> I found that, by a comparison of Scripture with history, all the prophecies as far as they have been fulfilled, had been fulfilled literally; that all the various figures, metaphors, parables, similitudes, &c., of the Bible, were either explained in their immediate connection, or the terms in which they were expressed were defined in other portions of the word; and, when thus explained, are to be literally understood in accordance with such explanation. . . .
>
> I saw that, as the events predicted to be fulfilled in prophetic days had been extended over about as many literal years; as God, in Num. 14:34, and Ezek. 4:4–6, had appointed each day for a year; as the seventy weeks to the Messiah were fulfilled in 490 years, and the 1260 prophetic days of the Papal supremacy in 1260 years; and as these prophetical days extending to the advent were given in connection with symbolic prophecy, I could only regard the time as symbolical, and as standing each day for a year, in accordance with the opinions of all the standard Protestant commentators. If, then, we could obtain any clue to the time of their commencement, I conceived we should be guided to the probable time of their termination; and, as God would not bestow upon us an useless revelation, I regarded them as conducting us to the time when we might confidently look for the coming of the Chiefest of ten thousand, One altogether lovely.[19]

That Miller fervently believed in the personal return of Christ need hardly be stressed. His emphasis upon the date of Christ's return — 1843 — is often erroneously said to

19. Ibid., 469, 473.

mark him off from the rest of the church and, more particularly, the other millenarian parties. In fact, the expectation that the year 1843 would bring the next great cataclysm was quite common among historicist premillenarians in both Britain and the United States.[20] Furthermore, Miller did not, until quite close to the date, place dogmatic and exclusive emphasis upon the date. He emphasized the imminence of Christ's coming but also accepted as associates and colleagues in the movement men who were unable to agree that 1843 ought to receive special prominence.[21] Millerite eschatology did differ from British premillennialism on two issues, however, and here Miller and his associates did not tolerate diversity.[22] The Millerites did not accept the restoration of the Jews to Palestine as a part of the prophetic timetable, nor were they willing to admit that biblical prophecy had any further promises to keep so far as the Jews were concerned. As Miller once bluntly put it, "The Jew has had his day." [23] Second, Miller did not expect any nonbelievers to survive the coming of Christ, which would be accompanied by fiery judgment. Quite obviously, there was no room in this forecast for the conversion of the Jews and their return to Palestine, the eventual conversion of the nations, and the triumph of Christianity anticipated by the British millenarians.[24] But Miller had not had the opportunity to read and be influenced by the literature of the British millenarian revival. He was left to his own logic and exegesis, and, when his convictions had matured, he remained unshakable.

20. The scholars of prophecy focused upon 1843 because they felt that the prophecy of the 2,300 days (Daniel 8) would be fulfilled about then, but there were other reasons unrelated to prophecy which created tension and expectation during these years (cf. Cross, *Burned-over District*, p. 321).

21. Henry Dana Ward was such a man (cf. Nichol, *Midnight Cry*, pp. 90–91).

22. Ibid., pp. 91–92.

23. Isaac C. Wellcome, *History of the Second Advent Message* (Boston, 1874), p. 165.

24. Miller was attacked for his views on these points in David Lord's *Theological and Literary Journal* 6 (1853) : 169–71; and in the *Quarterly Journal of Prophecy* 1 (1849) : 135 ff.; 4 (1852) : 102–7.

> I found it plainly taught in the Scriptures that
> Jesus Christ will again descend to this earth, coming
> in the clouds of heaven, in all the glory of his Father:
> that, at his coming, the kingdom and dominion
> under the whole heaven will be given to him and
> the saints of the Most High, who will possess it
> forever . . . , that, as the old world perished by the
> deluge, so the earth, that now is, is reserved unto fire,
> to be melted with fervent heat at Christ's coming.[25]

Millerite millenarianism did not differ from the British
millenarian tradition in doctrine alone. William Miller began
his ministry with no intention of creating a new denomination; his only interest was to spread the warning that Christ's
return was imminent. Apart from his millenarianism, Miller
taught no doctrines that set him off from his evangelical
neighbors and even his millenarianism was scarcely ever described by his critics as anything but a mistake or a delusion — not heresy. Disputes over baptism and eternal damna-
tion, for example, were often carried on with more venom
and sectarian dogmatism. But unlike their British contemporaries, the Millerite millenarians found themselves forced
willy-nilly into the business of organizing their movement
into a denomination. The first step was taken in 1840 with
the calling of the first of a series of ministerial conferences
on the second coming of Christ. Intended originally only as
one more device to publicize and strengthen the millenarian
cause, by the third conference in 1841 the Millerite leadership
was using these occasions for the purpose of examining and
approving millenarian preachers much as a denomination
licensed its ministers. All those attending the third general
conference also joined in celebration of the communion,
and at the fifth general conference (also 1841) Miller, Himes,
and three others were named to an executive committee that
functioned very much like a denominational board. In the
classic pattern of American denominationalism, the Millerites,
without formally breaking ties with their previous congregations, were constructing a parallel and potentially conflicting
institution. The Millerites published their own newspapers

25. Froom, *Prophetic Faith*, 4:471.

and magazines and their own hymnal — *The Millennial Harp*. When they won converts in their many camp meetings and revival services, these proselytes found themselves dissatisfied in nonmillenarian congregations. As the movement rushed to its disastrous climax, antagonism from the denominations began to grow more intensive and Millerite leaders such as Elon Galusha and Joseph Marsh were forced out of their denominational posts among the Baptists and Christians respectively. The Millerites responded by extending the interpretation of apostasy symbolized by the whore of Babylon to Protestant as well as Catholic and developing, in Charles Fitch's preaching particularly, a doctrine of the ruin of the church which resembles John Nelson Darby's. By the time the Millerites had fixed at last upon 22 October 1844 as the day of the second advent, their denominational organization was virtually complete.[26]

But on 22 October 1844 the sun sank as it had on every other day since creation, and Christ had not come. In retrospect the Millerite movement appears to have virtually destroyed premillennialism in America for a generation. The Millerite campaign was magnificently organized and addressed to the people who were eager to hear and ready to believe. Based upon the accepted standards of authority, equally balanced between mathematical calculation and apocatyptic immediatism, Miller's message was admirably suited to the United States in 1830–44. But in concentrating upon the year 1843, Miller had also introduced an element that would destroy the movement. There were, as we shall see, a few millenarians who owned the name and doctrine without joining Miller's cause. But most of those to whom a more diffuse millenarian movement (similar to that in Great Britain) might have appealed were reached instead by the Millerites

26. When 1843 had passed without the coming of Christ, Millerite leaders, reviewing their calculations, concluded that they had made a mistake. Some began advocating the more precise date 22 October 1844 and, although he was not at first convinced, Miller eventually accepted that view. For Fitch's doctrine of the ruin of the church cf. Nichol, *Midnight Cry*, pp. 148 ff.

and either converted and disillusioned or else disillusioned immediately. In the wake of the tragedy of 1844, who could lift up his head and proclaim the message of an imminent advent? Miller's success before 1844 is matched only by the difficulties he created for anyone brave enough to attempt to preach a millenarian message after 1844. It took a long time for Americans to forget William Miller.

ONLY AFTER 1840 did British millenarian thought begin to attract attention in the United States. In 1820 the American Society for Meliorating the Condition of the Jews was founded in New York City, the former London Jews Society leader, Joseph S. C. F. Frey, contributing the first spark. But the society seems to have been conducted without the millenarianism so prominent in its British counterpart.[27] Joel Jones, a lawyer, and Orrin Rogers, a publisher, both from Philadelphia, appear to have initiated the first republication of British millenarian literature. In 1840 they began a periodical entitled the *Literalist*, which simply reprinted the complete text of premillennial works by British authors. During the next two years, five issues of this strange journal appeared.[28] A more customary kind of millenarian periodical, the *American Millenarian and Prophetic Review*, was published during 1842–44 in New York City by the Reverend Isaac P. Labagh, rector of the Calvary Episcopal Church. Very much aware of the bibliography of British millenarianism, Labagh recommended British authors such as J. W. Brooks and offered to sell his readers copies of the *Literalist*. Ministerial support for the British views was quite small, and what there was came almost entirely from the Episcopal and Presbyterian denominations. The leading millenarians in the Episcopal church other than Labagh were Edward Winthrop, Saint Paul's Church, Cincinnati; Richard C. Shimeall, Saint Jude's Church, New York City; and John P. K. Henshaw, bishop of Rhode Island after 1843.

27. *Israel's Advocate* 1 (1823) : 3 ff.

28. Jones was also at one time mayor of Philadelphia and president of Girard College.

Winthrop published a series of *Lectures on the Second Advent* (1843) which were earlier delivered to a crowded church. His views, he claimed, were the same as those of Brooks, Bickersteth, Cuninghame, and other of the British millenarians.[29] Among the Presbyterians, millenarians were represented by such men as William Ramsey, pastor of the Cedar Street Church, Philadelphia, who was the author of the *Second Coming . . . before the Millennium* (1841). John Lillie, another Presbyterian, preached a sermon before the Premillennial Advent Association of New York in January 1842 and was hailed before the New York Presbytery for examination of his eschatology.[30] Probably the best-known non-Millerite premillennialist of this period was George Duffield, pastor of the First Presbyterian Church of Detroit. Duffield published two defenses of the historicist premillennial position. In *Millenarianism Defended* (1843) he attempted to justify his views against Moses Stuart's apology for postmillennialism. When *Dissertations on the Prophecies Relative to the Second Coming of Jesus Christ* was published in 1842, the *Methodist Quarterly Review* made this observation in its review:

> Dr. Duffield appears as the first conspicuous champion on this side of the Atlantic, so far as we know, of that modified form of Chiliasm which does not possess in its own absurdities the seeds of its own dissolution, and which, therefore, promises to become a part of the permanent belief of a portion of the American church.[31]

EVEN SO BRIEF a survey of the millenarian views of early nineteenth-century Americans provides enough data to raise some doubts about old generalizations and encourage think-

---

29. John P. K. Henshaw, *An Inquiry into the Meaning of the Prophecies Relating to the Second Advent of our Lord Jesus Christ* (Baltimore, 1842); Richard C. Shimeall, *Prophecy, Now in Course of Fulfillment* (New York, 1844). Winthrop was the only American millenarian in this period to reflect any knowledge of futurism.

30. John Lillie, *The Perpetuity of the Earth* (New York, 1842). For Lillie's trial see Froom, *Prophetic Faith*, 4:771.

31. *Methodist Quarterly Review* 25 (1843): 421.

ing about some new ones. In spite of the strong sectarian emphasis in American religion and the churchly character of the British, the two nations were not developing in isolation. American and British clergy were continually and vitally concerned with the state of their sister churches, and each felt the impact of the other's ecclesiastical history. While the British millenarian tradition was being imported into this country, British observers were commenting with interest on the developing Millerite movement and criticizing its theology and behavior.[32] At the same time, the Millerite adventists were winning converts in Great Britain, and, of course, the Disciples of Christ, Mormons, and American revivalists were also bringing American style religion to Britain.[33] American historians, encouraged for half a century by the Turner thesis to emphasize the uniqueness of the American experiment, have only just begun to take account of the very real sense of Anglo-American community that existed in the early nineteenth century.[34]

A comparison of the early nineteenth-century British and American millenarian traditions does more, however, than emphasize the passage of ideas back and forth across the Atlantic; it serves to point out how closely these two nations stayed in step quite apart from any significant transoceanic communication. What is most striking about William Miller in this context is the degree of similarity — in content, style, and timing — between his witness and that of the British millenarians. Is it only a coincidence that the excitement over the imminent second advent and the dawning millennium broke out in both Britain and America during 1828–32? Is it only a coincidence that a return to apostolic simplicity and power was being sought in both countries just at this time or that speaking in tongues and healing should become local sensations for a few months? Any account of these

32. *Quarterly Journal of Proph-ecy* 1 (1849) : 135.

33. Even the Millerites established a British base, as has been shown by Louis Billington, "The Millerite Adventists in Great Britain, 1840–1850,"

Journal of American Studies 1 (1967) : 191–212.

34. Frank Thistlethwaite, *The Anglo-American Connection in the Early Nineteenth Century* (Philadelphia, 1959).

phenomena ought to make clear that the British did not participate in these happenings or approve of these doctrines in the same proportions as did the Americans. But in spite of differences in degree, there are remarkable and provocative similarities between these two cultures — similarities which pose a real challenge to the kind of historical explanation customarily offered to account for the functioning of both societies. The outbreak of millenarian excitement during the years 1828–32, for example, is usually explained in British history as a symptom of reaction against the political developments of the day — Roman Catholic emancipation and the Reform Act. In American history, Miller's simultaneous success is usually attributed to the great revival of the 1830s and described within the context of the panic of 1837, to say nothing of imprecise references to the frontier and the relative backwardness of American clergymen. If the same kind of movement developed in the two countries during the same years, some broader and more comprehensive explanation seems to be necessary. This study has not provided adequate data for constructing such an explanation. There is a temptation to paper over the cracks in our understanding of this aspect of Anglo-American history with speculation, but it seems more honest simply to state that we know only enough at this time to cast doubt upon explanations limited only to Britain or America.

Owing largely to the great attraction of the native millenarian movement of William Miller, British millenarianism, although not unrepresented, made very little impact upon the United States before 1845. In both Britain and America, the millenarian revival was led by a man whose calling ultimately brought near ruin to the cause. Edward Irving, though his foray into tongues speaking brought great disrepute to the millenarian cause, did less damage. William Miller's misconception about the date of the second advent lay at the heart of his millenarian doctrine. The failure of his predictions disillusioned most of his followers and marked the whole millenarian cause, rightly or wrongly, with the stigma of fanaticism and quackery.

3

John Nelson Darby
and Dispensationalism

WILLIAM MILLER illustrated, with telling exaggeration, a fundamental dilemma of the historicist school of millenarians. Chronology formed the structure of their dogma; they had tied themselves to a prophetic timetable derived from the events predicted in the Bible, especially Revelation. Although the non-Millerite millenarians seldom became committed to a specific month and day, there was scarcely a year that passed without one or another millenarian expectation being disappointed. This was particularly true from 1843 to 1848 and again from 1867 to 1870, when prophetic calculation and civil unrest coincided to bring expectations to a boil. Some prophetic scholars seemed to possess an indestructible faith in their ability to predict the time of the next great fulfillment of prophecy; no sooner had their hopes for one date been dashed by the passing of time than they rushed into print with another prediction. Michael Baxter, a hardy British publicist, managed to predict incorrect dates from 1861 through 1908, presumably being saved only by death from an infinite series.[1] But few possessed Baxter's exuberance; most of the leaders of the historicist school thought such a prediction mania dangerous and even forbidden by Scrip-

1. This Baxter was the son of Robert Baxter, the disillusioned member of Edward Irving's congregation who wrote an attack upon the tongues movement. Michael Baxter was a missionary in Canada, itinerant lecturer in the United States, and editor of his own prophetic journal. He once predicted that the second coming would occur on 12 March 1903, between 2:30 and 3:00 P.M. (*Our Hope* 10 [1903–4]: 514–15). Cf. also the comments on Baxter in chap. 4.

ture. But no matter how cautiously they might behave, they were committed at least implicitly to some kind of schedule of expectations. By adopting the year-day theory of interpretation for the 1,260 days of Daniel and Revelation and identifying the tableaux of Revelation with contemporary events, these commentators found their credibility mortgaged to the future. The validity of interpretations could only be demonstrated by a continuing process of matching history and prophecy. To give only one illustration, James Hatley Frere published a book in 1846 identifying the organization of the Evangelical Alliance in that year with the harvest of the earth described in Revelation 14, and two years later claimed that the revolutions of 1848 marked the "expiration of the times of the Gentiles."[2] Although not as dramatic, this proved to be potentially as risky as William Miller's predictions of the end of the world. Sooner or later these timetables failed to predict a great world event (such as the defeat and exile of Napoleon III in 1870, which confounded many scholars' expectations that the emperor would prove to be the Antichrist) or predicted one that failed to appear on schedule. After 1844 the historicist's position began to lose the almost undisputed position that it had held during the first generation of the millenarian revival.

Futurism, the competing eschatology of Irish millenarians and the Plymouth Brethren, gradually became more prominent during the 1840s and eventually commanded the adherence of a great part of the British and, especially, the United States millenarians. In the next chapter we will trace the appearance and progress of futurism among British and American millenarian periodicals and associations, but as a preface to that discussion it is necessary first to describe the Darby-Newton controversy within the Plymouth Brethren and to analyze Darby's singular theological system, known since his day as dispensationalism. Since Darbyite dispensa-

2. J. H. Frere, *The Harvest of the Earth prior to the Vintage of Wrath, Considered as Symbolical of the Evangelical Alliance* (London, 1846) ; and *The Great Continental Revolution Marking the Expiration of the Times of the Gentiles* (London, 1848).

tionalism dominated late nineteenth-century American millenarianism, formed the substance and the structure for the
Scofield Reference Bible, and constituted one of the most
significant elements in the history of Fundamentalism, a
clear, factual description and analysis is of paramount importance for this study.[3]

The quarrel between John Nelson Darby and Benjamin
Wills Newton broke out in 1845 after Darby's return to Plymouth from a long mission in Switzerland. During the years
of the Powerscourt conferences the Brethren had possessed
little more identity and group unity than participants at a
summer camp. During the formative years immediately following the Powerscourt meetings, the character of the Brethren congregations tended to be shaped, as was natural, by the
previous experience of the members and, most significantly,
by the dominating personalities within each area.[4] Newton
had exercised leadership within the Brethren meeting at Plymouth for many years when Darby returned to that city from
Switzerland and mounted his challenge. Whether one judges
Darby to have been justified in his charges or not, there can
be no doubt that the ensuing turmoil almost destroyed the
struggling young sect and left a legacy of bitterness which
remained to blight the experience of Plymouth Brethren for
generations. Darby first accused Newton of attempting to
dominate the Plymouth meeting, to impose his will upon a
group of special followers, and to create a separate sect; but
within a few months he added a charge of heresy in respect
to the doctrine of Christ. Although there was a good deal of
truth in these charges, the vindictive and violent manner in
which they were brought and the persistence with which they
were pursued (Newton being hounded by them until his
death in 1899) create the impression that Darby was unable
to tolerate rivals to his leadership. The blowup at Plymouth
appears to have been inevitable once Darby discovered that

3. For a contemporary
dispensationalist's description of
the movement see Charles C.
Ryrie, *Dispensationalism Today*
(Chicago, 1965).

4. Edmund Gosse, *Father and
Son* (New York, 1907), illustrates
this phenomenon.

he could not dominate Newton or convert him to his own theology.[5]

As was noted in chapter 1, Newton's disagreement with Darby began as early as the third Powerscourt conference (1833). Newton refused to attend the 1834 conference but instead organized a competing conference at Plymouth, an act which Darby viewed as schismatic.[6] Although bold enough in explicating his views at the Powerscourt conferences, Darby does not seem to have synthesized them into a satisfying theology until his visit to Switzerland. Reminiscing about his beliefs during the Powerscourt period many years later, he remembered, "I was not able to put these things in their respective places or arrange them in order, as I can now."[7] During 1840 he delivered a series of eleven lectures at Lausanne in which he gave systematic exposition to his theology for the first time.[8]

The focus of their disagreement was Darby's teaching about the second coming of Christ, known at that time and since as the secret rapture and one of the most distinctive teachings of dispensationalism. Darby, in company with all the Plymouth Brethren, believed that the church could not be identified with any of the denominational and bureaucratic structures which historically had made and presently were making that claim. The true church, the bride of Christ as Darby often referred to it, could only exist as a spiritual fellowship. The consummation of the church would take place at the second coming of Christ when the members of the body of Christ, both living and dead, would be caught away to dwell with Christ in heaven. Darby's view of the premillennial advent contrasted with that held by the historicist millenarian school in two ways. First, Darby taught that the second advent would be secret, an event sensible only to those who participated

5. Darby's account of the dispute is found in "Narrative of Facts," in his *Collected Writings*, 2d ed. (London, 1967), 20:1 ff. For an impartial account see Rowdon, *Origins of the Brethren*, pp. 227 ff.

6. B. W. Newton and H. Borlase, *Answers to Questions Considered at a Meeting Held in Plymouth on September 15, 1834*, 2d ed. (Plymouth, 1847).

7. *Letters of J. N. D.*, 3:299.

8. *Collected Writings*, 2:278–83.

in it. Darby did not expect the kind of public and dramatic event so graphically described in Matt. 24:27: "For as the lightning comes from the east and shines as far as the west, so will be the coming of the Son of man." The character of the church required that the coming be secret and mystical.

> It is this conviction, that the church is properly heavenly, in its calling and relationship with Christ, forming no part of the course of events of the earth, which makes its rapture so simple and clear; and on the other hand, it shews how the denial of its rapture brings down the church to an earthly position, and destroys its whole spiritual character and position. Our calling is on high. Events are on earth. Prophecy does not relate to heaven. The Christian's hope is not a prophetic subject at all.[9]

There were, in effect, two "second comings" in Darby's eschatology. The church is first taken from the earth secretly and then, at a later time, Christ returns in a public second advent as described in Matthew 24. As Darby put, "The church's joining Christ has nothing to do with Christ's appearing or coming to earth."[10]

Second, Darby taught that the secret rapture could occur at any moment. In fact, the secret rapture is also often referred to as the doctrine of the any-moment coming. Unlike the historicist millenarians, Darby taught that the prophetic timetable had been interrupted at the founding of the church and that the unfulfilled biblical prophecies must all wait upon the rapture of the church. The church was a great parenthesis which Old Testament prophets had not had revealed to them. As was true of all futurists, of course, Darby maintained that none of the events foretold in the Revelation had yet occurred nor could they be expected until after the secret rapture of the church. Christ might come at any moment; the watchful believer might have been, and indeed should have been, waiting faithfully and patiently for that return,

9. Ibid., 11:156. The whole of that volume is helpful in understanding Darby's eschatology, especially the third in the series of lectures on the second coming of Christ (Ibid., pp. 241 ff.).

10. Ibid., pp. 153.

like the ten wise virgins in Jesus' parable, ever since the day of Christ's ascension. Darby avoided the pitfalls both of attempting to predict a time for Christ's second advent and of trying to make sense out of the contemporary alarms of European politics with the Revelation as his guidebook.

> To me the Lord's coming is not a question of prophecy, but my present hope. Events before His judging the quick are the subject of prophecy; His coming to receive the church is our present hope. There is no event between me and *heaven*.[11]

This expectation of the imminent advent, with no obstacle in the way of Christ's return, proved to be one of the greatest attractions of dispensational theology.

Darby never indicated any source for his ideas other than the Bible — indeed, he consistently affirmed that his only theological task was explicating the text of Scripture. The secret rapture was a distinctive development, however, and considerable interest has been aroused about the source of the doctrine. As late as 1843 or possibly even 1845, Darby was expressing doubts about the secret rapture.[12] In later years he seems to have felt that he was convinced about the doctrine as early as 1827.[13] Darby's opponents claimed that the doctrine originated in one of the outbursts of tongues in Edward Irving's church about 1832.[14] This seems to be a groundless and pernicious charge. Neither Irving nor any member of the Albury group advocated any doctrine resembling the secret rapture. As we have seen, they were all historicists, looking for the fulfillment of one or another prophecy in the Revelation as the next step in the divine

11. *Letters of J. N. D.*, 1:329–30.

12. Ibid., 1:59; and Rowdon, *Origins of the Brethren*, esp. p. 233.

13. *Letters of J. N. D.*, 1:344; and 3:298–99.

14. A wide variety of critics have made this claim, including Thomas Croskery (*Princeton Review* 1 [1872]:61–62), James

Grant (*End of All Things*, 1:107), and Robert Cameron (*Watchword and Truth* 24 [1902]:238). All such claims seem to depend ultimately, however, upon the charges of S. P. Tregelles (*Hope of Christ's Coming* [London, 1864], p. 26), who was a friend of B. W. Newton and antagonist of Darby.

timetable, anticipating the second coming of Christ soon but not immediately. After Irving's death the Catholic Apostolic church continued to teach historicist doctrines. It is true that among the English phrases pronounced by one or another of the illuminati in Irving's church there occurred fragments such as "Behold the bridegroom cometh," and "count the days one thousand three score and two hundred — 1,260 — . . . at the end of which the saints of the Lord's should go up to meet the Lord in the air," but such utterances can scarcely be considered as evidence for any doctrine and have, in any case, little reference to the secret rapture as Darby taught it. Since the clear intention of this charge is to discredit the doctrine by attributing its origin to fanaticism rather than Scripture, there seems little ground for giving it any credence.[15]

By 1840, B. W. Newton had begun what was to become a lifelong critique of the doctrine of the secret rapture and the theological implications associated with it. In his treatise *Five Letters on Events Predicted in Scripture as Antecedent to the Coming of the Lord* Newton posed the question, "Is the church directed in Scripture to expect a secret coming of the Lord Jesus Christ?" and answered with a resounding no. Claiming that it was a new doctrine, he stated, "the whole testimony of Scripture is against it."[16] The church had never anticipated the return of Christ at any moment, Newton argued, for the apostles themselves had clear intimations of intervening events, such as the predictions of Peter's death in John 21 and 2 Peter 1. Furthermore, the Scriptures themselves contain the refutation of the idea of a secret rapture, Newton claimed, and he turned by way of illustration to the parable of the wheat and the tares in Matthew 13 where Jesus had said, "Let both grow together until the harvest." If one accepted Darby's view of the secret rapture and any-moment coming, Newton pointed out, then many Gospel

15. For the Catholic Apostolic church, see Miller, *Irvingism*, 1:430–31. For the tongues in Irving's church, cf. Baxter, *Narrative of Facts*. This topic is discussed again in chap. 9.

16. *Five Letters* (London, 1877), pp. 72–73.

passages must be "renounced as not properly ours."[17] To anyone unacquainted with the theology of dispensationalism, this would appear to have been — in the context of nineteenth-century biblical literalism — a wholly unacceptable alternative. But in spite of his continuous and devout celebration of the Scripture as the sole source of truth in this world, this is precisely what Darby was prepared to do. Too traditional to admit that biblical authors might have contradicted each other, and too rationalist to admit that the prophetic maze defied penetration, Darby attempted a resolution of his exegetical dilemma by distinguishing between Scripture intended for the church and Scripture intended for Israel. Matthew 24, for example, is filled with signs foretelling the return of Christ which readers are urged to heed. In Darby's eschatology, as we have seen, there are no such signs which herald the rapture of the church — the whole event is shrouded in secrecy. Darby's difficulty was solved by assuming that the Gospels were addressed partly to Jews and partly to Christians.

> Now when Christ appears, we appear with Him. (Col. iii.4.) Matthew xii. 41, 43 only proves that, when the wicked are judged, the righteous *shine forth*; but they had been previously gathered into the garner, in order to do so. In verse 49 the judgment severs the wicked from among the just. This is not the rapture. Judgment leaves the just where they were; one is taken and the other left, as in Matthew xxiv. . . .
>
> The tares are declared to be *taken in hand* before the wheat is gathered into the garner; but, as we have seen, when the tares are burnt, the wheat is already in the garner and then shines forth. As regards the unparalleled tribulation in Matthew xxiv., and the passages from which that is taken, it is exclusively Jewish. There is no passage to prove there is such a tribulation but those which prove it is Jewish.[18]

The main tenets of Darby's theology should now be clear. His doctrine of the church seems to have acted as the catalytic

17. Ibid., p. 73.   18. *Letters of J. N. D.*, 3:334–35.

agent for the rest of his beliefs. Deeply distressed with a worldly Erastian establishment, Darby had declared that church to be in ruins and sought earnestly for the true church. The ecclesiology he proclaimed after 1827 seems to have been generated by reversing almost every position held by the Church of Ireland. In opposition to the worldliness of the church, Darby advocated a church so spiritual that it existed outside of history. The church in this new dispensation of grace was so much a mystery that it had been hidden even from the prophets of the Old Testament. Israel had been a worldly kingdom with material promises and blessings. The Messiah had come to fulfill that worldly kingdom but had been rejected by his people. When that happened, God had broken the continuity of history, stopped the prophetic clock, and instituted the church. When the church is raptured out of the world, this clock will start again and God will return to the task of dealing with the earthly problems of Israel. Only then will the final events predicted in Daniel — the events of the seventieth week — occur. Since for Darby the ministry of Jesus was divided into two parts (his early appeal to the Jews as earthly Messiah and his later role as founder of the church), the exegesis of the Gospels required a careful separation of passages referring to Jewish or to churchly promises and admonitions. The task of the expositor of the Bible was, in a phrase that became the hallmark of dispensationalism, "rightly dividing the word of truth." [19]

Like many of the millenarian scholars of his time, Darby had little patience or respect for other students of prophecy. His intolerant nature combined with confidence in the direction of the Holy Spirit to prevent Darby from appreciating how much this theology reflected the millenarian tradition from which he attempted to separate it. His preoccupation with prophecy, with the second advent, and with the restoration of the Jews to Palestine was shared by almost all participants in the millenarian revival. The exegetical problems which had forced him to adopt the radical solution of consigning

19. The phrase is found in 2 Tim. 2:15. It is also the title of a well-known pamphlet by Cyrus I. Scofield (New York, 1907).

some parts of the New Testament exclusively to the Jews and others exclusively to the church were created by the literalistic hermeneutics consistently adopted by the millenarians. One cannot read much of the literature of millenarianism without being struck by the fact that the same problems of biblical interpretation being faced by men such as Darby and Newton were being discussed and resolved on the basis of completely different presuppositions by advocates of higher criticism.

In addition to a common interest in prophecy and a common dedication to literalism in biblical interpretation, Darby also shared with other millenarians, and indeed with many nonmillenarian nineteenth-century thinkers, a philosophy of history which divided the past into a number of distinct eras in each of which the mode of God's operations, if not nature's, was unique. The eras were called dispensations. Most historians of the theology of dispensationalism have begun their descriptions of Darby's thought with an account of his philosophy of history and system of periodization. As we have seen, however, his theological development was sparked by his insights into the nature of the church. The system of dispensations is not primary in Darby's thought; and, furthermore, it is shared by many of Darby's opponents and by literally scores of others, some of whom were not millenarians at all. B. W. Newton, as we have seen, objected strenuously to Darby's doctrine of the secret rapture, his interpretation of the seventy prophetic weeks of Daniel, and his dichotomy between Jewish and Christian truth in the Gospels. But Newton retained a very clear system of dispensations in his exegesis of the Bible. In *Five Letters*, the treatise in which his opposition to Darby's eschatology was first enunciated, Newton alludes frequently to a system of dispensational interpretation:

> Those who are accustomed to read Scripture dispensationally are aware that the great characteristic of the present dispensation is this: that the Lord Jesus . . . has not yet assumed the power of his Kingdom.[20]

20. *Five Letters*, p. 69; cf. also   pp. 17, 25.

As late as 1897 Newton still considered the use of dispensations in the interpretation of Scripture so essential that he included an article on the subject in one of his creedal statements: "It is necessary to distinguish between the different periods of man's history as given in the Scripture."[21] In reading nineteenth-century religious literature one finds the word and associated philosophy of history in continual use — among millenarians and millennialists alike.[22] John Humphrey Noyes, the American perfectionist, used the term with great frequency and appears to have found the concept of considerable importance in making judgments about the past.[23] Even in Alexander Campbell's theology, dispensational distinctions were declared to be essential for a correct understanding of the Bible:

> It must always be remembered by him who would be a scribe, well instructed in the kingdom of heaven, that the whole Bible comprehends *three* distinct dispensations of religion, or three different administrations of mercy to the human race. These are the Patriarchal, Jewish, and Christian ages of the world.
>
> There are three high priesthoods, viz. — that of Melchizedek, that of Aaron, and that of Jesus the Messiah; and under each of these there will be found a different economy of things.[24]

Ironically, the name of Darby's theology does not denominate a distinctive feature of his teaching. What distinguished Darby's theology was not belief in a system of dispensations. Darby's distinctive beliefs were precisely those to which Newton took exception in *Five Letters*: the doctrine of the

21. Fromow, *B. W. Newton*, p. 57; cf. also p. 93.

22. Drummond utilized the concept in recounting the conclusions of the Albury conferences (see chap. 1). Another historicist, writing in the *Investigator* (2:267–71), found the term useful. For other references cf. F. W. Newman, *Phases of Faith*, p. 7; William Burgh, *Lectures on the Second Advent* (Dublin, 1832) ; or Josiah Priest, *A View of the Expected Christian Millennium . . . Embellished with a Chart of the Dispensations* (Albany, New York, 1831). Priest was a progressive millennialist.

23. *The Berean*, pp. 270, 271, 276, 316.

24. *Millennial Harbinger*, January 1846, p. 22.

secret rapture and the subsequent necessity to divide the New Testament into Jewish and churchly texts.

WITH THE ENERGY and personal magnetism with which he seems to have been so largely endowed, Darby might have been able to build the Plymouth Brethren into a formidable denomination — if he had been interested in building a denomination at all. After 1837, when he went to Lausanne, he probably spent as much time abroad as he did in Britain, living for considerable periods in Switzerland, Italy, France, Germany, Holland, Canada, the United States, the British West Indies, New Zealand, and Australia. The Plymouth Brethren in Britain never really flourished but seemed, instead, to live in an atmosphere of continual schism. The Newton-Darby controversy had badly split the Brethren, and episodes of this sort, only perhaps more tawdry and petty, continued to dog the history of the sect until schism, like the secret rapture, became its trademark. Darby, however, carried on, more or less indifferent to the outward success of the Brethren — as one might have expected. The church was never intended to become the great world network that was the boast of archbishops and prelates; that kind of success he considered a sign of apostasy. Darby seemed satisfied with a handful of followers. It was his constant refrain:

> Hitherto in infirmity and weakness the brethren have been a testimony, and are more and more publicly so. I do not expect this to be popular, especially in these last days; conversions may accompany it, and have, thank God, in many cases, as lately in Canada. But when it was not from the testimony and with it, the preaching left them in the world and in system [i.e., in denominations]. The Lord is over all: our part is to be faithful.[25]

This philosophy and style of life combined to spread Darby's teachings very widely and very thinly. More effective in person than through his books and pamphlets, Darby touched men in ways that are most difficult to assess. Nevertheless, in

25. *Letters of J. N. D.*, 1:538.

view of the extent and significance of the influence of Darby-ite dispensational theology in America and its impact upon the history of Fundamentalism, it seems necessary to make an effort.

Darby visited the United States and Canada seven times between 1862 and 1877, actually residing in and traveling through the two countries for nearly seven out of those sixteen years. His activities in North America began in Toronto during the autumn of 1862. Except for visits to Montreal and Ottawa, and one short trip to Halifax, Darby restricted his ministry to the area between London and Toronto, Ontario. The Brethren mission in this area had already been initiated when he arrived, and Darby gave credit to a Mr. R. Evans as "the founder of the work in Canada."[26] An annual summer conference for Brethren was begun in Guelph and proved to be a good occasion both for strengthening the faith of new converts and for winning additional converts. Darby seems to have been particularly fond of this conference, making the trip across the Atlantic in 1870 especially for the meetings, which he estimated about four hundred attended.

> The evangelists had brought so many younger converts, that the beginning of the conference gave less communion than earlier ones, but met the need of the moment. . . . Many came from different parts of the States, and all our evangelists were there, some under tents. The happiest spirit reigned throughout.[27]

Darby ventured into the United States for four weeks during his first American trip. He was not much impressed: his first reaction was, "The church is more worldly in America than anywhere you would find it, that is, the professing bodies, the world — professedly such — inordinately wicked."[28] Except for his journey from Chicago to San Francisco in the

26. Ibid., 1:335. Evans's name, which is, like so many others, omitted from the printed version of this correspondence, has been supplied from the Sibthorpe manuscripts.

27. Ibid., 2:87.

28. Ibid., 1:351.

spring of 1875, when he was traveling to New Zealand, and the return trip in June 1876, Darby appears to have confined his United States itineraries to the area from Detroit to Chicago to Saint Louis in the Midwest and to the area from Boston to New York in the East. He generally traveled from Chicago and Detroit to New York and Boston by way of Canada.

At first Darby was attracted to the United States by the number of his converts who had emigrated from Europe. In writing about his first United States trip in 1862 he explained:

> My object was to visit the French and Swiss brethren, which save in one locality, I through mercy effected, and was out in the prairies living among them as in old times, and glad indeed to see them as they are. . . . The system of coming to America, taking up land without being able to pay for it . . . had brought them spiritually low, pinching as they must to pay, or careless in paying. But they have felt it, and there has been a reaction in conscience, which has had a most healthful effect on them, and there is a lively desire of profiting by the word. Many neighbouring French came, and their meeting-house could not hold the people.[29]

He never gave up this ministry to the immigrant, but by 1873 Darby had found greater scope for his influence. Particularly in the larger cities of the Midwest and East, he began to preach publicly or, more frequently, to teach privately both laymen and ministers from the American denominations.

> The work in the States [in previous years] was essentially among settlers; my present, among real Americans, God opening the way distinctly. Some new gatherings are formed, weak, but still a testimony, and wholly of such, and I have had large readings, and some lectures in various places. . . . I have been able in various places and circumstances to bring the whole truth before ministers and people, and they interested in it.[30]

29. Ibid., 1:352. The community described was probably either Highland, Illinois, or Vinton, Iowa.

30. Ibid., 2:201. For further comment on the nature of these Bible readings, see below, pp. 136–39.

John Nelson Darby and Dispensationalism

Darby had great difficulty in convincing Americans to accept the whole of his theology. And what was worse, he was least successful in convincing Americans that acceptance of his doctrine of the ruin of Christendom obligated a minister or parishioner to abandon his former denomination to meet with the Brethren "gathered only in the name of the Lord."

> In the west [i.e., the Midwest] a good many Presbyterians, several ministers among them, teach the Lord's coming, the presence of the Holy Ghost, that all sects are wrong, but as yet few move from their place.[31]

Darby blamed the permissive and worldly state of the American churches for this difficult situation. "People join churches for respectability, but christian life is feebleness itself," he commented in 1863, and a few years later he observed, "Organization and work they like — outward effects that they can show — but a life with God and the truth they hardly think of."[32]

Slow and difficult though it was, the work of the Plymouth Brethren in the United States began to attract notice in the 1870s. As a result of proselyting in Chicago, Robert T. Grant, a Brethren evangelist, was able to report to Darby in 1868 that he had won some promising young men. "Moody," he noted, "is quite in a pet about so many of them leaving him who were his best workers."[33] The situation was apparently troublesome enough to lead the editors of the *Princeton Review* to publish a lengthy analysis and critique of the Plymouth Brethren by an Irishman. The author hit first at what he, along with many others, felt were the Brethren's unfair methods of winning converts.

> The aim of the Brethren is to "gather churches out of churches;" to disintegrate all existing bodies by opening a door in each, not for the exit of the faithless and false-hearted, but of the pious and the good; and, accordingly, they prowl unceasingly round all our churches, seeking to reap where they

31. Ibid., 2:182.
32. Ibid., 1:354; 2:190.

33. Robert T. Grant to J. N. Darby, 9 August 1868, Sibthorpe manuscripts.

have not sown, and leaving to the denominations generally the exclusive privilege of evangelizing the masses.[34]

Darby made his greatest impact in the United States, however, outside of the Brethren congregations in a few large cities — Saint Louis, Chicago, New York, and Boston. Since it is in just these centers that dispensationalist theology had the most effect upon American denominations and won its foremost champions among denominational leaders (as distinct from converts to the Plymouth Brethren), a detailed picture of Darby's activities in these cities ought to prove most helpful. Unfortunately, his correspondence does not reveal much about the details of his life, and we are left with the task of piecing together a picture from scraps of evidence. In Saint Louis Darby described his work in 1872 as "extremely difficult."

> In most places grace is hardly known, and mostly opposed: a few old school Presbyterians hold it, otherwise I know none — the state of things deplorable. The teacher of the Sunday school teachers openly denies the resurrection: so one of the pastors — everything as loose as it can be: only God is above it.[35]

But he also noted, a little earlier in the summer of 1872, that he "had good opportunities" in Saint Louis, "and I am in pretty full intercourse with those exercised, among whom are more than one official minister."[36] Whether Darby is referring to James Hall Brookes, pastor of the Walnut Street Presbyterian Church, remains an intriguing but unanswerable question. Brookes became a leader in American millenarian conferences soon after this visit and for most of the remainder of his life taught a dispensational theology. One historian of the Brethren, without citing the evidence for his remark,

34. Thomas Croskery, "The Plymouth Brethren," *Princeton Review* 1 (1872) : 48; an excellent article, based presumably upon primary sources or first-hand knowledge.

35. *Letters of J. N. D.*, 2:197. Darby made five trips to Saint Louis.

36. Ibid., 2:180.

claimed that Darby preached in Brookes's pulpit, but this is the only testimony we can cite to connect Darby and Brookes directly.[37]

In Chicago, which Darby visited on at least five occasions, the evidence is somewhat clearer. Once again Darby found what he considered appalling religious ignorance: "all is a beginning, everything has to be shown — the most elementary truths of Christianity."[38] And once again he found his most compatible audience among the Baptists and Presbyterians, particularly the Old School Presbyterians.[39] What most attracted him to the members of these denominations was their relatively rigorous Calvinistic stand on grace and works. "Work, not truth," Darby complained, "is the American line of things."[40] The Chicagoan who at this time most characterized this American style in religion was, of course, Dwight L. Moody, and Darby disagreed so strongly with that style that he referred derogatorily to Moody as "the active man at Chicago."[41] Since Moody had a hand in everything religious in Chicago, it is not surprising to discover that he and Darby met and exchanged views. Darby found Moody at this period shockingly ignorant of what Darby considered the first principles of the Gospel. Writing about Moody's first great revivalistic success in Edinburgh in 1873, Darby commented:

> As to the work at Edinburgh, I dare say there may have been conversions, and one must bless God for that. But Moody before he came to England denied openly all work of grace in conversion, and denounced it as diabolical in his own pulpit. . . . We discussed it at Chicago, and he held it there, namely, that no man is condemned for his sins, but for not coming to the refuge — sins are all borne and put away for everybody.[42]

By 1875 Darby had changed his opinion of Moody somewhat, but only because he felt that Moody had "greatly got on

37. H. A. Ironside, *Historical Sketch of the Brethren Movement* (Grand Rapids, 1942), pp. 196, 204.
38. *Letters of J. N. D.*, 2:189.
39. Ibid., 1:329, and 503; 2:193, 330.
40. Ibid., 2:189.
41. Ibid., 2:193.
42. Ibid., 2:259.

in the truth."[43] In addition, Darby's reputation in Chicago seems to have markedly improved; he noted in May 1875 "I am suddenly in great vogue with a certain number."[44] But the final estimate of Darby's influence must be left indefinite, and the extent to which Moody himself became an advocate of dispensational theology must await discussion in chapter 7.

Although Darby visited New York City at least nine times and stayed in the city for five months from October 1867 to February 1868 and for four months from November 1874 through February 1875, his letters reveal little about his activities. As usual, his first impressions were bleak; he found New York ecclesiastically in "complete confusion" on his first visit in 1865, and even a few years later he was able to write only that he had "gathered up a few more stray souls."[45]

> But the truth has spread after all considerably, and some fruits even now appear, not only in many souls who have found peace and see clear as to grace, . . . but the Lord's coming is planted in many souls, and that they have seen . . . its connection with the church. . . . Public meetings, I may say I have none, but I meet with people. People interested come in small numbers: I have reading meetings, and so on.[46]

One of the leaders of late nineteenth-century millenarianism, Robert Cameron, recalled first meeting Darby, whom he described as gracious and charitable, at a reading meeting in a humble kitchen in New York City.[47] But other than this kind of report, nothing is known. The extent of his influence must, apparently, remain vague.

Concerning Boston, happily Darby's correspondence is much more helpful. He traveled to Boston on at least eight occasions, settling down twice for periods of at least two months — during the first months of 1875 and the last few of 1876. During 1865 and for some years later, Darby reached a great many Millerite millenarians in the Boston area. As

43. Ibid., 2:369; and cf. 2:327.
44. Ibid., 2:346.
45. Ibid., 1:402, 475.
46. Ibid., 1:495.
47. *Watchword and Truth* 24 (1902) : 327 ff.

Darby described the situation, he was able to destroy their pretensions at prophetic interpretation and convince a good many of them that they were mistaken.

> Their grand array proved to be ignorance, and no more, and the foundations fell. This did every way much good: their whole relative position was altered. Their scraps of Greek and Hebrew I could meet and their calculations of dates for the Lord's coming only baffled them, and the word of God resumed its ascendency. But still it was only some deliverances, and an unfinished work. But a door was opened in Boston, and I was greatly begged to stay: one devoted man, I trust delivered from danger, having just now as I was leaving got a fine room, where he wants me to speak.[48]

In this instance we do know that Darby won a notable convert to the Plymouth Brethren from Millerite adventism. Mr. F. G. Brown, an elder in the Adventist church and, with Joshua V. Himes, a member of the English mission of 1846, was converted to the Brethren at about this time and opened a book and tract depot on Pemberton Square, Boston.[49]

Darby also spent much time combating two heresies which he found particularly prevalent in the Boston area — annihilationism and perfectionism. The doctrine that the wicked soul perishes at death began to gain a considerable following among evangelicals during the 1860s, particularly in the Boston area, if Darby's experience is representative.[50] Many of the adventists accepted this doctrine, thus creating a double challenge for Darby's evangelism. In later years Darby met Wesleyan Methodists rather regularly and became concerned about their doctrine of perfectionism. In 1875 he reported:

> A notion of perfectionism accompanied by a wild looking for the Spirit, is one thing one has to contend with — merely deliverance really, with a taint of Wesleyan perfectionism, but a good deal of pre-

48. *Letters of J. N. D.*, 1:402.
49. Ibid., 1:537; and a newspaper obituary of Brown found in the Sibthorpe manuscripts.

50. For other contemporary reaction, see D. M. Gilbert, "The Annihilation Theory Briefly Examined," *Lutheran Quarterly* 9 (1879): 613–48.

tension, and some good. . . . Yesterday I had the
two principal Wesleyan ministers and chief members, and some others, all the afternoon on deliverance from sin, full acceptance, the Lord's coming.
It was on the whole a satisfactory meeting, one of
the ministers was deeply interested in the truth, and
said he should return, also the chief Baptist
minister.[51]

In this last comment about the chief Baptist minister of Boston Darby has managed, as usual, to be tantalizingly imprecise. One of the chief Baptist ministers in Boston at that time
was Adoniram Judson Gordon, pastor of the Clarendon
Street Baptist Church from 1869 to 1895. He joined with
James Hall Brookes to lead the millenarian movement during
the last quarter of the nineteenth century. But this little hint
is the closest that the historian can come to showing that
Darby had any direct contact with A. J. Gordon.

Darby crossed the Atlantic for the last time in 1877, quite
sure, as he said, that "at my age [seventy-seven], I shall
hardly return to America."[52] In the last letter penned in
North America, Darby summarized for German Brethren his
impressions of his work in the western hemisphere.

I now propose to depart for Europe on Saturday,
God willing, embarking at Quebec, and if God in
His unfailing goodness grant a quiet passage, I
hope to obtain some rest. The position of the brethren is in some slight respects altered. There is an
acknowledgment here in the United States of their
acquaintance with the word such as nowhere else.
They are not the less opposed to us; but they buy
the books, and come in numbers to the Bible readings: they feel they must reckon with us, as they
say. The Presbyterians, the Methodists, the Baptists,
are minded to oppose. The first are unanimous, the
ministers, as everywhere, opposing our work, and
some write about it: the remainder study much
what this (to them) new movement means. The
godly ones are discontented with the sermons, and
some, like Moody, endeavour to help by a strenu-

51. *Letters of J. N. D.*, 2:330.
Darby also strongly opposed the
teachings of Robert Pearsall
Smith, the American perfectionist.
52. Ibid., 2:376.

ous effort of activity. . . . But I let all these movements pass. The truth is spreading; that truth of
the Holy Spirit's presence consequent upon the
Lord being glorified, for that He as Son of man
glorified God on the cross; and the coming of the
Lord. These are the fundamental truths of the
gospel. . . . But we are at the end of days. For
some time the coming of the Lord has wrought in
souls far and wide, and the doctrine is spreading
wonderfully.[53]

Such was Darby's estimate of his sixteen years of labor in
North America. The results, in view of his own intentions,
do not appear impressive.

At about this time there were eighty-eight Brethren meetings in existence, none of them large. The New York City
meeting, for example, counted about fifty members, Philadelphia a few more than twenty and Springfield, Illinois,
hardly ten.[54] Throughout his ministry in the United States,
Darby had been frustrated by his inability to arouse more
dissatisfaction among Americans with their denominations,
and during his last few years in America he lamented like
Jeremiah: "Eminent ministers preach the Lord's coming,
the ruin of the church, liberty of ministry, and avowedly
from brethren's books, and stay where they are, and there
is a general deadening of conscience."[55] Darby never understood the difference that the disestablishment of the church
had made in the United States or how much his own doctrine
of the ruin of the church had been shaped by early nineteenth-
century British social conditions. That Americans showed
little concern about abandoning their denominations remained the greatest puzzle of Darby's American experience.

But Darby did do much to publize his own brand of dispensational theology. Although Darby thought them inconsistent, many American ministers and laymen accepted his

53. Ibid., 2:395.
54. Brethren assemblies were
enumerated in *List of Gatherings
in the United States and Canada,
July, 1878* (Vinton, Iowa, n.d.).
The size of the congregations is
mentioned in W. Taylor to
J. N. Darby, 5 January 1881,
Sibthorpe manuscripts; *Letters
of J. N. D.*, 2:193, 342.
55. Ibid., 2:308.

theology without feeling obligated to join his sect. To determine precisely who these men were and how many of them were convinced by Darby has proved almost impossible. Nothing more than a few hints have rewarded a long search. After Darby left the United States, and even while he was there, others assisted him in the labor of spreading Brethren truth — men such as Robert T. Grant, Frederick W. Grant, George V. Wigram, and a number of American Brethren as well. Furthermore, not all the Plymouth Brethren labored under the burden of Darby's style. Brethren books by F. W. Grant, C. H. Mackintosh, William Kelly, and William Trotter became well known in the United States. But when everything has been said about the imperceptible and silent influence of Brethren teaching, when full account of the energies and skills of all the Brethren teachers and writers has been taken, something still seems to be lacking. We must return to a description of the mainstream of the millenarian movement in order to assess the extent of the impact of Darbyite dispensationalism and to explore the possibilities of other sources for the growing interest that millenarians were showing in the secret rapture and the any-moment coming.

4

The Second Phase of the Millenarian Revival in Britain and the United States 1845–78

WHEN THE FIRST number of the *Quarterly Journal of Prophecy* appeared in 1849, its editor, Horatius Bonar, stated, "The circle of inquirers is widening every day, — interest is rising, prejudices are breaking down, and even the unwilling are compelled to listen. . . . The increase of inquirers, especially in Scotland, during the last five years, is most cheering."[1] The founding of this journal occurred, in part, as a response to the quickening pace of millenarian activity after 1845 and served for the next twenty-five years as a weatherglass for the British millenarian movement. The resurgence of millenarian interest in Britain during the late 1840s coincides, as we have seen, with the collapse of the Millerite movement in the United States and the development of Darby's distinctive dispensational system of futurist interpretation. The happy coincidence of all of these events allows the historian to organize his narrative more easily, but it may reflect, as well, a deeper kind of periodicity within the millenarian movement and the society of Britain and America as a whole.

This period, which witnessed the climax and decline of the historicist school of millenarian interpretation within Britain, was inaugurated by the founding of yet another his-

1. *Quarterly Journal of Prophecy* 1 (1849) : iv.

toricist journal of prophecy — the short-lived *Prophetic Herald and Churchman's Witness for Christ*. The editor, Joseph Baylee, an Anglican, was (like so many other millenarians) educated at Trinity College, Dublin, and in 1845 was acting as principal of the Birkenhead Theological College. During the journal's two-year run many participants in the Albury conferences appeared regularly in the pages of the *Prophetic Herald* — Joseph Wolff, the indefatigable Jewish missionary-evangelist; George Montagu, by then the Duke of Manchester; James Hatley Frere, who seems to have acted as associate editor; and William Cuninghame, who as usual complained that his work was not being properly appreciated.[2]

But if the millenarian movement was to flourish, new men were needed, and, indeed, the historicists could boast some effective leaders who belonged to the second generation of the movement. Thomas Rawson Birks, son-in-law of Edward Bickersteth, published an attack upon futurism in 1843 and continued to write on prophetic subjects even after his appointment as professor of moral philosophy at Cambridge in 1872.[3] Edward Bishop Elliott, though actually a contemporary of many first-generation millenarians, did not become prominent until the publication of his monumental four-volume study of Revelation, *Horae Apocalypticae*, in 1844. Perhaps as a result of writing such a staggering work, Elliott never seemed able to express himself concisely, nor did he possess any measure of tolerance for other commentators' views. Elliott attempted to destroy the futurist position and, in his own interpretation of Revelation, stressed the significance of the year 1866 — until that year had passed. John Cumming followed in Edward Irving's footsteps, moving from Scotland to the National Scottish Church, Crown Court, London, and championing a curious combination of causes. He wrote a column in the *Times* on bee-keeping and advocated an eminently charitable scheme for relieving malnutrition among Irish Roman Catholic children in London, sug-

2. *Prophetic Herald* 1–2 (1845–47) ; see 1:426 for Cuninghame's complaints.

3. *First Elements of Sacred Prophecy* (London, 1843). See also Froom, *Prophetic Faith*, 3:706 ff.

gesting that they be provided a free meat meal every Friday.[4] Like Elliott, Cumming saw great significance in the years culminating in 1867; both authors, in effect, risked the credibility and authority of the millenarian movement on the fulfillment of their predictions for 1866–67. The failure of these historicist prophecies probably more than offset their attacks upon the futurist position.

Further evidence of the increasing prominence of the millenarian movement can be deduced from the antimillenarian literature that was published during this period. During the first phase of the millenarian revival, the public scarcely knew what the millenarians were advocating and the response of the skeptical was generally moderate and random. By 1845 there could be no doubt about the nature of this eschatology or about its vitality. Serious refutations of the millenarian position began to appear. David Brown's *Christ's Second Coming* (1846) seems to have attracted more attention from the millenarians than any of the other attacks. Brown must have understood the millenarian position well, for he had served as Edward Irving's assistant from 1828 to 1830. Horatius Bonar gave Brown, a fellow Scottish Free church minister, a backhanded compliment when he declared, "By the very skill and ability which he has displayed, the author [Brown] has made it manifest to not a few, that, behind the bulwarks of a plain common sense, scriptural hermeneutic, pre-millennialism has nothing to fear."[5] Samuel Waldegrave's 1854 Bampton lectures, *New Testament Millenarianism,* in contrast to Brown's book, were more cheered by the opponents of the millenarians than resented by the millenarians themselves.[6] Yet another Scottish Free church minister, Patrick Fairbairn, took his turn against the millenarian cause in *The Typology of Scripture Viewed in Connection with the Entire Scheme of the Divine Dispensations* (Edinburgh, 1845–47). Works like these tended to polarize

4. *New York Times*, 2 January 1869.

5. *QJP* 2 (1850) : 53.

6. See "Waldegrave's Lectures on New Testament Millenarianism," *Theological and Literary Journal* 9 (1857) : 529–82; and "Waldegrave on Millenarianism," *Biblical Repertory and Princeton Review* 28 (1856) : 524–51.

positions and create parties in the church, but they do not seem to have been effective as countermillenarian propaganda. A commentator in the *Eclectic and Congregational Review* in 1864 complained how melancholy it was to realize that in any omnibus heading home to Clapham of an evening (young stockbrokers on the upper deck and staid merchants inside), many kept a corner in their hearts for prophecy and could not be reasoned with.[7]

Horatius Bonar, editor of the *Quarterly Journal of Prophecy*, had first heard the millenarian message when Edward Irving lectured during Assembly week, 1828, in Edinburgh. During the 1843 schism in the Scottish Presbyterian church, Bonar seceded and eventually became minister of the Chalmers Memorial Church in Edinburgh. For twenty-five years, from 1849 through 1873, he conducted what must, journalistically speaking, be judged the best of the millenarian journals. In the fashion of nineteenth-century religious conventions, the *QJP* carried frequent appeals to Christian standards in controversy and indulged in much hand wringing over unchristlike and uncharitable attacks, each writer certain that he was more sinned against than sinning. And one also finds, as was typical in this kind of literature, a notable lack of engagement in argument, one respondent claiming to have demolished his opponent's position and the other answering that his whole argument had been ignored. During the last few years of its life, the quality of the periodical slipped noticeably. Bonar's own position does not emerge clearly from the pages of his journal, since he regularly allowed space in the paper for points of view with which he disagreed. But in 1849 he was described as a futurist. The correspondent, William Gibbs Barker of Bath, stated that there were a growing number of futurists, like himself and Horatius Bonar, who saw the confusion of competing historicist systems and were "waiting for further light."[8]

7. *Eclectic and Congregational Review* 6 (1864) : 54–69.

8. *QJP* 1 (1849) : 224; this reference must have been correct, for Bonar would not have printed an erroneous statement about himself. For Bonar's life see *Horatius Bonar, D.D., A Memorial* (London, 1889).

References to the Plymouth Brethren and to J. N. Darby in *QJP* are uniformly critical, not to say hostile. An 1853 review of one of Darby's books begins, "When a person undertakes to expound Scripture, it is supposed . . . that he can make himself understood." In 1859 a brief but very strong condemnation of the Brethren appeared in the form of a description of spiritual atrocities committed in Italy by Darby's followers. In 1862 the journal printed such a pointed assault that Darby felt obliged to break his own rule and answer his antagonists.[9] Furthermore, it is clear that Bonar, especially toward the end of his life, treated B. W. Newton respectfully, reviewed his books with approbation, and invited him to contribute notes on the Scripture to *QJP*. It is striking then that Bonar, in his last editorial comment, should come down closer to Darby's than to Newton's view of the second coming. He stated that he could not accept the secret rapture, but continued, "We are not of those who see anything interposed between us and the advent. There *may be* an interval still, but we are not prepared to affirm that there *must be*." [10] When one digs more deeply into the pages of the journal, he finds this paradox amplified.

In the first year of publication, *QJP* was the arena for a controversy between the historicist T. R. Birks, defending Elliott's *Horae Apocalypticae*, and James Kelly, who maintained a Darbyite dispensational position. Kelly, the minister of Charlotte Chapel, Pimlico, argued, exactly as Darby might have, that the prophecies of the Old Testament related to Israel, a history now suspended; that this dispensation forms a parenthesis about which the Hebrew prophets were ignorant; and that the Revelation did not contain a description of any events before the coming of Christ.

> Nations, as such, are not dealt with by God under this dispensation. . . . With the nations of Christendom, indeed, God is now dealing, but not as nations, but as aggregates of individuals.[11]

9. *QJP* 5 (1853) : 93; 11 (1859) : 371–74; 14 (1862) : 52–60. See, as well, *Letters of J. N. D.*, 1 : 335.

10. *QJP* 25 (1873) : 318.
11. *QJP* 1 (1849) : 42–43; see, as well, 1 : 216–22, 248–52.

The struggle between the conflicting positions was also revealed by an article called "The Difficulties of Extreme Futurism," in which Darby's position regarding the Apocalypse was rejected; and another entitled "The Dispensation of the Fulness of Times," which begins by affirming some dispensational distinctions between biblical eras but ends with a forthright denunciation of Darby's parenthesis thesis: "Some seem to be of the opinion, that all pre-millennialism labours under the vicious necessity of putting these Gospel-times within brackets, — of making the present age a mere parenthesis in the world's history."[12]

As was noted in the last chapter, the use of the concept of dispensations was not limited to Darby's disciples; the term should not be used as a shibboleth with which to distinguish Darbyites from other millenarians. The development of these age systems provided a potential foundation for the Darbyite theology (as indeed occurred in Darby's own experience), but did not commit anyone to his doctrine of the secret rapture or his exegesis of the Gospels. The concept of dispensations served as a necessary but not sufficient constituent of his theology. The great interest in dispensations revealed in the pages of the *QJP* cannot, therefore, be taken as evidence for the spread of Darbyite eschatology, but does provide evidence of a disposition on the part of many millenarians to take the first steps in that direction. Throughout 1858 and 1859 a correspondent gave a lengthy report of the meeting of a group called the Prophetical Alliance to the readers of *QJP*. The entire conference was devoted to discussing dispensations in the Scripture. The reporter warned his readers:

> There is a very practical, as well as very consolatory result attached to rightly dividing the Word of Truth; for we thereby get warning or comfort, as we need. . . . Unless we understand the different dispensations, we are in danger of misapplying truth in reference to them.[13]

12. *QJP* 1 (1849): 142–47, 412–24, with the quoted phrase found on p. 420.
13. *QJP* 10 (1858): 47. The Prophetical Alliance may have been an abbreviation for the Society for the Investigation of Prophecy.

During 1866–68 another series of articles on dispensational hermeneutics appeared from the pens of three anonymous authors all insisting upon the same principle: "Distinguish the dispensation and the laws that govern it," and following with their outline of the ages.[14]

Discussion of the distinctive element in Darby's eschatology, the secret rapture, did occur in *QJP* on several occasions. In 1864 the editor published an attack upon the secret rapture listing twenty-two reasons for believing that no such event would occur.[15] But in 1869 John R. Echlin of Lisburn, Ireland, gave a spirited defense of the doctrine. The second advent, Echlin argued, would consist of two parts: "The coming of the Lord to the AIR FOR His people . . . and, secondly, the coming of the Lord to the EARTH WITH His people."[16] In support of his position, Echlin cited the work of John Stevenson, vicar of Patrixbourne, Kent, and, in fact, Echlin had taken the phrase quoted above from Stevenson's book, *The Second Advent*, 2d ed. (London, 1864).

As a result of this survey of the pages of the *QJP*, we can see that historicism, though not unrepresented, did not retain its appeal and was not much represented after the middle sixties. Futurism became dominant, at least in the pages of this journal. Although the Plymouth Brethren and John Nelson Darby were anathematized, the hermeneutical use of the concept of dispensations and some of the critical distinctions of Darbyite theology — the church as a divine parenthesis and the secret rapture — were discussed and advocated.

The *Rainbow*, a minor millenarian periodical of this period, illustrates a variation on the theme discerned in the *QJP*. Edited by an Anglican, the Reverend Dr. William Leask of Islington, the *Rainbow* did not quite match the quality of *QJP*. In the first volume, R. A. Purdon discussed whether human happiness in the millennium did not imply that the weather in that wonderful era would "be very greatly improved."[17] Throughout the early numbers of the *Rainbow*,

14. *QJP* 19 (1867) : 94; 18 (1866) : 94–96, 160–72; 20 (1868) : 22–35.
15. *QJP* 16 (1864) : 54–62.

16. *QJP* 21 (1869) : 404–11.
17. *Rainbow: A Magazine of Christian Literature, with Special Reference to the Revealed*

contributors regularly advocated the Darbyite secret rapture without associating that teaching with the Plymouth Brethren. Most prominent of these was Robert Govett of Norwich, a perpetual controversialist and author of more than twenty books and tracts including *The Saints' Rapture to the Presence of the Lord Jesus* (London, 1864). In his contributions to the *Rainbow*, Govett framed his arguments in favor of the secret rapture as an antithesis to the work of B. W. Newton, but he claimed to be defending his own position and not Darby's. It might also be noted that editor William Leask in 1866, commenting upon a wave of anti-Darbyite books just then appearing, stated that he agreed with Darby's prophetic position and disagreed with Newton's.[18] In the *Rainbow*, then, one finds an eschatology not only reminiscent of but identical to Darby's being supported by an Anglican minister. Whether he, Govett, and the other correspondents of the *Rainbow* first learned these doctrines from Brethren teachers and books seems likely but is unproved.

During the summer of 1867, a three-day prophetic conference was held in London "for Prayer, and for Addresses on the subject of the Lord's Coming." The meeting seems to have been organized by futurists, most of whom had some connection with the Plymouth Brethren. In an address entitled "The Perils of Prophetic Study," a speaker focused upon the problems caused by historicist exegesis:

> We have now reached that stage in prophetic inquiry when we must either go forward or turn back. And I say this from past history, I say it from the

---

Future of the Church and the World 1–24 (London, 1864–87). The reference to the weather is found in 1 (1864) : 550. Purdon also edited his own millenarian periodical called *Last Vials* 1–23 (Torquay, 1846–72).

18. References to the secret rapture are found in the *Rainbow* in 1 (1864) : 88, 177–79, 292–95. Govett left the Anglican church to become pastor of an independent congregation in

Norwich. Grant (*End of All Things*, 1 : 315 ff.) gives Stevenson and Govett the principal credit for publicizing dispensational views. For Govett's views see *Rainbow* 1 (1864) : 257–65, 295–302; and for Leask's see ibid., 3 (1866) : 533–42. Leask became an annihilationist in 1869 and changed the character of his periodical as a result of this conversion.

history of the previous revival of prophetic study in the first quarter of this century. The leading men of that time were mightier men than we; and yet, when it came to the test, will they go forward or backward? . . . I find that that prophetic movement did subside, and persons, because of the difficulties and trials by the way, went back to what they found easier. Satan aimed at the highest of those gifted men; he turned them aside into speculation. We know what was the result, and therefore let us be warned. Let us take care, first of all, of false doctrine; and secondly, of attempting to construct anything of ourselves, for God will overturn, overturn, overturn it, till He comes whose right it is.

The conference continued then to listen to a well-developed presentation of Darby's doctrine of the secret rapture and spiritual church entitled "The Two Peoples."[19]

What, then, was the state of the millenarian movement in Britain by the 1870s? During its second generation the cause had continued to attract able, winning advocates within the evangelical party of the church in England and Scotland. Among dissenters only the Plymouth Brethren gave wholehearted support to the movement. This second phase of the movement had witnessed a great strengthening of the futurist faction at the expense of the older historicist party, and the emergence of Darby's dispensational theology as a distinctive type of futurism. The Brethren's own efforts to spread his eschatology were always connected with other aspects of his thought — his doctrine of the church and his disdain of ordained clergy, particularly. But millenarians who vehemently protested Darby's attacks upon the church, or at least rejected his anti-institutional views, still accepted and taught an eschatology almost indistinguishable from his life. This seems to be an anomalous situation, particularly in view of

19. The proceedings of this conference were published but have not been located in any library. The conference was reported in the *Prophetic Times*, however (5 [1867]: 74–77; the quote is on p. 74). The leaders of the conference were H. H. Snell, H. W. Soltau, J. L. Harris, Robert Howard, the Honorable W. Wellesley, Sir John Bell, and Granville Waldegrave, the third Baron Radstock.

the violent reaction against virtually everything Darby stood for. The emotional level found in the literature attacking the Brethren would be difficult to match in any age, though, it must be admitted, much of it was written by disenchanted or excommunicated Darbyite disciples. Yet the particular set of millenarian doctrines enunciated by Darby escaped this censure. The eschatological sections of Darby's theology seemed to exist as free elements in the religious atmosphere and were welcomed or banished according to criteria of verification that took no notice of the putative source. For whatever reason, the association of Darby with dispensationalism was not sufficient to destroy its attractiveness for non-Plymouth Brethren.

This line of reasoning raises a further question. Is it possible that one explanation for the disproportionate influence of this one aspect of Darby's theology upon other millenarians is that Darby was not alone in developing it? Is it possible that the doctrines of the secret rapture and parenthesis church were being taught simultaneously by several or even many prophetic students? If more were known about early nineteenth-century Irish Protestantism and, particularly, the intellectual history of Trinity College, Dublin, a clearer light might be thrown upon these puzzling and difficult points.

THE AMERICAN millenarian movement passed through a similar development in the second period, 1845–78: a resurgence of historicism followed by awakening interest in futurism and, among some, the adoption of Darbyite dispensationalism. The first sign of millenarian vitality after the failure of the second advent on 22 October 1844 was the founding of the *Theological and Literary Journal* in 1848 by David Nevins Lord. Lord's father, Nathan, was a Connecticut Congregationalist minister and was president of Dartmouth College from 1828 to 1863, and David Lord had hoped to enter the ministry himself until prevented by ill health. Instead, he spent his life in New York City as a dry goods importer and edited his journal as an expression of his true vocation. He was assisted by his brother Eleazar, who had also failed to fulfill his youthful ambition for the ministry and had become, instead, the first president of the Erie Railroad, and by Joel Jones, another son of Connecticut who during his eminent career was lawyer, judge, president of Girard College, and mayor of Philadelphia. Jones contributed a regular column of notes on Scripture to the *Theological and Literary Journal.* Lord's journal upheld a standard historicist position, though Lord was critical of almost every historicist commentator so far discussed in this book. Lord initiated his publication in an effort, he told his readers, to introduce some order into the interpretation of prophecy which he described as "wrenched by a thousand experimenters on the wheel of conjecture." As a result, Lord did not open the pages of his paper to conflict of opinion, but neither did he succeed in impressing his own interpretations upon many of his fellow millenarians.[20]

The *Christian Intelligencer*, the weekly newspaper of the Dutch Reformed church, was never intended to serve as an organ of the millenarian movement; but during the 1860s millenarianism became a cause of contention within the denomination and the *Intelligencer* became the arena of combat. As a preface to the controversy, two Reformed ministers had published tracts on opposite sides of the question. Robert Kirkwood published his *Lectures on the Millennium* — lectures first delivered at the Dutch Reformed Church of Yonkers, New York, in 1855.[21] Quite in contrast to the usual omniscient millenarian style, Kirkwood introduced his comments with the admission that he had been confused about the interpretation of prophecy, had read everything he could get his hands on, and had finally become a convinced millenarian. The answering salvo came from the Reverend Joseph F. Berg of Philadelphia. In *The Second Advent of Jesus Christ, Not Premillennial* (Philadelphia, 1859), Berg, on the eve of the Civil War, proved to be as optimistic about the future of the kingdom of God in America as were Alexander Camp-

---

20. *Theological and Literary Journal* 1–12 (New York, 1848–61). The quote is in 1 (1848) : 9.

See the *DAB* for biographical information.

21. They were published in New York, 1856.

bell and Samuel H. Cox in the 1840s. The discussion moved
to the pages of the *Intelligencer* in November 1863, when
John Terhune Demarest read an essay on the premillennial
advent to his ministerial association and was then urged to
submit his remarks for publication.[22] Within a few weeks
a paper war commenced. The Reverend William Fulton attacked Demarest's position for its overly literal scriptural
exegesis and denigration of the power of the Gospel. This
last point, one of the most common raised against the millenarians, was based upon the argument that the Gospel
must be considered a failure if the world ended in wickedness
and rejection of Christ, as the millenarians contended, rather
than in the conversion of all peoples to Christianity. Before
the end of December the Reverend W. R. Gordon had joined
the battle in defense of the millenarian cause in general and
Demarest in particular, though his own share in the controversy soon surpassed everyone's. In editorial comment in
the last issue of 1863, Elbert S. Porter, the editor, offered
to continue printing contributions to the debate but stated that
he could not undertake to publish anything like the "mass
of manuscripts" which "a score or more" correspondents
had poured into his office. Porter must have decided to limit
himself to the three contributors already engaged, for no
new names appeared during the next year. Twenty-eight articles appeared during 1864 and January 1865, in which
Gordon and Demarest attempted to show that their millenarian position was supported both by Scripture and by the
early church fathers and accused Fulton of defending a doctrinal novelty. Fulton, aided on a few occasions by Porter,
accused the millenarians of violating their ministerial oaths
and of teaching doctrines contrary to the creedal standards
of the Dutch Reformed church, but by the end of March he
seems to have lost his taste for combat and retired from the
struggle, leaving the field to the millenarians for the remainder of 1864. Eventually Gordon and Demarest published

22. *Christian Intelligencer,*
19 November and 17 December
1863. Demarest was for most of
his life pastor of a Reformed
church in Ulster County, New
York; Berg was a professor at
the New Brunswick Seminary.

their group of essays, somewhat supplemented, under the peculiar title, *Christocracy* (New York, 1867). Their millenarianism reflected the standard historicist stance without any hint of Darbyite influence. In reviewing the book for the *Intelligencer*, Porter observed that very few Dutch Reformed ministers had accepted the millenarian position.

The *Christian Intelligencer* debate attracted considerable comment in the millenarian press, where it was treated as an encounter of some note.[23] The controversy serves as an example of the manner in which the millenarian cause in the United States grew within the denominations and also helps to illustrate the degree to which millenarian interest and activity had increased during the 1850s and 1860s in contrast to the nadir reached with the disappointment of Miller's followers in 1844. The list of books and articles threatens to become tediously long. William Ramsey, Richard C. Shimeall, and Isaac P. Labagh, who wrote during the first phase of the movement, remained active. Jacob J. Janeway, professor of theology at (Presbyterian) Western Seminary, published a millenarian treatise on the restoration of the Jews, and Joseph L. Lord wrote *Briefs on Prophetic Themes* (Boston, 1864) in which he acknowledged the influence of B. W. Newton.[24] Presbyterian theological journals attempted to alert the denomination's ministers to the nature of the millenarian threat and to educate them concerning the history of eschatology. Similar concern was evident among Lutheran and Episcopalian journals. A Moravian bishop warned the Reverend E. E. Reinke to cease preaching the premillennial advent or face censure.[25]

23. See the first two articles of *QJP* 17 (1865), which were reprinted from the *Christian Intelligencer*; G. S. Bishop, "The Question of the Second Advent," *Waymarks in the Wilderness* 9 (1871):73–96; and W. R. Gordon, "The Hope of the Church," *Prophetic Times* 10 (1872):169 ff.

24. William Ramsey, *Messiah's Reign* (Philadelphia, 1857); R. C. Shimeall, *Christ's Second Coming: Is It Pre-millennial or Post-millennial? (The Great Question of the Day)* (New York, 1865); Isaac P. Labagh, *Twelve Lectures on the Great Events of Unfulfilled Prophecy* (New York, 1859); J. J. Janeway, *Hope for the Jews* (New Brunswick, 1853).

25. "The Fulfillment of Prophecy," *The Princeton Review* 23 (January 1861); "History of

Beginning in 1863 the American millenarian cause found new focus and scope of expression within the pages of the *Prophetic Times*, a monthly periodical which remains the best source of information about the development of millenarianism in this period.[26] During the years of their common publication, the *Prophetic Times* and the *Quarterly Journal of Prophecy* played similar roles of leadership in the United States and Britain. On the title page of the first number the *Prophetic Times* was described as "A New Serial devoted to the exposition and inculcation of the doctrine of the speedy coming and reign of the Lord Jesus Christ, and related subjects," and the editors listed as the Reverend Drs. Seiss, Newton, Duffield, and others. The complete roll of editors indicates to some extent the denominational penetration of millenarianism.

Joseph A. Seiss	Philadelphia, Pennsylvania	Lutheran
Richard Newton	Philadelphia, Pennsylvania	Episcopal
George Duffield	Detroit, Michigan	Presbyterian (New School)
John Forsyth	Newburg, New York	Dutch Reformed
E. E. Reinke	Olney, Illinois	Moravian
Robert Adair	Philadelphia, Pennsylvania	Presbyterian (New School)
William Newton	Gambier, Ohio	Episcopal
C. Colgrove	Sardinia, New York	Baptist
L. C. Baker	Camden, New Jersey	Presbyterian (Old School)
B. B. Leacock	Harrisburg, Pennsylvania	Episcopal

Opinions Respecting the Millennium," *American Theological Review* 1 (1859) : 655 ff.; *Presbyterian Quarterly Review* 1 (1853) : 529–48; 2 (1853) : 19–40; J. A. Brown, "The Second Advent and the Creeds of Christendom," *Bibliotheca Sacra* 24 (1867) : 629–51; *Evangelical Quarterly Review* 12 (1860–61) : 242–55, 341–401; J. I. T. Coolidge, "Looking for the Advent," *Church Monthly* 3 (1862) : 2–3. For the warning to Reinke, see *Prophetic Times* 1 (1863) : 4–7.

26. *Prophetic Times* 1–12 (Philadelphia, 1863–74) ; new series, 1–4 (1875–78) ; and third series, 1–3 (1879–81).

| Samuel Laird | Lancaster, Pennsylvania | Lutheran |

In spite of this impressive list, the burden of the editorial work fell upon Joseph A. Seiss, one of the most remarkable figures in the history of American Lutheranism. The millenarian cause often absorbed most of the energy of its advocates, but Seiss seemed capable of remarkable breadth and capacity. In addition to his work as editor of the *Prophetic Times*, he wrote dozens of books — at least seven on millenarian subjects — ministered to a Philadelphia congregation described as the largest English Lutheran church in America, served from 1867 to 1879 as editor of the *Lutheran*, and was president of the board of the Philadelphia Lutheran Theological Seminary from 1865 until his death in 1902.[27] In the first number of the *Prophetic Times* the editors published their creed: "We believe," they stated:

1. That we are living in the last periods of the present dispensation.
2. That Christ will soon reappear upon earth, to avenge His elect, and fulfill His covenant to them.
3. That the expectation of a Millennium of universal righteousness and peace before the return of the Saviour, is an unchristian delusion.
4. That the Church will remain under the cross until Christ comes; and that the present dispensation is only preparatory to another.
5. That the personal return of the Lord Jesus is the great hope of the Church, to which, and not to the triumph of present institutions, we are to look for the fulfilment of the great promises of the world's ultimate blessedness.
6. That when Christ comes, it will not be to depopulate, annihilate, or destroy the earth, but to renovate it by judicial administrations, and to bless it with a new and heavenly rule.
7. That the saints shall rise first, and together with such of the living as shall be accounted worthy of such honor,

27. *DAB.* It is possible that he lost some of his millenarian fervor in the last decades of his life.

be received up in the glorified state, to share with Christ in His subsequent dealings with our world, and its inhabitants.

8. That Christ is to reign in glorious empire over all the earth, sending forth His law from Jerusalem; an earnest of the glory of which was furnished on the Mount of Transfiguration.

9. That great judgments are pending over Christendom, and that all present systems in Church and State shall be revolutionized by them, if not quite destroyed.

10. That in the new order of things to come, the house of Israel, or Jewish race, shall again occupy their own land, and hold the first place among the nations, under their proper King, the Son of David, forever.

11. That the earth, and the heavens enveloping it, are to be renovated by Him who is to have the dominion; and that the heavens and earth which are now, shall be made into new heavens and earth, as the natural man by regeneration is made into the new man.

12. That only those who are properly awake to these truths, and watchful, and waiting, and looking for the Lord's speedy return, and prepare accordingly, shall escape the dreadful tribulations which are to mark the last years of this dispensation, or secure the high and peculiar honors in reservation for the wise and faithful.[28]

A good deal about the eschatology of the editors can be learned from this creedal statement, but much remains obscure in spite of it. In the first article there occurs one of those casual uses of the term dispensation that tells one nothing — the operative words in that article are "last periods." Articles 3 and 5 distinguish nicely between the millenarian and the millennial cause. The sixth is aimed at excluding Millerite adventists. But whether the periodical is going to support historicist or futurist millenarianism is nowhere stated. However, there is quite a hint that the *Prophetic Times* will advocate the secret, any-moment rapture of the

28. *Prophetic Times* 1 (1863) : 13–14.

church, the critical element in Darby's eschatology. Article 9 is not explicit, but does sound something like Darby, though this may be mostly caused by the use of the word "systems" in that context. However, the twelfth article clearly intimates the doctrine of the secret rapture.

The general tone of the *Prophetic Times* was mature, the editing was competent, the articles were restrained and conservative. The British millenarian periodicals, the *Quarterly Journal of Prophecy*, the *Rainbow*, and the *Last Vials* were frequently cited and often quoted, as were well-known millenarians such as John Cumming, Edward Bickersteth, and Henry Dana Ward. Whether or not the Civil War had any role in the founding of the *Prophetic Times* was not made clear by the editors, but the war was mentioned in its columns. One correspondent inquired, "What is going to become of us as a nation?" The war had begun with expectations of quick victory for the North, but these hopes had given way to despair. "We have been long expecting and predicting that the rotten and tottering dynasties of the Old World would fall," but not "our government, so free, so just, so liberal, so enlighted, so Christian." Now, in 1863, he continued, the permanent separation of North and South seemed likely and anarchy or military rule in the North itself appeared possible. If this happened, what could "reconcile us so well to such calamities, as the belief that Christ is coming to set up his long-prayed-for kingdom upon earth."[29]

But although the Civil War might push some despairing believers into the millenarian camp, the events of that domestic tragedy did not elicit a fraction of the interest lavished upon Napoleon III. The mystique of the Napoleonic legend so clouded millenarian eyes that many of them were convinced that he was destined for more than mere mortality; he was usually picked out for the greater role of the Antichrist. Whatever difficulties the emperor fell into, the millenarian press was prompt to excuse him — one writer, on the eve of Napoleon's fall, penned the ultimate compliment to boundless faith: "He has acted for years with that con-

29. Ibid., 1 (1863): 22.

summate prudence which superficial men have mistaken for imbecility."[30] No one did more to spread the Napoleonic legend than Michael P. Baxter, the peripatetic sensationalist who first appeared in millenarian periodicals as a Church of England missionary in Onondaga, Canada. During 1859–60 he toured North America delivering lectures in Montreal, Boston, Philadelphia, Baltimore, Washington, and other United States cities, which he ultimately published as *The Coming Battle, and the Appalling National Convulsions Foreshown in Prophecy Immediately to Occur during the Period 1861–67* . . . (London, 1860). In unlikely combination, Baxter managed to combine a historicist millenarian position with advocacy of the secret rapture. As the period of crisis moved on toward culmination, Baxter published a book entitled *Louis Napoleon, the Destined Monarch of the World and Personal Antichrist* (Philadelphia, 1866) and founded a periodical of his own (in 1867 in London) called *Signs of Our Times*. When the Franco-Prussian war broke out, he confidently predicted victory for the French. The sudden and simultaneous collapse of the French empire and of their prophetic hopes at the battle of Sedan sobered the editors of the *Prophetic Times* greatly and would appear to have caused them to move away from historicism — indeed, this was the general result of the disappointments of the years 1867 to 1870, as has been noted previously. But Baxter was a true believer: he is found writing in *Signs of Our Times*, "The man who walks at Torquay will one day . . . ."[31]

As we noted in discussing the creedal statement of the *Prophetic Times*, the editors hinted but did not make clear whether or not they would support the doctrine of the secret rapture of the church. This position seems to have confused readers as well, for a correspondent wrote in 1866 that he could find no difficulty with "your excellent monthly but this one point, the silent stealing away of the righteous at

30. Ibid., 7 (1869) : 23.
31. *Signs of the Times* 1 October 1871. Baxter wrote his own biography under the pseudonym Nathaniel Wiseman (*Michael Paget Baxter* [London, 1923]).

the end of this dispensation." The editor then proceeded
to explain and defend the Darbyite doctrine of the secret
coming; he concluded:

> We thus find nothing in the references of our cor-
> respondent to interpose the slightest difficulty to the
> doctrine of a coming of Christ to steal away His
> saints from their graves and from their compan-
> ions. . . . Harmony throughout is what we seek,
> and harmony throughout really exists, but upon no
> theory except that which presents Christ as coming
> first invisibly *for* His saints, before He is openly re-
> vealed *with* His saints in the destruction of Anti-
> christ and his hosts.[32]

This was not a passing fad in exegesis on the part of the
editors, and many other articles supporting this doctrine and
its implications appeared in subsequent issues — especially
in 1871 under the initials of the Reverend E. E. Reinke, the
Moravian from Illinois, and in 1875 in an article with
J. A. Seiss's byline. Furthermore, a long series devoted to
"Israel and the Church" appeared in 1869 in which Darby's
distinctive definitions informed the whole discussion.[33] Is
this evidence of the spread of Plymouth Brethren theology
among American millenarians? Again, the answer is am-
biguous. The ideas are present, unmistakably, but no source
for those ideas is offered save the Scripture, and no discussion of Plymouth Brethren theology as such can be found.
However, in our next source we find, at last, a clear-cut
statement of the problem.

Waymarks in the Wilderness never occupied or pretended
to occupy a place among millenarians like the *Prophetic
Times* or the *Quarterly Journal of Prophecy.* A wandering
periodical of limited circulation, it boasted no impressive
editorial board or wide denominational representation. Ironically, this minor journal provides great insight into the nature of millenarianism during this period and throws much

32. *Prophetic Times* 4
(1866) : 174–75.
33. Ibid., 9 (1871) : 59 ff.;
second series, 1 (1875) : 52 ff.;
and 7 (1869) : 1 ff., 17 ff., 33 ff.,
49 ff., 65 ff., and 81 ff.

light on a significant transition in its history. Looking back
from the end of the nineteenth century, several prominent
millenarians stated that the editor of *Waymarks in the Wilderness*, James Inglis, was the creative spirit behind the rise
of the prophetic conference movement in which they had
spent their lives.[34] Born in Scotland in 1813, Inglis had emigrated to Michigan in 1848. After being converted by a
Scottish Baptist minister at Adrian, Michigan, he began
training for the ministry himself and became pastor of the
First Baptist Church of Detroit. While in Detroit, in May
1854, he first published *Waymarks* with the help of his
brother, David Inglis of Montreal, and James Hogg of Hamilton. He then moved, first to Saint Louis and then to New
York, where in 1864 he refounded the journal and continued
it until his death in 1872.[35] Inglis taught an eschatology
which is unmistakably and consistently Darbyite dispensational, though some contributors who did not agree with
this point of view were also represented. Although Plymouth
Brethren writers seldom appeared as contributors to the
journal, the works of Brethren and former Brethren were
continually reviewed and referred to — Darby, William
Kelly, Andrew Jukes, J. G. Bellett, B. W. Newton, and Samuel
P. Tregelles, for example.[36] This influence was so obvious, apparently, that *Waymarks* was attacked in another periodical
(in the course of some general review of the pernicious influence of the Brethren upon the American churches, it may
be assumed) as an agent of Darbyite theology. Inglis felt
obliged to defend himself. Referring to the Plymouth Brethren he wrote:

34. G. C. Needham said this in
Watchword 13 (1891) : 59, and
Robert Cameron in *Watchword
and Truth* 24 (1902) : 136.

35. *Waymarks in the Wilderness* 1–2 (Detroit and Saint Louis,
1854–57) ; and 1–10 (New York,
1864–72). He also published
a magazine called the *Witness*.

Biographical information is
contained in his obituaries
(*Waymarks in the Wilderness* 10
(1872) : 197 ff., 297 ff. David
Inglis was professor of theology
at Knox College, Toronto.

36. Ibid., 9 (1871) : 73–96; 2
(1865) : 41 ff.; 4 (1867) : 267 ff.

No one connected with that sect ever wrote a line for its [*Waymarks'*] pages. Our contributors are chiefly "pastors of our Reformed Churches," most of them well known, though they do not claim the consideration for what they write on ecclesiastical grounds. So far from being "the doctrinal representative of the Plymouth Brethren," while we gratefully own our indebtedness to them under God for the testimony they have borne to our standing in Christ and the hope of our calling, we have been constrained to testify against nearly everything in their theology which distinguishes them from the other men of God named in the review which occasions this statement.[37]

This defense clarifies a great deal. Inglis, and the millenarians he represented, were well acquainted with the works of Darby and the others connected with the Plymouth Brethren. But they had rejected their distinctive beliefs, presumably the sectarian and separatist elements of Darby's teachings which would have required the Americans to sever their denominational associations had they been convinced by him. Inglis, in other words, was testifying to the truth of Darby's continual lament that the Americans took what they wanted from his theological bag but refused to forsake their positions within the denominations. What the Americans appreciated in Darbyism is equally clear — his doctrine of grace ("our standing in Christ") and his doctrine of the secret rapture ("the hope of our calling"). We know that Inglis strenuously opposed the growth of perfectionist teaching in the American churches (even as Darby did), and it is perfectly evident in the pages of *Waymarks* that he taught the any-moment secret rapture.[38] What may be even more revealing is the fact that Inglis, when charged with purveying a doctrinal system associated with the Plymouth Brethren, did not deny that some of his theology did, in fact, have its source with Darby and his followers. Although it cannot be proved

37. Ibid., 10 (1872) : 187. One Canadian Plymouth brother, W. C. Baynes, did write for *Waymarks*, but Inglis may have been unaware of his denominational affiliation.

38. On perfectionism see, for example, ibid., 7 (1869) : 352 ff.

that Darby's eschatology did not have earlier and different advocates from whom it might possibly have been learned by British millenarians, there is no evidence of another possible source for American advocates of the Darbyite eschatology. Although not willing to admit their affiliation with his denominational views, Americans raided Darby's treasuries and carried off his teachings as their own.

 **5**

Biblical Literalism:
Millenarianism and
the Princeton Theology

A FIRM TRUST and belief in every word of the Bible in an age when skepticism was the rule and not the exception — this has been both the pride and the scandal of Fundamentalism. Faith in an inerrant Bible as much as an expectation of the second advent of Christ has been the hallmark of the Fundamentalist. In the preceding chapters we have often noted the reverence and honor in which the millenarians held the text of Scripture and the literalistic method of interpretation which they consistently utilized, but we have not yet discussed this aspect of their thought in the context of the nineteenth-century crisis over biblical authority.

The history of modern Western civilization has been a history of secularization. Since the Reformation and the rise of science, the external supports of the Christian faith have gradually fallen away. Legal compulsion first disappeared, toleration gradually gaining ground until the United States achieved complete religious freedom and the British, with the exception of Roman Catholics, enjoyed virtually the same liberty. During the seventeenth and eighteenth centuries the power and prestige of the clergy declined drastically; where they performed religious duties they often faced competition from a dissenting minister or could be ignored; and where they still possessed legal powers — as in the conduct of parish and vestry business — they acted as agents of the state and exercised small spiritual authority. In the United States even these limited legal powers were eliminated by the nineteenth century. Behind these institutional changes lay an intellectual revolution characterized by empirical methods and mechanical models which left little room for revelation. As scientific experimentation began to produce results of intellectual and economic significance, fears of the unknown and hope for eternity gave way to a new philosophy of human progress. Christianity survived, but few of the traditional bulwarks of Christian faith remained. The church was too divided in doctrine and too shrunken in power to enforce its own teachings. The United States constitution had stipulated that Congress "make no law respecting an establishment of religion, or prohibiting the free exercise thereof." According to Newtonian physics, God might well have taken leave of the world, and philosophers such as Hume had established that he had, so far as rational demonstration of his existence was concerned.

Thus by the eighteenth century Christian faith no longer served as the necessary and inescapable cosmology of Western man, and the Christian who hoped to remain faithful to the church found his faith more weakened than supported by contemporary social and intellectual forces. As a Protestant he based his beliefs increasingly on revelation and miracle, in an age which doubted the value if not the possibility of both. The Bible, the embodiment of revelation and the epitome of miracle, was not immune from attack. For many, empirical investigation and reason provided surer grounds of knowledge than revelation, and much of the Bible's loss of influence occurred because of the rise of science and not because of direct assaults upon the credibility of Scripture. But the attacks did come. They were often, like those of Voltaire, satiric and diffuse, in which case they were painful but seldom fatal to believers. Most devout Christians were warned away and would never have dreamed of reading such literature. The other type of attack — that of Tom Paine, for example — now seems like a kind of primitive biblical criticism, often intentionally defamatory and frequently misconceived. But though the skeptics may have been wrong in suggesting, for example, that the disciples were illiterate or that Jesus never lived at all, their doubts were more deeply grounded and more widely representative than churchmen were willing to acknowledge. The critics deserved better treatment than they received.

The church's answer to this onslaught was provided through a voluminous body of writing on Christian evidences, all aimed at demonstrating that the Bible was a trustworthy record of the workings of God among men.[1] The youthful experience of Archibald Alexander, the first professor of Princeton Seminary, illustrates the role played by this body of apologetic literature. Tutoring away from home, he had begun to fall prey to doubts about the truth of Christianity when a book accidentally fell into his hands.

> On looking at the title-page, I observed the word "Evidences," and it struck me immediately that it was possibly something in favour of Christianity. On further inspection, I saw that I was not mistaken, for the whole title was "Internal Evidences of the Christian Religion, by Soame Jenyns, Esq." I was rejoiced; and as all the family had gone to church, I sat down and began to read. At every step conviction flashed across my mind, with such bright and overwhelming evidence, that when I ceased to read, the room had the appearance of being illuminated.[2]

In harness with this kind of defense of the Bible the eighteenth-century apologists placed stout denunciations of French thought and Jacobinism. Jefferson and Tom Paine, for example, were pictured as unethical if not diabolical men whose nefarious intentions deprived them of anything but contempt and condemnation. In the hands of controversialists such as Timothy Dwight, these attacks degenerated into character assassination.

By the early nineteenth century the Protestant churchmen of Britain and the United States had been forced into the position of assuming that the Bible was the main bulwark of

---

1. Frederic Relton and John H. Overton, *The English Church from the Accession of George I to the End of the Eighteenth Century* (London, 1906). The most popular of these works was William Paley, *Evidences of Christianity* (1794).

2. James W. Alexander, *The Life of Archibald Alexander* (New York, 1857), p. 43.

Christianity and that criticism of the Bible should be treated as the equivalent of blasphemy and infidelity. This was not a promising heritage for a century that was to witness a serious theological debate concerning the nature of biblical authority. Most twentieth-century Fundamentalists and many twentieth-century historians have mistakenly assumed that Protestantism possessed a strong, fully integrated theology of biblical authority which was attacked by advocates of the higher criticism. As we shall see, no such theology existed before 1850. What did exist was a great deal of popular reverence for the Bible, the eighteenth-century literature defending the authenticity of the Scriptures and providing "evidences" of their supernatural origin — all of which was beside the point — and an apologetic stance which had conditioned defenders of the faith to respond to any challenge to the Bible with the cry "heresy." A systematic theology of biblical authority which defended the common evangelical faith in the infallibility of the Bible had to be created in the midst of the nineteenth-century controversy. The formation of this theology in association with the growth of the millenarian movement determined the character of Fundamentalism.

The future of Christianity did not hang on the infallibility of the Scriptures, as many nineteenth-century Christians believed and as most twentieth-century Fundamentalists affirm. In the Oxford movement, Newman and Keble developed a doctrine of the church that was designed to provide escape from the biblicist dilemma, and liberal theology supplied another solution. Since all Evangelicals insisted that conversion was prerequisite to Christian faith, that only those who had passed through the experience of the "new birth" could consider themselves Christians, there is reason to doubt whether the Bible functioned as the foundation of religion even for these believers. The Protestant church, as a whole, though severely troubled by the debate over biblical authority and the discoveries of biblical critics, managed to reconcile itself to a new view of the Bible while maintaining a vigorous outreach. The lives of Harry Emerson Fosdick and William Newton Clarke, for instance, perfectly illustrate this process of accommodation.[3] A minority of Evangelicals rushed to the defense of the Bible convinced that their faith could not stand if the infallibility of the Bible was undermined. George S. Bishop expressed the point vividly:

> Verbal and direct inspiration is, therefore, the "Thermopylae" of Biblical and Scriptural faith. . . . No book, no religion.[4]

When many others carried on, supported by their personal experience or faith in the church, why did some Christians demand an inerrant Bible? This is the central question of Fundamentalist historiography. The understanding of millenarian hermeneutics — the manner in which the millenarians interpreted the Bible — and the theology of biblical authority developed at Princeton Seminary in the nineteenth century can help to answer this question.

An American commentator in 1853, after having analyzed the millenarians quite perceptively, summarized their views on biblical interpretation:

> Millenarianism has grown out of a new "school of Scripture interpretation;" and its laws of interpretation are so different from the old, that the Bible may almost be said to wear a new visage and speak with a new tongue — a tongue not very intelligible, in many of its utterances, to the uninitiated. The central law of interpretation by which millenarians profess always to be guided, is that of giving the literal sense.[5]

James Grant, another Scottish contribution to the nineteenth-century London scene, wrote a series of three critiques of the millenarians in which he too commented upon millenarian literalism. "A literal interpretation is, indeed," he wrote, "the basis on which the Millennial edifice chiefly rests."

> Nor do Millenarians hesitate to make an admission of the fact. On the contrary, they are forward to

3. H. E. Fosdick, *The Living of These Days* (New York, 1956), and W. N. Clarke, *Sixty Years with the Bible* (New York, 1912).
4. G. S. Bishop, "The Testimony of the Scriptures to Themselves," in *The Fundamentals* (Chicago, 1910–15), 7:39.
5. *Princeton Review* 25 (1853) : 68.

confess that, if they cannot prove that we are bound, in connection with the question of Christ's second coming to the earth, to accept a literal rendering of the Word of God, they are not in a position to make out a case for their faith in the personal reign of our Lord.[6]

The millenarians were most zealous in defense of this position — zealous to the point of intolerance and uncharitableness, Grant stated. In conversation with an eminent and gentle Christian lady Grant had challenged the soundness of her literal interpretation of a biblical passage and found himself asked, "What! Do you refuse to believe God himself when he speaks in his Word?" Grant commented, "That, let me here observe, is not the right way in which to put the case."[7]

Although Grant was unimpressed by this approach, millenarians won a great many nineteenth-century converts by forcing this alternative upon their opponents. Allegory has provided both crutch and sword to many a theologian. Figurative exegesis has been utilized to bolster a theological point of view which literal interpretation would not support, and it has also aided the commentator in interpreting passages he could not understand literally — either because his historical understanding of the Bible was inadequate or because his cultural or philosophical position prevented him from grasping the meaning of the passage. It was possible to utilize this type of interpretation, however, only so long as believers were willing to accept allegory as the equivalent of history, spiritual truth as the equivalent of literal. By the late eighteenth century the scientific revolution had begun to weight the balance in favor of fact, even within the church. The millenarians of the early nineteenth century won converts to their cause simply by showing that their position was based upon a literal exegesis and their opponents' upon a figurative.[8] In argument the millenarian possessed considerable tactical advantage in showing that he accepted the literal sense of the Bible whereas his opponent did not. In an 1828 tract entitled

6. Grant, *End of All Things*, 1:199.
7. Ibid., 1:200.

8. See, for example, Birks, *Memoir of Edward Bickersteth*, 2:45–46.

A Defense of the Students of Prophecy, Henry Drummond, the millenarian who convened the Albury prophetic conferences, made this kind of attack upon the Reverend William Hamilton, and must have made the Scottish theologian very uncomfortable. "You will give him [Christ] no credit for ability to accomplish his promise," Drummond charged, "unless, in your judgment also, it shall seem feasible."[9]

But did the millenarians consistently affirm that every passage of Scripture must be interpreted literally? Some millenarian expositors attempted this feat, but with results more ludicrous than credible. Isaac P. Labagh, editor of the *American Millenarian*, struggled with the problem in connection with Revelation 20, "And I saw an angel come down from heaven, having the key of the bottomless pit and a great chain in his hand."

> Those who are opposed to the literal interpretation of Scripture amuse themselves, as they think, at the expense of those who advocate the literal interpretation by asking, with a jeer, what kind of a chain was this, — brass or iron? and what kind of a key, — steel or copper? and what kind of a pit is a bottomless pit? and where can such a thing be found?

Defiantly declaring that if God had affirmed the existence of a chain with which to bind Satan he would believe that it existed, Labagh plunged into the problem of the bottomless pit. The center of the earth has neither top nor bottom, since it is constantly revolving. If Satan were thrown into the center of the earth, Labagh triumphantly concluded, he would indeed be confined within "a vast abyss! a bottomless pit!"[10] But most millenarians, to their great credit, refused to follow their literalistic interpretation to quite such extremes. In fact, spiritualizing and allegorizing of some parts of the Old Testament was consistently practiced by most millenarians.[11] Critics

9. Henry Drummond, *Defense of the Students of Prophecy* (London, 1828), p. 30.
10. Quoted in Grant, *End of All Things*, 1:278–81.

11. None of them, for instance, interpreted the Song of Solomon literally, or failed to find references to Christ in the Psalms.

like James Grant concluded that the millenarians simply applied the literalistic interpretation whenever it suited their fancy.

> This, we repeat, is unreasonable. It is asking more than they have a right to claim. Were we to acquiesce in their claim to this capricious mode of construing the Scriptures, they could of course make out a case for Millenarianism, or for almost anything else.[12]

What was needed was an exegetical method that could distinguish between the literal and figurative passages of Scripture. But one looks in vain for this kind of methodological discussion. Instead, one finds this kind of statement:

> The *Literalist* (so called) is not one who denies that figurative language, that *symbols*, are used in prophecy, nor does he deny that great *spiritual* truths are set forth therein; his position is, simply, that the prophecies are to be *normally* interpreted (i.e., according to the received laws of language) as any other utterances are interpreted — that which is manifestly literal being regarded as literal, that which is manifestly figurative being so regarded.[13]

The author seems to assume that no method for distinguishing between literal and figurative passages need be constructed. In fact, the word "manifestly" operates as an excuse for method. Unfortunately, this simple dependence upon common-sense criteria was characteristic of the whole millenarian movement. There is no evidence that the literalistic interpretation followed by the millenarians was grounded in any new understanding of the biblical text. Their new-found zeal for the literal sense was dictated more by the apparent success of some commentators in matching prophetic and historic events, and by the popular belief that factual, empirical, and literal statements were more true than spiritual, allegorical,

12. Grant, *End of All Things*, 1:202.
13. Elijah R. Craven added this editorial note to the American edition of J. P. Lange's commentary on Revelation (*Commentary on the Holy Scripture* [New York, 1874], 25:98).

and figurative, than by any new grasp of the intention of the biblical authors. In fact, this was the greatest weakness of the millenarians — they had inherited such a view of the nature of biblical inspiration that they were incapable of asking questions about the intention of the author or the character of his literary mode. This is not to say that the millenarians behaved hypocritically about the Bible. They were serious students of the text of the Scripture. It is no accident that some of the finest textual criticism of the nineteenth century was produced by such millenarians as Samuel P. Tregelles. But the millenarians assumed that divine inspiration had so controlled the writing of the Bible that the resultant text was free of error or fallibility and that this freedom guaranteed them a divine, not a human, source of truth — an immediate and not a mediated revelation. As one biblical apologist wrote:

> If the Bible is a book partly human and partly divine, it cannot, as a whole, be the word of God, nor be justly ascribed to Him as its sole author. . . . To be God's book, it must be His in matter and in words, in substance and in form.[14]

As a result, the millenarians built their movement upon a literalistic method of biblical interpretation which gave them considerable apologetic advantage. They could confront churchmen who at least tacitly accepted the infallibility of the Scripture and urge them to become serious enough about their biblical faith to believe what was quite literally prophesied. As the swelling rolls of the millenarian ranks demonstrate, this appeal could be quite persuasive. But this was a most hazardous venture. Hazardous, first, because its hermeneutical foundation was insecure. The millenarian utilized a literalistic approach to prophecy not because the author's intention was literalistic — a point of paramount significance and one which the millenarians neglected — but because the climate of opinion in that day offered more support for a literalist than a figurative interpretation. And hazardous, second, because it

14. Alexander Carson, *The Inspiration of the Scriptures* (London, 1830), pp. 13, 31.

tied the future of millenarianism to the maintenance of an inerrant and infallible text. The millenarians could not give up belief in the single-level, totally divine document postulated in their theory of interpretation without sacrificing their faith. Thomas Carlyle recognized this total dedication to the book in Edward Irving and tried to convince him of his peril.

> I stated plainly to him that he must permit me a few words for relief of my conscience before leaving him for we know not what length of time, on a course which I could not but regard as full of danger to him. That the 13*th of the Corinthians* to which he always appealed, was surely too narrow a basis for so high a tower as he was building upon it, a high lean tower, or quasi-*mast*, piece added to piece, till it soared far above all human science and experience, and flatly contradicted all that, founded solely on a little text of *writing* in an ancient book! No sound judgment on such warranty could venture on such an enterprise.[15]

But Irving did venture, and so did all the millenarians. They ventured this in a century in which their assumptions about the Bible would be subjected to critical examination and rejected by most biblical scholars and by the majority of the church in Britain and America. In this situation they searched for theological justification for their doctrine of inspiration.

Writing to the editor of the millenarian periodical, the *Investigator*, a correspondent thanked him for his review of two books supporting verbal inspiration and stated:

> Habitually reverencing the Bible as the Word of God, I yet often detected with pain a latent scepticism in my mind, regarding its plenary inspiration. . . . What the mind craves . . . is *proof*, and nothing less than proof.[16]

The two books, Alexander Carson, *The Inspiration of the Scriptures* and Robert Haldane, *The Books of the Old and New Testaments Proved to Be Canonical*, were published in 1830 as a complementary set of arguments. Carson's book,

15. Carlyle, *Reminiscences*, p. 159.

16. *Investigator* 1 (1831) : 180.

actually a collection of essays, did little more than spar with antipathetic authorities and state the most exaggerated claims for the power of inspiration.

> But, verily, if the Scriptures contained one rule of poetry or oratory, that rule must be a legitimate one, or the Bible is a forgery. And if it tells one historical untruth it must forfeit its pretensions in every thing, seeing its pretensions extend to every thing in the book. The inspired writers may have been as ignorant of natural philosophy, as the most ignorant of British peasants, without affecting their inspiration. But, verily, if they have delivered one philosophical dogma, it must either be true or the Scriptures as a whole are false.[17]

Haldane, in discussing the problem of canonicity, was audacious enough to claim that the critic had no right to examine the book itself if its position in the canon were not in doubt.

> If, then, in a book recognised by the canon, as the Song of Solomon, we find matter which to our wisdom does not appear to be worthy of inspiration, we may be assured that we mistake.[18]

These two works, though often quoted and referred to admiringly by millenarians, did not receive the volume of praise heaped upon the most quoted defense of verbal inspiration, Louis Gaussen's *Theopneustia*. Although written originally in French, this work was quickly translated and widely distributed in the English-speaking world, its argument being quoted in the United States by 1842. Gaussen's main points are often repeated in other defenses of the doctrine of inspiration and his position may be considered typical of early nineteenth-century attempts to construct a theology of biblical infallibility.[19]

Theopneustia is not so much a systematic argument as a

17. Carson, *Inspiration of the Scriptures*, pp. 34–35.

18. Robert Haldane, *The Books of the Old and New Testaments Proved to be Canonical* (London, 1830), p. 105. Neither Carson nor Haldane was a millenarian.

19. The British Museum catalog lists a London edition of 1841. Edward Withrop, an American millenarian, referred to an 1842 New York edition (*Lectures on the Second Advent* [Cincinnati, 1843], p. 39).

horiatory and comforting sermon. In opening the discussion of his subject, Gaussen warned his readers to adopt a properly reverent and acquiescent attitude before the teaching of Scripture. If you question the Scripture, God will never reveal the truths of his Word to you. If you doubt the total divinity of the Bible, you set yourself up as the source of authority. He closed his preface by applying Jesus' warning to the doctrine of inspiration: "Whosoever hath not [that is, belief in inspiration], from him shall be taken even that which he seemeth to have [that is, the Bible]" (Luke 8:18). Gaussen defined inspiration as "that inexplicable power which the Divine Spirit put forth of old on the authors of holy Scripture" to guide them "even in the employment of the words they used, and to preserve them alike from all error and from all omission."[20] This definition of inspiration he defended by reference to the Bible. This did not amount to a circular argument, Gaussen contended, because he was addressing himself to men who already admitted the veracity of the Bible. This is as near as Gaussen ventured to supplying a structured argument in defense of verbal inspiration. Such a book obviously could and did provide comfort to those who were worried by news of biblical criticism but whose basic reverence and trust of the Bible were unshaken. But what of the honest inquirer? If one had never assimilated the traditional Christian reverence for the text or if one's trust was seriously upset by confrontation with the discoveries of the higher critics, where did he turn then? Although the millenarians searched for a defender to match swords with the critics, they found none in their own ranks. But in the work of the theologians of Princeton Seminary inerrancy did find qualified defenders.

THE PRINCETON THEOLOGY was born with the seminary in 1811, fathered by Archibald Alexander, its first professor. Although he was a warm-hearted preacher of evangelical convictions, Alexander built a curriculum that was quite old-fashioned and rigorously rationalistic according to the model

20. Quoted from Gaussen, *Theopneustia*, rev. ed. (Chicago, n.d.), p. 34.

of scholastic Calvinism. Alexander admired Locke, was influenced by the Scottish common-sense philosophers, and required his students to study theology from the *Institutes* of Frances Turretin, a Genevan theologian of the seventeenth century. This rationalist style continued to mark the work of Alexander's most famous student and successor, Charles Hodge. A voluminous writer and controversialist, Hodge edited the *Biblical Repertory and Princeton Review* for over forty years. He worked throughout his life to complete a synthetic statement of the Princeton position, finally publishing his three-volume *Systematic Theology* in 1872–73. The consistency with which the Princeton Theology was maintained was due in part to the fact that two sons and one grandson of Charles Hodge held chairs in the seminary. The other notable figure in this tradition was Benjamin B. Warfield, possibly the most intellectually gifted professor ever to teach on that faculty. Throughout the nineteenth century none of the professors at Princeton was willing to concede that the faculty had indeed created an identifiable theology. At the seminary's centennial celebration, President Francis L. Patton remarked:

> Princeton Seminary . . . had no oddities of manner, no shibboleths, no pet phrases, no theological labels, no trademark. She simply taught the old Calvinistic Theology without modification. . . . There has been a New Haven theology and an Andover theology; but there never was a distinctively Princeton theology. Princeton's boast . . . is her unswerving fidelity to the theology of the Reformation.[21]

As we shall see, this mistaken conviction reflected both a failure to understand the Reformation and also a lack of appreciation for the development occurring in Princeton thought as a result of the controversies of the nineteenth century.[22]

21. *The Centennial Celebration of the Theological Seminary* (Princeton, 1912), pp. 349–50.
22. The best treatments of the history of the Princeton Theology will be found in John Oliver Nelson, "The Rise of the Princeton Theology," (unpublished

Although the Princeton professors conceived of themselves as traditional Calvinist theologians, their fundamental
assumptions about the theological task were derived from
eighteenth-century models. They took their stand between two
movements, deism and enthusiasm (or mysticism as they preferred to call it), and, with the orthodox party in England
represented by such leaders as Bishop Joseph Butler, labored
to demonstrate the insufficiency of natural religion against the
deists, while convincing mystics that the Scriptures contained
God's absolutely complete and final revelation. Charles Hodge
began his *Systematic Theology* by defining the right use of
reason, attacking its perversion by the deists and refuting its
abandonment by the mystics. Even when not systematically
delineated, this background could push its way into an argument unexpectedly, as in Warfield's discussion of "The Church
Doctrine of Inspiration":

> In the whole history of the church there have been
> but two movements of thought, tending to a lower
> conception of inspiration and authority of Scrip-
> ture. . . . The first of these may be called the
> Rationalistic view. . . . The second of the lowered
> views of inspiration may be called the Mystical
> view.[23]

Although opposed to both these adversaries, the Princeton
theologians did not stand equidistant from them on some
neutral epistemological ground, but as many commentators
have noticed, occupied exactly the same stance as their deist
rivals.[24] Although Princeton theologians were not ignorant

Ph.D. dissertation, Yale University, 1935) ; William D. Livingstone, "The Princeton Apologetic
as Exemplified by the Work of
Benjamin B. Warfield and
J. Gresham Machen" (unpublished Ph.D. dissertation, Yale
University, 1948) ; and Lefferts A.
Loetscher, *The Broadening
Church* (Philadelphia, 1957).
   23. Benjamin B. Warfield, *The
Inspiration and Authority of
the Bible* (Philadelphia, 1948),
pp. 112–13.

24. Sidney Ahlstrom has
pointed out that the Scottish
common sense and not Lockean
philosophy was taught at
Princeton after the days of John
Witherspoon, who came to the
presidency of the college from
Scotland in 1768 ("The Scottish
Philosophy and American
Theology," *Church History* 24
[1955]: 257 ff). The dualism of
the Scottish common-sense
philosophy is not, however,
noticeable in the Princeton The-

of Kant and included him in their own private Inferno, no influence of his *Critique of Pure Reason* can be seen in their writings. Their dependence upon reason, though carefully guarded, was complete. Hodge remarked in the introduction to his *Systematic Theology*:

> If natural science be concerned with the facts and laws of nature, theology is concerned with the facts and the principles of the Bible. If the object of the one be to arrange and systematize the facts of the external world, and to ascertain the laws by which they are determined; the object of the other is to systematize the facts of the Bible, and ascertain the principles or general truths which those facts involve.[25]

Hodge evidently thought of the theologian working with the data of the Scriptures on the analogy of the scientist. He seems guilty of what Whitehead has called the fallacy of misplaced concreteness:

> The seventeenth century had finally produced a scheme of scientific thought framed by mathematicians, for the use of mathematicians. . . . The enormous success of the scientific abstractions, yielding on the one hand *matter* with its *simple location* in space and time, on the other hand *mind*, perceiving, suffering, reasoning, but not interfering, has foisted onto philosophy the task of accepting them as the most concrete rendering of fact.
>
> Thereby, modern philosophy has been ruined. It has oscillated in a complex manner between three extremes. There are the dualists, who accept matter and mind as on an equal basis, and the two varieties of monists, those who put mind inside matter, and those who put matter inside mind. But this juggling with abstractions can never overcome

ology after the time of Archibald Alexander. The first words of his book *Thoughts On Religious Experience* are, "There are two kinds of religious knowledge, which though intimately connected as cause and effect, may nevertheless be distinguished. These are the knowledge of the truth as it is revealed in the Holy Scriptures, and the impression which the truth makes on the human mind when rightly apprehended" (Philadelphia, 1841).

25. Charles Hodge, *Systematic Theology* (New York, 1874) 1:18.

the inherent confusion introduced by the ascription
of *misplaced concreteness* to the scientific scheme
of the seventeenth century.[26]

Theologically, Charles Hodge and the Princeton Theology
certainly fit within this categorization as monists — continually insisting that the experiential element, the witness of the
Spirit, the mystical strain, be subordinated to the matter of
theological science, the Scriptures. This attempt to adapt
theology to the methodology of Newtonian science produced
a wooden, mechanical discipline as well as a rigorously logical one. The witness of the Spirit, though not overlooked, cannot be said to play any important role in Princeton thought.
It is with the external not the internal, the objective not the
subjective, that they deal.

As is true of the whole Princeton Theology, the Princeton
doctrine of inspiration was characterized by a concentration
upon external verifications to the neglect of the internal — a
prejudice extremely serious for those who make such a show
of orthodoxy, for the emphasis in the Westminster Confession is, though judiciously balanced, decidedly in favor of
internal proofs. Charles Hodge's position was expressed succinctly:

> The infallibility and divine authority of the Scrip-
> tures are due to the fact that they are the word of
> God; and they are the word of God because they
> were given by the inspiration of the Holy Ghost.[27]

The most relevant passage in the Westminster Confession
reads:

> We may be moved and induced by the testimony of
> the Church to an high and reverent esteem of the
> holy scripture; and the heavenliness of the matter,
> the efficacy of the doctrine, the majesty of the style,
> the consent of all the parts, the scope of the whole
> (which is to give all glory to God), the full dis-
> covery it makes, of the only way of man's salvation,
> the many other incomparable excellencies, and the

26. Alfred North Whitehead,
Science and the Modern World
(New York, 1960), p. 56.

27. Hodge, *Systematic Theology*, 1:153.

entire perfection thereof, are arguments whereby it
doth abundantly evidence itself to be the Word of
God; yet, notwithstanding, our full persuasion and
assurance of the infallible truth, and divine authority thereof, is from the inward work of the Holy
Spirit, bearing witness by and with the Word in our
hearts.[28]

As comparison of these texts shows, both are agreed that the
Scriptures are authoritative because they come from God and
are the Word of God. The Confession, however, insists that
only the witness of the Holy Spirit can convince any man
that this is so, whereas Hodge prefers to argue that the Scriptures are the Word of God because they are inspired. Hodge
has substituted a doctrine of inspiration for the witness of the
Spirit. This crucial distinction was perpetuated by every other
Princeton theologian, and, in fact, the later history of this
doctrine of the Scriptures becomes the story of the desperate
dilemma into which the Princeton professors were thrust
by this distinction, and the manner in which they attempted
to reconcile the problem.

We might anticipate that Hodge would follow his assertion
that the Scriptures are authoritative because inspired with a
defense of the doctrine of inspiration, but he did not. Instead
he immediately entered into a discussion of the biblical doctrine of inspiration. The nature of inspiration was explained
by the Bible itself, he stated. But what if the Bible is not true?
That question cannot be addressed to the Christian theologian,
answered Hodge. "It is his business to set forth what the
Bible teaches. If the sacred writers assert that they are the
organs of God . . . then, if we believe their divine mission,
we must believe what they teach as to the nature of the influence under which they spoke and wrote."[29] This looks
very much like letting the witness of the Spirit in by the back
door. If one does not already believe the Bible, Hodge's argument will not convince him. The Princeton position, at this
stage of development, resembles that of the millenarian apolo-

28. Philip Schaff, *The Creeds of Christendom* (New York, 1877), 3:602–3.

29. Hodge, *Systematic Theology*, 1:166.

gists for biblical infallibility — especially Louis Gaussen. Hodge seems more guilty of carelessness than heterodoxy. But even if it could be demonstrated that Hodge's discussion of inspiration coincided with the Presbyterian standards, the pressure of biblical criticism after 1870 became so strong that later Princeton scholars in reaction to that pressure made important modifications which moved the Princeton Theology still further from the reformed tradition.

For Charles Hodge's dependence upon previously acquired biblical reverence, B. B. Warfield substituted the externally verified credibility of the apostles as teachers of doctrine. This does not appear to be a substantial change. Quite obviously, someone who rejected the Scriptures completely would not hesitate to deny the authority of the apostles. It appears to be a debater's point: it was in that context that all of Warfield's work was done. He found it useful to point out that one could not accept the apostolic doctrine concerning the resurrection, for instance, and reject the apostolic (i.e., the Princeton) doctrine of inspiration. "If we refuse them trust here, we have in principle refused them trust everywhere."[30] But it is also more than a debater's point. Warfield's substantiation of the credibility of the apostles as teachers of doctrine did not depend upon previously established biblical reverence. That is, Warfield did not simply insert another step in Hodge's equation, though in some of Warfield's work that is what appears to have happened. "It is not on some shadowy and doubtful evidence that the doctrine is based . . . but first on the confidence which we have in the writers of the New Testament as doctrinal guides, and ultimately on whatever evidence of whatever kind and force exists to justify that confidence."[31] As Warfield drew out the implications of the Princeton position, the veracity of the

---

30. Warfield, *Inspiration and Authority*, p. 212.

31. Ibid., p. 214. Warfield's dependence upon external verification has been shown by Edward Dowey to be directly contradictory to Calvin's own doctrine of internal testimony. It was, in fact, "the very thing Calvin was trying to avoid" (Edward A. Dowey, Jr., *The Knowledge of God in Calvin's Theology* [New York, 1952], p. 115).

biblical authors, their skill as historians, their accuracy as scientists — all these fell within the compass of "whatever evidence" and were to be used to defend the credibility of the apostles as teachers of doctrine. Thus Warfield subtly shifted the ground on which Charles Hodge had established the proof of the doctrine of inspiration and made Princeton's dependence upon external authority complete.

The Scriptures were authoritative because inspired. The nature of this inspiration was described by the Scriptures themselves and must be accepted because of the credibility of the apostles as teachers of doctrine. Ultimately the credibility of the apostles depended upon the establishment of their general trustworthiness. When one recognizes that this apologetic took such a shape, in part at least, because of the pressures of higher criticism, the whole structure takes on an air of bravado. As doubts began to arise in the minds of many Christians concerning the accuracy of biblical history, geography, or science, these Princeton theologians refused to retreat from the ramparts of an externally verified Bible to what they felt was the quagmire of an inner light. The apologetic, however, was only the setting in which the Princeton scholars placed the jewel they called the biblical doctrine of inspiration.

To understand the Princeton analysis of the biblical doctrine of inspiration requires an intellectual journal of some distance. It is not that the logic is so involved, but that the mode of thought seems so foreign to contemporary theology. Here one finds the emphasis upon system building, the dependence upon a text so reminiscent of the later schoolmen, and a notable lack of historical perspective. The difficulties are all summed up, I believe, in this question: How is it possible for the Princeton theologians to assume a biblical *doctrine* of inspiration? Warfield in one of his discussions of inspiration gave a very clear answer to that question. After mentioning that not all of the teachings of Scripture are supported "with equal clearness, with equal explicitness or with equal frequency," he stated: "When exegesis has once done its work and shown that they are taught by the Biblical writers,

[121]

all these doctrines stand as supported by the same weight and amount of evidence — the evidence of the trustworthiness of the Biblical writers as teachers of doctrine."[32] Thus we see how literally limitless was Warfield's dependence upon his own methodology — to what extent he was willing to use the claims of biblical authority to cover his own doctrinal formulations. The Princeton Theology, especially in its latter days, continually fell victim to this besetting sin of pride, unable to make any distinction between Paul and Princeton. This is tragic, but more than that, almost inexplicable. These men were well trained and capable. They warned others of the peril of the traps into which they themselves fell. Earlier in the article just quoted, Warfield explained that the new attitude of dogmatics toward the Scriptures

> commended justly to us by the whole body of modern scholarship, is, as Schleiermacher puts it, to seek "a form of Scripture proof on a larger scale than can be got from single texts," to build our systematic theology, in a word, on the basis, not of the occasional dogmatic statements of Scripture alone, taken separately and, as it were, in shreds, but on the basis of the theologies of the Scripture — to reproduce first the theological thought of each writer or group of writers and then to combine these several theologies (each according to its due historical place) into the one consistent system, consentaneous parts of which they are found to be.[33]

When one first reads this, he must blink in surprise. Is Warfield also among the prophets — and quoting Schleiermacher at that? How then does he get back to the position quoted earlier? The answer lies, as it did in the case of Hodge, with Warfield's inability to understand history. For him, "each according to his due historical place" seems only to reflect an interest in chronological ordering. But the historian does not only arrange events chronologically. He must, moreover, do more than discover lost documents, rehabilitate maligned men, and resurrect lost causes. He must also understand the

32. Warfield, *Inspiration and Authority*, p. 209. 33. Ibid., pp. 198–99.

extent to which the past is irrecoverable. Warfield saw the
relevance of the Scriptures and thanked history for ordering
its contents correctly. But he missed the paradox in historical
method: that events cannot be seen only as undeniably relevant; they must also be seen as irremediably removed. This
is only another way of saying that the Princeton scholars
thought of theology from above, from God's point of view,
and used the past as though it shared God's attributes and
was in no way tarnished by time or fashioned by the cosmos.
The valiant struggle which they put up against the higher
criticism was intended to deny that conclusion and to retain
the data of their scientific theology, like Democritus' atoms,
indissoluble and indestructible.

But to return to the point, the Princeton theologians did believe that they had constructed the biblical doctrine of inspiration. This doctrine, they argued, had been taught in the
Scriptures and believed in the church from apostolic times to
the present. Warfield defined it in this way:

> The church has always believed her Scriptures to be
> the book of God, of which God was in such a sense
> the author that every one of its affirmations of what-
> ever kind is to be esteemed as the utterance of God,
> of infallible truth and authority.[34]

Behind such brief statements lay a great deal of exegesis and
analysis which there is not space to discuss. The essence of
this work will emerge, however, in an analysis of the three
distinctive emphases of the doctrine. First, the Princeton
theologians agreed that "the inspiration of the Scriptures
extends to the words."[35] Archibald Alexander did not feel
obliged to be dogmatic about the point, but after Charles
Hodge adopted the position, no change occurred at Princeton regarding verbal inspiration.[36] Many commentators have

34. Ibid., p. 112.
35. Hodge, *Systematic Theology*, 1:164.
36. "In the narration of well-
known facts, the writer did not
need a continual suggestion of
every idea, but only to be so
superintended, as to be preserved
from error; so in the use of
language in recording such
familiar things, there existed no
necessity that every word should

noticed the similarity of this theory to the seventeenth-century mechanical dictation theory of inspiration. There was a close connection between that school of theologians and Princeton through Turretin's *Institutes*, which were used for many years as the theology text at the seminary. The Princeton theologians, however, were quite explicit in their denial of any dictation theory. Hodge and Warfield went so far as to argue that even the seventeenth century Calvinists did not hold to it.[37] Princeton scholars particularly objected to the suggestion that God used the biblical authors as robots, for they were well aware of stylistic differences and other reflections of the authors' personalities. In spite of their disavowal, however, this charge has since frequently reappeared and been rejected with increasing irritation by contemporary defenders of the doctrine. In this case the Princeton Theology seems to have been innocent. A crucial distinction between the mode and effect of inspiration, always carefully guarded by Princeton scholars, lies at the bottom of this prolonged bickering. The Princeton position was intended as an assertion of the fullness of inspiration; all of Scripture was inspired — every book and every word in every book. They based their belief primarily upon those passages (e.g., Jer. 1:9) which asserted that God had placed his words in the writers' mouths. But this

be inspired; but there was the same need of a directing and superintending influence, as in regard to the things themselves" (Archibald Alexander, *Evidences of the Authenticity, Inspiration and Canonical Authority* [Philadelphia, n.d.], pp. 226–27). The whole chapter ought to be read, not only to see how far Charles Hodge moved from the rather liberal position of his teacher and colleague, but also to see how different Alexander's treatment of inspiration is from that of Francis Turretin's *Institutio Theologiae Elencticae*, which was used as a text at the seminary until the publication of Charles

Hodge's *Systematic Theology*. It may be that later Princeton figures, reading Turretin as students, were more influenced by him. Whatever the truth in that regard, it is quite clear that Alexander's originality has not been appreciated.

37. Warfield's remark was, "The reformed churches have never held such a [mechanical dictation] theory: though dishonest, careless, ignorant or overeager controverters of its doctrines have often brought the charge" (*Inspiration and Authority*, p. 421). See as well, Hodge, *Systematic Theology*, 1:157.

did not involve mode. That was inscrutable.[38] But in spite of the fact that they made this point clear on some occasions, it must be admitted that the discussion of the question was not always so lucid. Hodge, for instance, remarked that the biblical writers "were controlled by Him in the words which they used."[39] Is not the logical implication of that statement (to steal one of Princeton's tricks) some form of dictation? It is not difficult to see why the charge refuses to die.

Second, Princeton argued that the Scriptures taught their own inerrancy.[40] Here we find one of the interesting cases in which later Princeton scholars altered the emphasis of Hodge's theology. Hodge was firm enough in enunciating the infallibility of the Bible, but, as we have seen, his own faith in the inspiration of the Bible did not depend upon inerrancy. As a result, in his discussion of the possibility of errors in the Scriptures Hodge was relaxed and quite calm. In a famous passage he remarked:

> The errors in matters of fact which skeptics search out bear no proportion to the whole. No sane man would deny that the Parthenon was built of marble, even if here and there a speck of sandstone should be detected in its structure. Not less unreasonable is to deny the inspiration of such a book as the

38. Warfield, *Inspiration and Authority*, p. 420.

39. Hodge, *Systematic Theology*, 1:164. In the hands of careless writers, the words become even more indefensible: "God wrote the Bible, the whole Bible, and the Bible as a whole. He wrote each word of it as truly as He wrote the Decalogue on the tables of stone" (Bishop, *The Fundamentals*, 7:53).

40. The choice of words was not accidental — the Princeton vocabulary was precise. The word "plenary" was occasionally applied to inspiration, but the connotations were not exact enough to suit theologians. "Infallibility" was also used, occasionally as a synonym for

"inerrant," but most Princeton writers seem to feel the word to be too limited. "Inerrancy," however, fitted the Princeton mind perfectly, resting as it did upon a rationalist definition of truth. They seemed to believe that a Bible free of errors, contradictions, paradoxes, or inconsistencies would be a perfect revelation. That this involved a definition of the nature of God as well as truth Warfield made clear on one occasion, writing that the superintendence of the Holy Spirit in inspiration was of such a nature as to preserve the Scriptures from "everything inconsistent with a divine authorship" (*Inspiration and Authority*, p. 173).

Bible, because one sacred writer says that on a given occasion twenty-four thousand, and another says that twenty-three thousand, men were slain. Surely a Christian may be allowed to tread such objections under his feet.[41]

Again Warfield changed this argument, not so much in substance as in tone — and again though the change is subtle, it is significant. It occurs because of that other subtle shift in emphasis noticed previously when Warfield substituted the credibility of the apostles for Hodge's internally verified faith in the Bible. There can be little doubt that biblical criticism was responsible for the hardening of the Princeton position. A. A. Hodge and B. B. Warfield first expressed these new views in the *Presbyterian Review* (April 1881), possibly stirred to this sharpening of their apologetic weapons by a letter from Charles A. Briggs, who wrote, "If you could . . . keep in mind the difficulties that face those whose attention is given mainly to the original text and critical study of the various passages, you will do a great, a *very great* service to the Church." [42] Whether this particular critic was responsible or not, after this date the Princeton Theology took a much firmer position on the inerrancy of Scriptures. A. A. Hodge in his half of the article declared that "all the affirmations of Scripture of all kinds whether of spiritual doctrine or duty, or of physical or historical fact, or of psychological or philosophical principle, are without any error." Warfield, in the strongest statement in the article, wrote: "A proved error in Scripture contradicts not only our doctrine, but the Scripture claims and, therefore, its inspiration in making those claims." [43] Princeton in this article took its stand upon the absolute inerrancy of the Bible and, in a sense, seemed to risk the whole Christian faith upon one proved error. But the Princeton masters were very careful not to suggest that Christianity depended upon inspiration. On a number of occasions they declared that there could have been a Christian church

41. Hodge, *Systematic Theology*, 1:170.
42. Loetscher, *Broadening Church*, p. 30.
43. A. A. Hodge and B. B. Warfield, "Inspiration," *Presbyterian Review* 2 (1881) : 238, 245.

without inspiration. Warfield once stated: "The verities of our faith would remain historically proven to us . . . even had we no Bible."[44] These are remarkable words and have seemed to some to open up a possible area of compromise between criticism and conservatism, but the hope was never a real one. In these few passages we glimpse, as if through a partly opened door, a new side of Warfield's personality; but the door quickly swings shut, and the inexorable apologist and polemicist turns back to his task. It is possible, Warfield stated, that Christianity might have existed without an inspired Bible, but we are not discussing possibilities. Did the apostles teach inerrancy? They did, Warfield unhesitatingly replied. Then the critics are rejecting apostolic authority in denying inerrancy. Warfield has constructed his apologetic in such a way that Princeton may eat its cake and have it, too. He recognized the possibility of Christian faith without the Scriptures, but spun a logical net around the doctrine of inspiration that was designed to trap the critical "fly." Warfield can be accused of telling the critics that *his* orthodoxy was secure without inspiration but theirs was not. The Princeton Theology was a dangerous adversary, as Professor Briggs was to discover.

The Princeton position on the inerrancy of the Scriptures, seemingly heroic in its defense of truth, thus appears less risky when analyzed in terms of its apologetic intentions. In a discussion of the third distinctive emphasis of the Princeton doctrine of the Scriptures, belief in the inspiration of the "original autographs," we can see an even stronger defense against the possibility of one "proved error." Verbal and inerrant inspiration was claimed not for the Bible as we now find it, but for the books of the Bible as they came from the hands of the authors — the original autographs. This emphasis upon the original manuscripts is another example of the way in which the Princeton doctrine of the Scriptures was refined and tightened in the face of growing critical opposition. A. A. Hodge said nothing of the original autographs in the first (1860) edition of his *Outlines of Theology*, but saw fit

44. Warfield, *Inspiration and Authority*, p. 211.

to introduce it into the 1879 edition.[45] The collaborative article of A. A. Hodge and B. B. Warfield in the *Princeton Review* (1881) elevated the concept to an especially prominent place in the Princeton doctrine of inspiration.[46] That this concept of the original autographs had been recently added to their apologetic was never mentioned by Warfield and Hodge. Their silence might seem to imply that they did not view the new refinement as significant. But what might seem to be a casual change was in fact a significant retreat.

This new emphasis was introduced just at the time that the number of biblical errors or discrepancies turned up by the critics was growing too large to be ignored. One could no longer dismiss them as had Charles Hodge — as flecks of sandstone in the Parthenon marble. Hodge and Warfield retreated. In the first place, they stated that their theory of inspiration did not cover the *preservation* of the accuracy of the biblical manuscripts; inerrancy was claimed for the manuscripts only as they came from the hands of their authors. Copyists' errors could not invalidate the inerrancy of the Bible. Even this much hedging on the part of the Princeton professors has been widely criticized. As we have seen, the Princeton theory of inspiration served to define and describe the way in which God had provided an inerrant source of knowledge concerning Christianity. But what possible good can a nineteenth-century Christian derive from a Bible which, although once inerrant, is now riddled with mistakes through the carelessness of copyists? The Princeton claim to an inerrant Bible was maintained only by recourse to lost and completely useless original autographs. Once again the completely scholastic, theoretical nature of the Princeton mind is illustrated. And once again Princeton is caught propagating a dogma which is flatly contradicted by the Westminster Confession. In that creed the Scriptures are declared to be authentic not only at the moment of their description but now:

45. A. A. Hodge, *Outlines of Theology* (New York, 1860) and 2d edition (New York, 1879), pp. 66, 75.

46. Hodge and Warfield, "Inspiration," pp. 226, 237, 238, 242, 245, 246.

The Old Testament in Hebrew . . . and the New
Testament in Greek . . . being immediately inspired by God, and by his singular care and
providence kept pure in all ages, are therefore
authentical.[47]

The fact that later generations of biblical literalists were to
treat their own leather-bound Bibles as though they were the
original autographs does not improve the Princeton argument.

There is a second and even more important sense in which
the original autograph theory marked a retreat for the
Princeton apologetic. Warfield in particular phrased his defense of the inerrancy of the original autographs in such a
way that no further discussion was possible. In retreating to
the original autographs, Warfield, whether intentionally or
not, brought the Princeton apologetic to a triumphant conclusion. Although he continued to remark, with apparent
sincerity, that every biblical scholar must continue to examine the evidence turned up by critical investigation, he so
defined the problem that no possible error could be discovered.

With these presumptions, and in this spirit, let (1)
it be proved that each alleged discrepant statement
certainly occurred in the original autograph of the
sacred book in which it is said to be found. (2) Let
it be proved that the interpretation which occasions
the apparent discrepancy is the one which the passage was evidently intended to bear. It is not sufficient to show a difficulty, which may spring out of
our defective knowledge of the circumstances. The
true meaning must be definitely and certainly ascertained, and then shown to be irreconcilable with
other known truth. (3) Let it be proved that the
true sense of some part of the original autograph is
directly and necessarily inconsistent with some certainly known fact of history, or truth of science, or
some other statement of Scripture certainly ascertained and interpreted. We believe that it can be
shown that this has never yet been successfully done
in the case of one single alleged instance of error in
the WORD OF GOD.[48]

47. Schaff, *Creeds of Christendom*, 3:604.

48. Hodge and Warfield,
"Inspiration," p. 242.

Warfield was much too modest. Since in order to prove the Bible in error it now became necessary to find the original manuscripts, Warfield might have concluded this section by announcing that inerrancy could never be denied. The original manuscripts had been lost, and therefore the critic might just as well turn his attention to Homer or the Koran for all the effect his work would have upon the followers of the Princeton orthodoxy.

This was the shape of the Princeton doctrine of the Scriptures — one of the forms of biblical literalism in late nineteenth-century Protestantism. The problems raised by biblical criticism demanded a new formulation of the doctrine of the Scriptures. Both conservatives and liberals worked at the theological task, but the Princeton professors' insistence that they were doing nothing new, while creating a unique apologetic which flew in the face of the standards they were claiming to protect, cannot be judged as a historically honest or laudable program. The heart of their position was the argument that God could not, would not, convey truth through an errant document. The years of disputation never shook their confidence in that position. After a reading of much of the literature produced by the school one cannot avoid the feeling that the Princeton scholars seldom listened to their opponents with any view to modifying their own position. The gravest charge that can be leveled at the Princeton Theology is that it was not so much a theology as an apologetic, not so much an approach to be discussed as a position to be defended. Thus the antideist stance which characterized the founding of Princeton can be seen recurring in each Princeton generation. But whereas there was some justification for viewing some deists as outside the Christian camp, the continuing tendency to treat every opponent of the Princeton Theology as an atheist or non-Christian created a barrier of distrust and suspicion which prevented fruitful discourse and eventually friendly disagreement.

What kind of relationship existed between the Princeton Theology and the millenarian movement? It ought to be noticed that the effect of the Princeton doctrine of the Scriptures and the millenarian literalistic method of interpreting the Scriptures was very much the same. Both Princeton and the millenarians had staked their entire conception of Christianity upon a particular view of the Bible based ultimately upon eighteenth-century standards of rationality. Both of these schools of thought had vowed to defend the Bible or die in the attempt. In the next chapters the separate histories of these two movements will be searched to determine whether their similarity of interest ever developed into a real alliance.

6

The Prophecy
and Bible Conference
Movement

DURING the last quarter of the nineteenth century, the millenarian movement assumed a different form and, especially in the United States, began to organize and proselyte through a series of newly founded prophetic and Bible conferences. These conferences furnished an opportunity for the broader dissemination of the millenarian message, but also provided occasions at which friendships could be formed and personal leadership could develop. Millenarianism, though not for a moment forgetting the need to proclaim the imminent second advent of Christ, became something more after 1875. At its center, among the true initiates, it became a spiritual home, a community. Doctrinal interests other than millenarianism began to receive attention. A group of respected and beloved leaders emerged and extended their influence through personal association. American millenarianism was transformed into a protodenominational fellowship movement with enlarged doctrinal concerns, though the springs of its energy still rose from second advent sources.

The Niagara Bible Conference was the mother of them all — the Monte Cassino and Port Royal of the movement. Known during its first years as the Believers' Meeting for Bible Study, this conference can properly be called the earliest, most representative, most influential, and most difficult to describe. One of its long-time members wrote in 1897:

> To an uninitiated on-looker, Niagara Convention
> must be something of a mystery. In the quietest

and sweetest of retreats, without ostentation and
with only the nearest semblance of advertising; with
no attractions of singing or musical instruments,
without badges, salutes, mottoes, sensational oratory, or any of the usual accessories of a modern
conventicle, a large company of sober, cultivated,
well-mannered people come together, year after
year, ostensibly to study concerning "the things of
the Kingdom of God." . . . But what is Niagara
Convention?

To answer is both hard and easy. In Apostolic
days the name "Believer" stood for all that involved
separation unto Christ, and the reproach of His
cross. The name "Christian" to-day is lost in an
accretion of worldly maxims and practices. The
Niagara company are simply aiming to manifest
the primitive, New Testament idea of an ecclesia.[1]

The conference originated with a group of men associated
with the millenarian periodical, *Waymarks in the Wilderness*.
James Inglis, David Inglis, Charles Campbell, George S.
Bishop, George O. Barnes, Benjamin Douglas, L. C. Baker,
and George C. Needham held an informal private conference
in New York City in 1868. The first three men on this list
served as editors of *Waymarks*; George S. Bishop, who had
recently graduated from Princeton Seminary, was the pastor
of the First Reformed Church of Orange, New Jersey, from
1875 to 1906; L. C. Baker, who had been a member of the
editorial board of the *Prophetic Times*, was minister of the
Presbyterian Church in Camden, New Jersey; Needham had
only recently emigrated from Ireland. In the next few years
these men planned a group of conferences in Philadelphia,
Saint Louis, and Galt, Ontario. George Needham claimed
that the idea for such meetings originated in Ireland earlier
in the century and stated that the conferences emphasized
"the doctrines of the verbal inspiration of the Bible, the personality of the Holy Spirit, the atonement of sacrifice, the
priesthood of Christ, the two natures in the believer, and the
personal imminent return of our Lord from heaven."[2] Early
in the seventies, James Inglis and several other leaders of

1. *Watchword* 19 (1897) : 144.   2. Ibid., 13 (1891) : 60; see also
Northfield Echoes 1 (1894) : 92.

this group died, and the meetings were interrupted for several years until younger men took up the task. After refounding in 1875 in Chicago, the conference met annually for one or two weeks in the summer, usually in a resort setting. From 1883 to 1897 the conference met at Niagara-on-the-Lake, Ontario, and thus acquired its customary name.[3]

Virtually everyone of any significance in the history of the American millenarian movement during this period attended the Niagara conference. The names of over 120 leaders and speakers are known from the published proceedings and descriptions. The founding father and controlling spirit of the conference was the Reverend James Hall Brookes (1830–97), a Presbyterian minister from Saint Louis, Missouri. Ordained in 1854 after one year at Princeton Seminary, Brookes had moved to Saint Louis in 1858, where he remained pastor of the Walnut Street Presbyterian Church until his death. He was known to millenarians through his writing in *Waymarks in the Wilderness*; he had spoken at early pre-Niagara conferences arranged by James Inglis. When the Believers' Meeting was begun in 1875, Brookes was sought as the principal speaker; he attended almost every one after that date until his death, serving as the president of the conference. Also in 1875 Brookes began publishing his own periodical, the *Truth*, which he edited and almost entirely wrote during the twenty-three remaining years of his life. Like other millenarian magazines, it had very limited circulation and today is quite difficult to locate, but the *Truth* served, along with one other journal, as the unofficial organ of the millenarian movement during the last years of the nineteenth century.[4] George C. Needham (1840–1902), another millenarian leader of the Believers' Meeting, was raised in Ireland where he preached

3. The conference itinerated as follows: 1875, Chicago; 1876, Swampscott, Massachusetts; 1877, Watkin's Glen, New York; 1878, 1879, 1880, Clifton Springs, New York; 1881, Old Orchard, Maine; 1882, Mackinac Island, Michigan; 1883–97, Niagara-on-the-Lake, Ontario; 1898, 1899, Point Chautauqua, New York; 1900, Asbury Park, New Jersey.
4. *Truth* 1–23 (Saint Louis, 1875–97). The Moody Bible Institute library holds a complete file. David R. Williams, *James H. Brookes: A Memoir* (Saint Louis, 1897).

among the Plymouth Brethren. When he arrived in this country he came to know James Inglis and played a part in the conferences of 1868–71. During later life he joined the Baptists but worked primarily as an evangelist and conference speaker, maintaining a home in Manchester, Massachusetts.[5] William J. Erdman (1834–1923) played a less conspicuous but highly significant role in the Bible conference movement. Ordained as a Presbyterian minister in 1860 after graduating from Union Theological Seminary in New York, Erdman served a large number of pastorates, including Moody's Chicago Avenue Church, 1875–78; Jamestown, New York, 1878–85; Boston, 1886–88; and Asheville, North Carolina, 1888–95. He was particularly appreciated for his knowledge of the Bible and his skill in giving expository Bible readings, which were a feature of the Niagara conferences.[6] Leander W. Munhall (1843–1934), another evangelist and leader of the Niagara conference, was one of the few Methodists associated with the millenarian movement. A popular speaker and vigorous apologist, he was mostly self-educated.

What were the Niagara conferences like? To those who have spent a summer week at a church camp the format and arrangements will not seem unusual. Brookes described the 1892 conference in these words:

> The meeting this year, commencing July 7 and closing on the evening of July 13, was more largely attended than ever before. Often every seat in the pavilion was occupied, and the porches were filled with eager hearers of the Word. The place too becomes more beautiful as the years go by, and it would be difficult to find a spot better suited to the quiet and prayerful study of the Sacred Scriptures. The building in which the Conference meets, overlooking lake Ontario and the river Niagara, and surrounded by green trees, is secluded from the noise of the world; and so excellent were the arrange-

5. G. C. Needham, *Preach the Word* (New York, 1892), pp. 15–22; and Wm. McLoughlin, *Modern Revivalism* (New York, 1959), pp. 159–60.
6. Considerable biographical information relating to W. J. Erdman may be found in the Charles R. Erdman papers in the library of Princeton Theological Seminary.

ments for the accommodation of the guests, both in Queen's Royal Hotel and in the boarding houses of the village, that not a word of complaint was heard from any one.[7]

The conference opened with a Wednesday evening prayer meeting and for the following seven days the participants generally heard two addresses in the morning, two addresses in the afternoon, and a fifth speaker in the evening. On Sunday there was a gospel address in the morning, a communion service in the afternoon, and a missionary message in the evening.

What, then, lent such attraction and freshness to the Niagara meetings? Niagara was, of course, virtually the first Bible conference in the United States; but Americans had had a great deal of previous experiences in outdoor religious services such as the camp meetings and tents of the evangelists. Yet in the format and spirit of Niagara many felt they found some new ingredients. This spirit was alluded to earlier in the chapter by the correspondent who wrote about the Niagara company "aiming to manifest the primitive, New Testament idea of an ecclesia." To put it more concretely, the Niagara conference represented J. N. Darby's concept of the church adapted to the American environment. Although they were intrigued by much of Darby's theology, as we saw in chapters 3 and 4, most American ministers could not follow Darby in his denunciation of "systems" — that is, denominations. Although they might agree with Darby's dour assessment of contemporary Christianity, they could not bring themselves to drop out of their churches. But at Niagara denominations could be and were consistently ignored; the minister became the Bible teacher and the sermon was transformed into the Bible reading. Bible teacher and Bible reading were not simply different names for the same thing. We have seen in the last chapter how strongly and seriously the millenarians advocated the literal interpretation of the verbally inerrant Scripture. The Scriptures were God's word, they declared, and were their own best interpreter. The real

7. *Truth* 18 (1892) : 936.

need of every man was to listen to God's word, and the first requirement for every preacher was that he not substitute his own thoughts for God's word. The method of exegesis which resulted from this line of reasoning was the Bible reading. In an age in which American pulpit oratory reached its zenith with such fashionable ministers as T. Dewitt Talmadge, Henry Ward Beecher, Joseph Cook, and Phillips Brooks, the Bible teacher conceived of himself not only as teaching a different gospel but as teaching it in a wholly contrasting fashion. George C. Needham said about his own preaching, "By no means advertise me as being sensational, or magnetic, or eloquent, or scholarly, or smart, or any such thing, but only as a plain man, telling a plain story, in a plain manner."[8]

Although American historians have not often noticed the development of this new form of exposition, it did not pass unnoticed in the seminaries of that day. Francis L. Patton of Princeton Seminary, in a lecture on homiletics, warned his students about it:

> Then there is what is called a Bible-reading; very good too in its way, but a very poor substitute for a sermon. I suppose that the Bible-reading is a feature of the school of thought of which Mr. Moody is such a distinguished leader. With some of the theology of some of the members of this school I have no sympathy; and I particularly object to their arbitrary and unhistorical system of interpretation. But we cannot too much admire the earnestness of these men; their reverence for the Divine Word; their profound faith in the blood of Christ; and their working familiarity with the English Bible. But few, I fear, know the English Bible as they do. I advise you to learn their secret in this regard, but do not adopt their shibboleths; and I warn you against supposing that you have given an adequate substitute for a sermon when, with the help of Cruden's Concordance, you have chased a word through the Bible, making a comment or two on the passages as you go along.[9]

8. Needham, *Preach the Word*, pp. 15 ff.
9. *Presbyterian and Reformed Review* 1 (1890) : 36–37; see as well, McLoughlin, *Modern Revivalism*, p. 159.

Patton referred to the Bible reading as a product of Moody's influence, but in this case Moody was a follower and not a leader. He was greatly influenced in his style of preaching by the English Plymouth Brethren evangelist Harry Moorhouse, who astounded Moody by preaching for a whole week from the same text. One of Moody's biographers described the addresses, all based upon John 3:16, as "not a sermon so much as a string of related texts or passages briefly commented upon to form what came to be known, rather oddly, as a 'Bible Reading.'" [10] About that series of sermons Fleming Revell, Moody's brother-in-law, wrote, "D. L. Moody had great power before, but nothing like what he had after dear Harry Moorhouse came into our lives and changed the character of the teaching and preaching in the chapel." [11] That the Bible reading was popularized if not invented by the Plymouth Brethren seems quite clear. Darby, as noted previously, preferred private reading meetings to preaching and carried out his most successful work through this form of teaching, very frequently in homes rather than churches. Every Brethren teacher and evangelist used this method; its popularity is both contemporaneous with Brethren expansion to North America and coexistence with those millenarians which the Brethren were known to have influenced. Furthermore, as in Moody's case, the American ministers' adoption of the Bible reading can often be directly traced to an encounter with a Brethren preacher.

Bible readings were the consistent fare at the Niagara conference. In reporting the success of the 1882 conference, held that year on Mackinac Island, Brookes declared:

> These results have been produced, not by exciting exhortations nor by learned discourses, nor by new and startling themes, but by simple Bible-readings, in which the Sacred Scriptures have been their own interpreter.[12]

Brookes, for example, divided an address on the second coming into seven points, supporting each point by a group of

10. J. C. Pollock, *Moody* (New York, 1963), p. 73.

11. As quoted in ibid., p. 74.
12. *Truth* 8 (1882) : 385.

texts to which he expected his audience to turn in their own Bibles as he gave them a brief exegesis. The first point (It is a personal coming) Brookes supported by reference to passages in Matthew, Mark, Luke, John, Acts, 1 Thessalonians, and Revelation. In this fashion Brookes discussed the other six points.

> It is the hope set before us in the gospel.
> It is held forth as a powerful motive and incentive.
> It is presented as our consolation amid sorrow and trial.
> The state of the world at the time of our Lord's return, and during the entire interval of His absence from the earth, shows the folly of the common expectation of a spiritual millennium, or the conversion of the nations by the Church.
> This personal coming of the Lord may occur at any moment.
> The judgments.[13]

From this outline it is quite apparent that Brookes was teaching not only by the Brethren method, but also the Darbyite any-moment coming. In Brookes's other writings it is clear that he accepted most of Darby's dispensationalism, including the secret rapture of the church and the distinction between the spiritual role of the church in this age and the earthly role of the Jewish nation. Brookes never acknowledged any intellectual debt to the Plymouth Brethren, suggesting only that he became a premillennialist by reading the prophetic passages of the Bible. However, in his periodical the *Truth* he regularly recommended the writings of the Brethren, and he did visit B. W. Newton in about 1862 on his only European visit. We have already discussed the possibility that Brookes may have met Darby on one of Darby's visits to Saint Louis.[14]

Brookes was not alone in advocating the theology of dispensationalism at the Niagara conference. Although not every Niagara participant can automatically be assumed to have accepted these views, most of the speakers and leaders of the con-

13. Ibid., p. 403.
14. For his eschatology see *Maranatha*, 5th ed. (Saint Louis, 1878) ; *Truth* 18 (1892) : 516; and a series entitled "Israel and the Church," ibid., 8 (1882) : *passim*. For his biographical remarks see *Things to Come* 3 (1897) : 68.

ference do seem to have accepted the Darbyite view of the second coming for a time at least. One of the members of the executive committee, Robert Cameron, a Brantford, Ontario, Baptist pastor, stated that the 1884 conference witnessed a special emphasis upon the doctrine of the any-moment coming.

> At the 1884 Conference it came to be the "fashion" of every speaker to "ring the changes" on the possibility of Christ coming any moment — before the morning dawned, before the meeting closed, and even before the speaker had completed his address.[15]

The leaders at Niagara followed Darby's lead, furthermore, in strenuously opposing the doctrines of the perfectionists and annihilationists. Needham stated that James Inglis initiated the pre-Niagara conferences in order to warn against the perfectionism which had become popular since the revival of 1858.[16] During the first few conferences in the Niagara series, millenarians who maintained the annihilationist position — that the wicked soul perishes with death, and Christ grants eternal life only to believers — seem to have attended and participated. After the 1877 conference, where controversy seems to have broken out over these issues, Brookes drew up a creed which he published in the *Truth* with the comment, "If they (who oppose) do not stand upon it, and yet choose to attend, they are expected to keep silent. We do not deny the right of those who hold that what are known as 'annihilation views,' to assemble when and where they please." He also intimated that nonmillenarians were not welcome to express their views. The next conference would be much better, he promised, because "controversy hereafter will not be allowed under any circumstances."[17] The creed which Brookes drew up in 1878 served, apparently, as an unofficial guide to the teachings of the Niagara conference until 1890 when it was officially adopted.[18] The creed must have

15. Robert Cameron, *Scriptural Truth about the Lord's Return* (New York, 1922), pp. 145–46.
16. *Watchword* 13 (1891) : 60.
17. *Truth* 4 (1878) : 405. The creed is printed in full in Appendix A.
18. *Truth* 18 (1892) : 393; and W. J. Erdman, "The Niagara Conference," a privately printed

done its work, for Brookes happily reported that at the 1882 conference "no countenance whatever has been given to the unscriptural and mischievous notions, now so widely spread, of annihilation, soul-sleeping, restoration of the wicked, and perfectionism in the flesh."[19]

The fourteen-point Niagara creed (Appendix A) provides an index to the concerns of the millenarians. Bracketed between the first article affirming the verbal inerrancy of the original autographs and the last affirming the premillennial second advent, Brookes placed a very conservative Calvinistically oriented group of articles affirming human depravity (Arts. 3 and 4) and salvation by faith in the blood of Christ (Arts. 5, 6, 7), combined, however, with a derogation of the church and the sacraments characteristic of nineteenth-century evangelicalism (Arts. 5, 6, and 10). Although it seems odd to find it in a creed, Brookes felt it necessary to affirm his own method of biblical interpretation in a separate article (Art. 9). All of the Bible, including the Old Testament, Brookes affirmed, centered on Christ and all of it was designed to convey "practical instruction" to the reader. Articles 11 and 12 emphasized the personality of the Holy Spirit and the need for personal holiness, both of which will receive more extended treatment in chapter 7. The millenarian article (14) is quite general and does not commit the Niagara participant to any particular Darbyite or futurist position, but affirms simply that the world cannot be expected to improve, that Christ will return personally and premillennially, and that Israel will be restored to Palestine.

Although the Niagara creed was tolerant of various millenarian beliefs, the leaders and speakers at the conference consistently advocated the doctrine of the any-moment coming of Christ and followed Darby's interpretation of prophecy until the 1890s. One of these long-time leaders of the Niagara conference was Henry M. Parsons (1828–1913), who served

pamphlet. Cole was mistaken in stating that Niagara adopted a five-point creed in 1895. From that error has stemmed much of the confusion over the identification of Fundamentalism with a five-point creed (*History of Fundamentalism*, p. 34).

19. *Truth* 8 (1882) : 385.

a Presbyterian church in Buffalo, New York, during the 1870s and moved to Knox Presbyterian Church in Toronto in the 1880s. Parsons, who participated in almost all the Niagara conferences and in many of the other conferences which stemmed from Niagara, was only one of many Canadian Presbyterian, Baptist, and Anglican clergymen active in the conference.[20] William G. Moorehead (1836–1914), a corresponding editor of Brookes's periodical, the *Truth*, as well as a regular leader and speaker at the Niagara conferences, graduated from Allegheny Seminary and served as a missionary in Italy from 1862 to 1869 before becoming professor of New Testament in 1873 and in 1899 president of the United Presbyterian Seminary at Xenia, Ohio. Nathaniel West (1826–1906), also a Presbyterian, emigrated from England as a boy, graduated from the University of Michigan in 1846, and held pastorates in Cincinnati from 1855 to 1862, Brooklyn from 1862 to 1869, Detroit from 1883 to 1884, and Louisville from 1884 to at least 1898, as well as teaching at Danville Theological Seminary, Kentucky, during 1869–75. West, Moorehead, and W. J. Erdman held the reputation for possessing the best knowledge of theology and the Bible among all the ministers who taught at Niagara.

Adoniram Judson Gordon (1836–95), though not as active in Niagara as the preceding figures, played such a prominent role in the millenarian movement as a whole that he cannot be overlooked. Gordon, a Baptist, was trained at Newton Seminary and served as pastor of the Clarendon Street Church, Boston, from 1869 until his death. Like Brookes, he edited a periodical, called the *Watchword*, which shared with the *Truth* the role of unofficial organ of the millenarian movement. Like many other evangelicals of his time, Gordon was concerned about foreign missions and founded a training

20. Other Canadian participants in the Niagara conferences were the Reverend Thomas Wardrope, one-time moderator of the Canadian Presbyterian church; the Reverend William Stewart, principal of the Toronto Bible Training School; the Reverend Maurice S. Baldwin, bishop of Huron; the Reverend Robert Cameron, the Reverend Elmore Harris, and quite a number of laymen.

school in the Clarendon Street Church to help supply the need for laymen and laywomen who could serve the church both at home and overseas. Unlike many of the other millenarians, Gordon was quite frank in paying tribute to the influence of the Plymouth Brethren on his own theology. He taught the any-moment coming and read virtually every Brethren author. In regard to the Brethren he wrote:

> Such, we believe, after much thought and careful investigation and frequent conversations with those best qualified to judge, is the real spring of the present evangelistic movement. It demands fearless candor to concede it, but we believe that truth requires us to confess that we owe a great debt, both in literature and in life, to the leaders of this ultra-Protestant movement. And we are glad to believe that the light which it has thrown out by its immense biblical study and research has been appropriated by many of the best preachers and evangelists in our Protestant churches.[21]

Arthur Tappan Pierson (1837–1911), one of the most prominent evangelical clergymen of his day, a prolific author and vigorous missionary advocate, also spoke regularly at Niagara. Pierson, after graduation from Union Seminary in New York, served Presbyterian congregations in Detroit and Indianapolis and Wannamaker's Bethany Tabernacle in Philadelphia. He became a premillennialist in 1878 because of the influence of George Müller, the Bristol minister and orphan-master who had spent his early ministerial career among the Plymouth Brethren. In later life Pierson did not often hold a settled pastorate but made a career of writing and

21. *Watchword* 1–19 (Boston, 1878–97). Gordon's words are quoted in Ernest B. Gordon, *A. J. Gordon* (New York, 1896), p. 88. In the preface to *Ecce Venit* (New York, 1889), Gordon revealed that he was "nourished and brought up" in futurism, but later became a historicist — an unusual kind of conversion. Quite confusingly, however, Gordon does not seem to have adopted all of the historicist positions, for he still argued that "the Church will be raptured away to join the Lord on His advancing way, and escort Him back to earth" (ibid., p. 242). Gordon apparently believed, in spite of his historicist conversion, that the second coming would be a secret coming and that the church would escape the tribulation.

conference preaching. Influenced greatly by his friendship with A. J. Gordon, Pierson was rebaptized and became in fact, if not in name, a Baptist.[22] These men, along with Brookes, Erdman, Needham, and Munhall, are representative of the kind of converts the millenarian movement was winning during the last half of the nineteenth century. Moreover, all of these men embraced and taught, at least for a few years, the millenarian views identified earlier with Darby's dispensational theology. We will trace the manner in which Niagara's small witness was amplified by the founding of more popular and publicized conferences, but even if its influence had not been extended indirectly, Niagara would have deserved to be known as the source of a new method of Bible teaching, a new zeal for the defense of the Bible, and a new wave of enthusiasm for dispensational millenarianism.

In assessing the influence of the conference, one must add to the list of methods and doctrines some notice of the new spirit of Niagara—the manifestation of "the primitive, New Testament idea of an ecclesia." Much of this spirit was generated by the personal contact and delightful atmosphere of the summer conference by the lake. But whether intentionally or not, the Niagara conference leaders taught their millenarian views as a part of a coherent theology, not as a special emphasis or single-issue movement, and they taught them as part of a complete theology—the foundation for a new sect. By the later years of the century, when the turmoil of higher criticism had alarmed and discouraged many ministers, Niagara was able to offer an alternative view of both the church and the world. The report of the 1898 Niagara conference carried this testimony:

> The Rev. Mr. Ayers, from Illinois, mentioned how he had wandered through the mazes of the higher criticism until he came to disbelieve in what he had held dear, and finally began to consider the question of leaving the ministry. But God was very gracious to him and sent the showers of his Holy Spirit upon

22. Delavan L. Pierson, *Arthur Tappan Pierson* (New York, 1912) and Arthur T. Pierson, *Forward Movements of the Last Half Century* (New York, 1900).

his dry heart. He told of the refreshment of his spirit, his acceptance of premillennial truth, the full inspiration of the Bible, the coming back of his love for the Word, and his faith in all he had previously held dear, and now he was continually preaching the doctrine of the premillennial coming of the Lord.[23]

When we have come this far, the foundations of Fundamentalism have already been laid.

IN 1878 A GROUP of eight millenarians, drawn almost entirely from the leadership of the Niagara conference, published a call for the convening of a public conference in New York City to "listen to a series of carefully prepared papers on the pre-Millennial advent of the Lord Jesus Christ and connected truths, and to participate in such discussions as the topics may suggest." "It has seemed desirable," they wrote, "that those who . . . are 'looking for that blessed hope,' should meet together in conference, as our honored brethren in England have recently done." Once again, the British millenarians were leading the American.[24]

The Plymouth Brethren held a conference in 1867 which drew some attention in the United States; another more widely representative but little-noticed conference was convened in 1873, but the conference to which the Americans referred was undoubtedly the first of three held at Mildmay Park in 1878, 1879, and 1886.[25] The Reverend William Pennefather began to hold regular missionary conferences at Barnet, Hertfordshire, beginning in 1856; and moving to Mildmay Park near London, where he became perpetual curate of Saint Jude's in 1864, he worked to secure a tract of land and to raise funds for the construction of a special conference

23. *Watchword and Truth* 20 (1898) : 283.

24. Nathaniel West, ed., *Premillennial Essays* (New York, 1879), p. 12.

25. *Prophetic Times* 5 (1867) : 74; Froom, *Prophetic Faith*, 4:1193; Mildmay Second Advent Conference, *"Our God Shall Come"* (London, 1878) ; Mildmay Second Advent Conference, *The Sure Word of Prophecy* (London, 1879) ; Mildmay Second Advent Conference, *"Things That Shall Come to Pass"* (London, 1886).

hall which when completed in 1870 seated twenty-three hundred people.[26] The first of these Mildmay Second Advent conferences was convened by a group of respected and prominent millenarians, such as William R. Fremantle, dean of Ripon and president of the Prophecy Investigation Society; Horatius Bonar, editor of the *Quarterly Journal of Prophecy*; Edward Auriol, prebendary of Saint Paul's; and the London Plymouth Brethren preacher, Joseph Denham Smith. The conferences consisted of a series of addresses emphasizing the basic elements of the millenarian faith and skirting the areas of controversy. They represented, apparently, an attempt to put up an impressive united front and to awaken nonmillenarian churchmen to the cardinal points of this "neglected truth." In 1878 Edward Auriol, Horatius Bonar, Claremont Skrine, vicar of Emmanuel Church, Wimbledon, Andrew R. Fausett, biblical commentator and rector of Saint Cuthbert's, York, Dr. William P. Mackay, pastor of the Prospect Street Presbyterian Church, Hull, and the Earl of Shaftesbury offered variations on the familiar theme that the world could only be expected to grow worse and not better until the second advent. Canon Edward Hoare and several others spoke about the restoration of Israel, and four Bible readings were given. In 1879 the lectures became more specialized with such topics announced as, "Christ's Own Testimony Concerning His Second Coming," "The Two Advents Often Combined in Old Testament Scripture," and "The Two Resurrections." Captain R. Moreton, who served as chairman of one session in 1879, attended the 1892 Niagara conference where he served as chairman for the entire week's program. The 1886 conference offered much the same fare. Fifty-six millenarians sponsored and spoke at these three conferences at Mildmay Park, and almost half of them (twenty-six) can be identified as clergy of the Church of England. Denominational affiliation for sixteen participants has not been ascertained; many were laymen and probably were Anglicans. Only one other denomination contributed significantly to the conference —

26. *DNB*, and H. J. Owen, "Days in London: Mildmay Park," *Presbyterian*, 5 August 1876, p. 4.

the Plymouth Brethren, who were represented at least by the Earl of Cavan, Sir Robert Anderson, J. Denham Smith, T. Shuldham Henry, Theodore Howard, and Henry Varley. A wide variety of eschatologies was represented among the participants. H. Grattan Guinness was a champion of the historicist position; many, such as William P. Mackay, taught dispensationalist doctrine; G. H. Pember advocated a partial rapture theory; and Frank II. White had become an annihilationist. Perhaps as a result of these conferences, the *British Weekly* published throughout the summer of 1887 a debate on the question, "The Second Advent: Will It Be before the Millennium?" Canon A. R. Fausset and H. Grattan Guinness defended the millenarian cause with help from the Swiss evangelical Frederic Louis Godet. In 1888 the Scots held a conference of their own in Edinburgh where twenty-three speakers supported the millenarian position.[27]

These British conferences obviously influenced American millenarians. When writing about the 1867 millenarian conference in London conducted by the Plymouth Brethren, Joseph A. Seiss, editor of the *Prophetic Times,* had commented:

> We should be glad to see a free convention of those who hold with our doctrines in this country, but we should like it to be a meeting for more vigorous and aggressive work than common prayer and mutual exhortation alone. There are great questions in stern dispute among good men which need to be sifted, and the truth set out with all possible strength and scriptural proof. And there are important points in which it would be very desirable better to understand each other, and on which a solid and united public testimony would be of great force. Much prudence, and very thorough and prayerful preparation would, however, be necessary to make such a meeting, or deliverance, a real success. We are in hope of seeing it some day, if the Lord will.[28]

THE NIAGARA CONFERENCES obviously met some of this need, but the desire for a dignified but resounding public testimony

27. *Personal and Premillennial Coming of . . . Christ* (Edinburgh, 1888).

28. *Prophetic Times* 5 (1867) :74.

to the vigor of the millenarian forces and authority of their message prompted the Niagara leaders to put out a call for the First American Bible and Prophetic Conference. The conference call did not mention the serious social turmoil then troubling the United States — the depression that had begun with the panic of 1873, the labor unrest culminating in the ominous and alarming violence of the railroad strike in 1877, and the confusion within the political life of the country brought about by the contested election of 1876. But the later reaction of one of the prominent millenarians of the conference illustrates that theology and current events were not necessarily insulated.

> It is one of the ruling ideas of the century that man is fully capable of self-government, and that he is sure yet to work out — at least with the beneficent aid of Christianity — the great problem of government by the people for the people's good. To this confident anticipation of our democratic age premillennialism everywhere opposes the distasteful declaration that, according to the Scripture, all these hopes are doomed to disappointment; and that already, in the counsels of God, Mene, Tekel, Upharsin, is written concerning modern democracies no less than concerning Babylon of old.[29]

In this atmosphere, what the New York *Tribune* called a novel religious conference was called to order at 10 A.M., 30 October 1878, in New York's Holy Trinity Episcopal Church by its rector, Stephen H. Tyng, Jr.[30] Although there was some rain in the morning, people crowded into the large church and, by the afternoon session, had well filled the building. Five papers were read during the three sessions which occupied that first day, and although some exceeded ninety minutes and were closely argued, the *Tribune* reporter ob-

29. *Bibliotheca Sacra* 45 (1888) : 273. Kellogg (1839–99), a graduate of Princeton Seminary, missionary to India from 1865 to 1876 and again at the end of his life from 1893 to 1899, served as professor of theology at Western Theological Seminary from 1877 to 1886.

30. The New York *Tribune* printed a special edition of the paper for the conference. The proceedings were published as West, *Premillennial Essays.*

served that the audience was unusually attentive. On the evening of the second day, Philip Schaff attended the conference and was asked to pray. During two of the evening sessions the English Presbyterian minister, Dr. William P. Mackay, the dispensationalist millenarian who had spoken at the Mildmay conference earlier in the year, preached rather informally. Letters from other British millenarians, such as Horatius Bonar, were read to the audience. The titles of the addresses read like a litany of millenarianism, with basic points being made in a restrained and noncombative manner.

The committee which organized the conference included many familiar names — James H. Brookes, William G. Moorehead, A. J. Gordon, H. M. Parsons. Stephen H. Tyng, Jr., rector of Holy Trinity, does not seem to have attended the Niagara conferences, but had already made a reputation as a millenarian with a book entitled *He Will Come* (1877). William R. Nicholson (1822–1901) had joined the 1873 secession from the Protestant Episcopal church and become a bishop in the tiny Reformed Episcopal church. In light of the disproportionately large number of millenarians who joined this splinter group, there is reason to believe that issues associated with the millenarian movement may have played a hitherto unnoticed role in that schism. Certainly the type of intercommunion championed by W. R. Nicholson in his defense of his own departure from the Episcopal church was identical to that special brand of spiritual ecumenicism so prized among the Plymouth Brethren and at the Niagara conference.[31] Nicholson was active in millenarian conferences in 1886, 1887, 1890, and 1895. Maurice S. Baldwin (1836–1904) also became a bishop — the bishop of Huron in the Anglican church of Canada after 1883. In 1878 he was rector of Christ Church Cathedral, Montreal. The last clergyman on the committee was Rufus W. Clark, pastor of the

31. W. R. Nicholson, *Reasons Why I Became a Reformed Episcopalian* (Philadelphia, 1875). Kellogg (*Bibliotheca Sacra* 45 [1888]: 253) said that half the Episcopalians at the conference were Reformed Episcopalians. See also Paul Carter, "The Reformed Episcopal Schism of 1873," *Historical Magazine of the Protestant Episcopal Church* 33 (1964) : 225–38.

Reformed Dutch Church, Albany, New York. Both Baldwin and Clark spoke regularly at Niagara.

Since the 1878 conference was intended to put up a common front of millenarian witness against postmillennial and non-millennial clergymen, most of the speakers emphasized the common elements of the millenarian creed and talked often of unity. But a rather strenuous effort was made to dissociate the conference from Millerite adventism, in spite of the fact that Adventists joined in the call for the conference and attended the sessions. Rather than bringing their ascension robes with them, the New York *Tribune* reporter declared, the millenarians were attempting to weaken the Millerite tradition and to stimulate "holy living and spirituality." [32] The conference adopted a creedal statement, again designed to place some distance between themselves and the specter of William Miller, containing the following article:

> This second coming of the Lord Jesus is everywhere in the Scriptures represented as imminent, and may occur at any moment; yet the precise day and hour thereof is unknown to man, and known only to God. [33]

Not too much weight ought to be given to the fact that, in denying Millerite doctrine, the conference went on record as supporting dispensationalist doctrine. But if not everyone attending the conference caught the significance of Article 3, certainly the committee members introduced the words as the reflection of their own position.

Quite in contrast to their previous practice, millenarian speakers at the 1878 conference frequently referred to European scholars for support of their positions — a practice that persisted for the next two decades and then disappeared. There was an extensive tradition of continental millenarianism, to be sure, but before the 1878 conference the Americans seemed to have been ignorant of it. We have already

32. New York *Tribune*, 25 October 1878, p. 4.

33. West, *Premillennial Essays*, p. 8. This creedal statement was reaffirmed in 1886.

traced the close relationship between British and American millenarians. But aside from some evangelistic work among continental Jews and slight contact with Swiss pietists, the British and American millenarians had behaved previously as though there were no Europe. Nathaniel West and Samuel H. Kellogg, however, cited continental scholars, Kellogg at one time arguing that the nineteenth-century millenarian revival was due largely to European theologians such as Frederic L. Godet, Franz Delitzsch, and J. J. Van Osterzee. West cited Bengel and dozens of other German "authorities." These Americans may have learned from the men they cited, and there is no question about their familiarity with the literature. But there was an unavoidable sense of pretentiousness about elaborate references to literature most of which was no more authoritative than the articles published in American millenarian journals and much of which qualified as millenarian only when quoted in a very selective and discriminating fashion.[34]

Most of those associated with the 1878 conference resided in the northeastern part of the United States. Only one non-American speaker was present (Mackay) and only four Canadians signed the call for the conference. Of the 122 millenarians who signed that call, the great majority were from New York, New Jersey, Pennsylvania, and New England; eight from border states signed (none from the deep South, significantly), thirty-two from the Midwest (sixteen of those from Illinois), and one Presbyterian pastor from San Francisco. Analysis of the denominational representation on that call illustrates how selective was the appeal of the millenarian movement in North America.[35]

34. Godet, Auberlen, and the sources quoted in the 1878 appendix were not particularly authoritative; Delitzsch's and Lange's commentaries were not millenarian at all but were made to appear to support that position.

35. The denominational membership estimates were taken from Edwin W. Gaustad, *Historical Atlas of Religion in America* (New York, 1962). The Episcopalian attendance at the 1878 conference represents a combined total of Episcopal and Reformed Episcopal. The lone Lutheran was Joseph Seiss.

1878 Conference Call		1878 Denominational Membership	
Presbyterians	47	Methodists	3,000,000
Baptists	26	Baptists	2,000,000
Episcopalians	16	Presbyterians	900,000
Congregationalists	7	Lutherans	550,000
Methodists	6	Disciples	550,000
Adventists	5	Congregationalists	350,000
Dutch Reformed	4	Episcopalians	300,000
Lutherans	1		
Not identified	10		

Presbyterians and Episcopalians seem to be disproportionately represented, whereas Methodists, Lutherans, and Disciples of Christ appear to be greatly underrepresented. This result may be attributed in part to the influence of British Anglican and Presbyterian millenarians upon the American scene, but is probably also due to the strong stand millenarians took on such doctrines as free will, human depravity, and substitutionary atonement. The millenarian movement was providing a refuge for those whose basic orientation to Christianity was formed through the Calvinist theological heritage.

If publicity for the millenarian cause was one of their aims, the conveners of the 1878 conference succeeded handsomely. The reports and discussions of denominational newspapers and theological journals raised public awareness of the movement and its doctrines, but the reaction was not entirely beneficial or comforting to the millenarians. The *Christian Advocate*, the leading Methodist weekly, before the 1878 conference described millenarianism as a "fanciful theory" but harmless; after the conference, however, the editor devoted considerable space to its refutation.[36] The *Watchman*, a Boston Baptist paper, confessed "that we look with some anxiety upon the spread of the view represented at the so-called Prophetic Conference held in New York." Premillennialism, the editor prophesied, would sap all missionary initiative. He guessed that the greatest part of the millenarians were drawn from Roman Catholics and Episcopalians who despaired of evangelizing the world. None of the evangelical

36. *Christian Advocate* 53 (1878) : 691, 712.

denominations, he thought, would ever succumb to this doctrine while they remained prosperous.[37] Substitute the word "worldly" for "prosperous" and the millenarian would, no doubt, have agreed. "The modern easy-living, card-playing, theatre-going, dancing type of Christian, is very rarely found to be one who has learned to look for his Lord's premillennial advent," Samuel H. Kellogg wrote and then quoted Harnack in his defense:

> A genuine and living revival of chiliast hopes is always a sign that the church at large has become secularized to such a degree that tender consciences can no longer feel sure of their faith within her.[38]

Another Baptist paper, the Chicago *Standard*, although initially antagonistic to the millenarians, over a period of eight years considerably softened its attitude. In three articles written during the preconference days, the *Standard*'s New York correspondent displayed caution and concern over the "second advent excitement." The stories covering the conference itself, however, were mellower. He expressed surprise over the large number of reputable scholars who had agreed in their support of premillennialism. By 1886, when the second conference was held in Chicago, the *Standard*, though not a convert, spoke with a great deal more respect:

> It was in 1878 that the first "Bible and Prophetic Conference" was held in the city of New York. At that time the discussions were widely read and attracted to themselves large attention among Christian people. Taking up the promise of our Lord's coming, looked forward to by all, and considering the doctrine of the second advent from no sectarian stand-point, a freedom of speech and of hearing was granted, which would not otherwise in all probability have obtained. A new impulse was thereby given to subjects of prophetic study, the religious press of the country gave larger and larger space to the treatment of the intimations of the book of Revelation and kindred Scriptures, and new advo-

37. *Watchman* 59 (7, 14 November, 5 December 1878: 356, 364, 388.

38. *Bibliotheca Sacra* 45 (1888): 273.

cates of the theories suggested in the New York meeting, came to the front. One of the prominent participants in the programme which was announced for the second meeting in Chicago, Nov. 16–21, 1886, suggested that it seemed a strange thing that he should be a speaker in the meetings of today, whereas, at the time of the former session he was inclined to ridicule the doctrine. Pre-Millennial views, whatever may be said of them, have become so widespread in the various denominations, not excluding the Baptists, that it is folly to ignore this mode of Christian thinking, or to attempt to silence the discussion which is in progress.[39]

But attempts were made. It is common knowledge that biblical critics and liberals were charged with heresy during these decades and that some clergymen, such as Charles A. Briggs, were forced to leave their denominations. The threats of exclusion were not mounted against Liberalism alone, however. In 1882 Samuel H. Kellogg had an article entitled, "Is the Advent Pre-Millennial?" published in the *Presbyterian Review*.[40] For an article which contained nothing unusual, James H. Brookes's response was surprising. Brookes broke in on one of his own essays to report very excitedly that he had just seen Kellogg's article.

> It is well that the article of Prof. Kellogg was admitted, for when the rationalistic views of Prof. Briggs and Prof. Henry [Preserved] Smith were spread broadcast throughout the church, and the testimony of pre-millennialists was excluded, . . . a storm of indignation was gathering in the breasts of thousands, which would have made itself heard as of a rushing mighty wind.[41]

Other of Brookes's statements indicate that he feared that Presbyterian millenarians were in danger of being attacked and prosecuted as heretics. R. M. Patterson, in an article about the millenarians in the *Princeton Review*, although

---

39. *Standard* 26 (26 September, 24 October, 7 and 14 November 1878); and 34 (25 November 1886).

40. *Presbyterian Review* 3 (1882): 475–502.

41. *Truth* 8 (1882): 388–89.

criticizing them, pointed out that this form of eschatology had been accepted by too many Christians and was supported by too many biblical texts to be called heresy. He did not believe that the Presbyterian church could initiate discipline against premillennialists, although "some would have us believe the judicial axe is being sharpened."[42] Much of this turmoil seems to have been stirred up, ironically, by Charles A. Briggs. In reaction to the conference of 1878, Briggs wrote an article on "The Origin and History of Premillenarianism," in which he characteristically swashbuckled through patristic eschatology, arguing that millenarian church fathers of the second century were minor figures whose views of the last times were not accepted by the church as a whole. "Christian scholars are called upon once more," he said, "to meet this ancient and oft exploded error on the historic ground." The millenarians of the 1878 conference reminded him, Briggs said, of the "Anabaptists of the Reformation, and the Fifth Monarchy men of the English Revolution. . . . We see their culmination in the Zion of Münster."[43] Briggs expressed himself even more provocatively in the New York *Evangelist.*

> It depends entirely upon themselves what the future is to bring forth. If they will *abandon* their organization, *disband* their committee, *stop* their Bible and Prophetic Conferences, we doubt not that there will soon be a calm again, and they will remain undisturbed in their ecclesiastical relations; *but if* they are determined to go on in their aggressive movement, they will have only themselves to blame *if the storm should become a whirlwind that will constrain them to depart from the orthodox churches, and form another heretical sect.*[44]

These comments now echo with intimations of Briggs's own heresy trial and the later Fundamentalist schism within the Presbyterian church. But in the light of this developing con-

42. *Princeton Review*, Series 4, 2 (1879) : 415–34.
43. *Lutheran Quarterly* 9 (1879) : 207–45; quotes taken from pp. 208 and 245.
44. Quoted in G. N. H. Peters, *Theocratic Kingdom* (New York, 1884), 1: 481.

flict of the millenarians with their antagonists, it is not so clear as the traditional historiography of Fundamentalism has claimed which side in the controversy was the aggressor and which side the protector of orthodoxy.

Even J. N. Darby, traveling through France, heard of the 1878 conference and raised the question of heresy, although his views hardly coincided with Briggs's.

> In the congress at New York there was the positive good of bringing the coming of the Lord publicly forward; but there were all sorts of heretics there, and persons deliberately hindering the truth in seeking to connect it with the world and the camp — avowing it, if the account is to be believed — leaving out the essential point of the presence of the Holy Ghost. Let us be content to be little and despised, but give out the full truth.[45]

No one known to be affiliated with the Plymouth Brethren signed the call or attended the 1878 conference, in contrast to Mildmay, where they were relatively prominent; but Darby's views were being more widely represented than he realized. The Chicago *Interior*, a Presbyterian paper, carried an open letter on 20 March 1879, in which a man described as a distinguished Presbyterian minister reproached a correspondent for taking the position that "the professing Church is apostate and needs to be 'converted.'" "Plymouthism" is more dangerous than postmillennialism, this minister argued, although he himself supported the premillennial position.

> In answer to your question, "What shall be the relation and attitude toward the professing Church of those that wait for the Lord's appearing?" I can only speak for myself. . . . I am not going out of the Church of my fathers until I am cast out, unless that Church should, by some formal, official act, depart from the truth as set forth in its own standards.

The editors of the *Interior*, offering their own comments, suggested that the line separating millenarianism from "Plymouthism" was "very narrow and very easy to cross."

45. *Letters of J. N. D.*, 2:499.

> Our earnest, zealous brethren, in this new discussion of Millenarianism, cannot well be too cautious how they suffer their enthusiasm for what they deem new discoveries of truth, to unmoor them from the safe old shore line of orthodoxy and drift them out into this deep sea. Once afloat on the wide uncertain ocean of Plymouthism, and we know not where they will again find moorings.[46]

The conveners of the 1878 conference, thus, succeeded beyond their expectations in alerting American Protestants to the nature of their movement. Whether they had anticipated the volume of criticism that would accompany the publicity or had calculated the risks of attacks upon their party from antagonists such as Briggs is not known. But once initiated into the struggle, these leaders of millenarianism did not flinch or turn back, although faced with the threat of schism. They were utterly convinced that they were right. In the next decades their public conferences spread until they become an embarrassment to the historian.

THE SECOND American Bible and Prophetic Conference, 16–20 November 1886, extended over a longer period than the first but does not convey the same impression of good planning and serious thought, perhaps because of the rapidity with which the published report of the conference was issued. The addresses were taken down by stenographers, published the next morning in the Chicago *Inter Ocean*, and then bound at the end of the conference. Copies were on sale by the end of November.[47] Thirty-four millenarians either spoke at the conference or signed the call. Of these nineteen had been associated at the Niagara conference, twenty had participated in the 1878 conference and twenty-one would remain active in future conferences. Once again familiar names head the list: Brookes, Gordon, Baldwin, Nicholson, Parsons, Moorehead, Clark, Erdman, Needham, West, Kellogg, Munhall. As at the 1878 conference, Presbyterians dominated the proceedings,

46. *Interior*, 20 March 1879.
47. G. C. Needham, ed., *Prophetic Studies of the International Prophetic Conference* (Chicago, 1886).

with a large number of Baptists also represented. But surprisingly, very few Episcopalians participated (only Baldwin and Nicholson), possibly because the bulk of their churches were located farther east; and an unusually large number of Methodists (six) took part. Two of these Methodists, William Nast and E. F. Stroeter, belonged to the German Methodists, who seemed more open to millenarian influence than the English-speaking mother church. Munhall and Blackstone were actually independents with a Methodist heritage. J. S. Kennedy and Henry Lummis were not active in the movement after 1886. No Lutherans or Disciples of Christ were represented. J. M. Orrock, editor of the Boston Adventist paper *Messiah's Herald*, attended the 1886 conference as he had the 1878, and in 1886 delivered an address which contained a good many intimations of his Millerite heritage. Norman Kraus has argued that there are more indications of divergencies between interpreters at this conference than the previous one and that many more speakers give evidence of well-developed dispensational affinities (both of which points seem to be true). Kraus concludes that dispensational truth must have made great conquests between 1878 and 1886 (a conclusion not supported by the evidence cited).[48] The prevalence of dispensationalists at the 1886 conference resulted, more probably, from accidental factors such as the choice of speakers and the more informal, less apologetic stance of the proceedings. Without question, however, advocates of dispensationalism were prominently represented there. As mentioned previously, all of the participants at the conference accepted the 1878 premillennial creed, which included the affirmation of the any-moment coming. Periodical reaction to the conference was relatively slight. If the millenarians had hoped to equal their success in 1878, they must have been disappointed. In originating this series of conferences, the millenarians had planned with a double intention — to publicize their views among unbelievers and to strengthen the convictions of the converts. By 1886 the first

48. Norman Kraus, *Dispensationalism in America* (Richmond, 1958), pp. 89 ff.

of these intentions seems to have been slipping into the background, largely because the unbelievers were no longer listening — not, at least, beyond the outskirts of Chicago.

With the third conference in the series, this trend became even more exaggerated. Held in two Presbyterian churches in Allegheny, Pennsylvania, 3–6 December 1895, it aroused virtually no comment in the press and functioned very literally as a school of the prophets.[49] Although A. J. Gordon had died and J. H. Brookes was too ill to attend, almost all of the other participants were regular Niagara leaders. This trend was not, however, symptomatic of declining vigor among the millenarians. The 1878 conference functioned as the coming-out party of millenarianism, and one can only be a debutante once. It was natural that these second and third conferences not attract attention as had the first. Far from feeling discouraged by their experience with these later conferences, one must conclude that they were viewed as capital successes, for other conferences organized by the Niagara nucleus could be found all over America in the years following 1886. Two of the most significant were the Bible Inspiration Conference held in Chambers Church, Philadelphia, 15–18 November 1887, and the Bible Conference on the Holy Spirit held in the Mount Vernon Place Methodist Episcopal Church, Baltimore, 29 October and following days, 1890.[50] The leaders of both of these conferences belonged to the Niagara old guard. At the inspiration conference W. R. Nicholson acted as chairman, G. C. Needham as secretary, and A. T. Pierson edited the proceedings. Among the speakers were J. H. Brookes, J. M. Stifler, George S. Bishop, and W. G. Moorehead. The 1890 conference was organized by G. C. Needham and Amzi C. Dixon, a

49. Wm. S. Miller and Joseph Kyle, eds., *Addresses on the Second Coming of the Lord* (Pittsburgh, 1896). The Reverend Dr. John H. Prugh, in paying tribute to the teachers of the conference during the final session, stated, "Some of these Doctors were our teachers in other days, and we loved them then. And, during these past four days having sat at their feet again, and at the feet of those who companied with them, we delight, to-night, to pay honor to them all" (ibid., p. 219).

50. A. T. Pierson, ed., *The Inspired Word* (New York, 1888) ; and A. C. Dixon, ed., *The Person and Ministry of the Holy Spirit* (London, 1891).

younger Baptist minister from Baltimore who had spoken at Niagara. Among the speakers were Bishop, Erdman, Munhall, Nicholson, and D. M. Stearns — all familiar faces on the Niagara platform. That this association was not accidental is made clear by Dixon's statement that the conference on the Holy Spirit belonged to the series begun in New York and continued in Chicago and Philadelphia. In the two conferences of 1887 and 1890 the millenarian movement almost belied its name, wearing in public view the more comprehensive theological dress that we have examined already in its private manifestation at the Niagara conferences. As will be remembered, the doctrines of inspiration and the role of the Holy Spirit had been given prominent place at Niagara, both on the platform and in the creed drawn up by Brookes. The millenarian was becoming the complete Christian.

With the founding of the Baptist Society for Bible Study we discover a different puzzle. We have just commented upon millenarian conferences in which prophecy was not discussed. The Baptist Society for Bible Study was a denominational organization which declared itself nonsectarian. Sources for the history of the BSBS are sketchy, but it is known that the group was organized in the spring of 1890, named A. J. Gordon president, held a conference 18–21 November 1890 in Centennial Baptist Church, Brooklyn, and adopted Gordon's paper, the *Watchword*, as its official journal. Although yearly meetings were projected, no other meeting of this group is known except for a conference held 12–16 November 1900 in the Hanson Place Baptist Church, Brooklyn. In the light of the history of the earlier Bible conference movement, it is evident that this society was only another manifestation of Niagara. The BSBS was composed of millenarians associated with Niagara, many of them dispensationalists who also happened to be Baptists. And indeed, being Baptist hardly seemed to matter. The prospectus read:

> The constituency of this Society is made up of Baptist brethren, who believe in the pre-millennial coming of our Lord. . . . All who are in sympathy with our purpose are cordially invited. Christians

of every evangelical school we welcome to our gatherings.[51]

When Gordon reported that the BSBS had selected the *Watchword* as the "organ to which their support and cooperation are pledged," he promised that the paper in the future would "not be denominational, but strictly spiritual, not sectarian, but scriptural."[52] As might be expected, the roster of this organization reads like an index to Baptist millenarians; most of the speakers at the 1890 conference were alumni of one or more of the conferences previously discussed.

51. The quote was found on a sheet inserted between pp. 280 and 281 of *Watchword* 12 (Nov. 1890); the conference proceedings were published as G. C. Needham, ed., *Primitive Paths in Prophecy* (Chicago, 1891).

52. *Watchword* 12 (1890): 309.

7

The Millenarian Meridian

THE MILLENARIANS within the United States never grew large enough to overawe any of the denominations to which they belonged. Their conception of the church seemed to dissolve any ambitions toward denominational leadership — at least few of them held administrative positions. They preached to their congregations and on the burgeoning conference circuit, they wrote for their periodicals, and they published books. Their cause had developed from a midcentury interest in prophecy and the premillennial advent into a unified but multifaceted concept of Christianity, supported by some display of scholarship and a great deal of personal, interdenominational leadership. Their aims were first of all evangelical. Millenarian faith, W. E. Blackstone wrote, "gives us a view of the world, as a wrecked vessel, and stimulates us to work with all our might that we may save some." [1] This involved revivalism, but particularly foreign missions. Second, they worked to arrest the alarming progress of apostasy within Protestantism, even though they recognized such degeneration as a part of the pattern of events predicted for the last days. Because they did not expect to save the world or the church, historians have assumed that they did not want to succeed and have failed to ask what — other than the second advent — they might have accepted as the fulfillment of their aims. To understand the Fundamentalism of the twentieth century we must first recognize that these fathers of the Fundamentalists at the end of the nineteenth century came very close to impressing their vision of the church and the world upon at least one segment of evangelical Protestantism.

1. *Jesus Is Coming* (New York, 1898), pp. 18–19.

The Millenarian Meridian

As we have seen, the millenarians were never in a position to exert equal influence upon all sections of the United States or upon all the denominations represented there. Never rural or in any sense a grass-roots sentiment arising from the congregations, millenarianism had taken hold first among urban pastors, particularly in New York, Boston, Philadelphia, and Chicago and their surrounding areas. Their conference retreats to the lakeside, the seaside, or the countryside were no more the reflection of an agrarian mentality than are fresh-air camps for ghetto children. During the nineteenth century millenarianism had not penetrated very far into the South or grown with any extraordinary rapidity in the West.

A surprising number of denominations remained virtually untouched by millenarianism. No representative of the Disciples of Christ is known to have attended any of the conferences or to have written for any of the periodicals sponsored by them. Although the Lutherans had been well represented in the earlier part of the century, by Joseph A. Seiss especially, they disappeared completely after 1878, probably because of the surge of Scandinavian and German immigrants whose confessional and liturgical orientation and lack of English language swamped the syncretistic tendencies in the more Americanized part of the denomination.[2] Few Methodists were influenced by millenarianism and many of those that were seemed, inexplicably, to leave the denomination as their allegiance to millenarianism increased. L. W. Munhall, E. F. Stroeter, Arno C. Gaebelein, and W. E. Blackstone all either formally or practically severed their connections with Methodism, and when they were counted out, few Methodist millenarians remained. Why the Methodists should feel obliged to forsake their denomination when Presbyterians and Baptists did not remains a riddle. Episcopalians played a prominent role in the establishment of millenarianism in the United States, but at the end of the century their participation had been greatly reduced, probably in direct proportion to the success of the broad churchmanship of such leaders as Phil-

2. For one branch of Lutheranism see Milton L. Rudnick, *Fundamentalism and the Missouri Synod* (Saint Louis, 1966).

lips Brooks and the growing popularity of the Oxford movement. The Reformed Episcopalians, however, continued to play a prominant part in millenarianism.

As early as 1864–65 the Dutch Reformed church had witnessed controversy over the teachings of the millenarians in the debate carried on in the columns of the *Christian Intelligencer*. But after that time very little interest seemed to arise. Demarest, indeed, never made another appearance among the millenarians, although he lived until 1897. W. R. Gordon participated in the founding of the Niagara conference and signed the call for the 1878 conference, but from that date until his death, also in 1897, he too disappeared from millenarian circles. Only George S. Bishop remained active, and he had been trained at Princeton and ordained a Presbyterian. No German Reformed millenarians are known. Congregationalists were just as scarce; only Edward P. Goodwin, pastor of the First Congregational Church of Chicago, played an active role, unless one counts the itinerating and in effect nondenominational Reuben A. Torrey and Cyrus I. Scofield.

In fact, by the end of the nineteenth century, only the Baptists and Presbyterians were providing substantial support for the millenarian movement, but they were providing strong support indeed. The death of A. J. Gordon in 1895 deprived the millenarians of the greatest Baptist leader in the movement's history, but his influence lived on in the *Watchword*, the Boston Missionary Training School, and the Clarendon Street Church, and in the careers of many devoted followers such as F. L. Chapell and James M. Gray. But great as his influence was, not even his prestige was able to awaken Andover and Newton to the importance of the millenarian message. Baptist seminaries with one exception remained unimpressed by the millenarian campaign. Millenarian James M. Stifler (1839–1902) served as professor of New Testament at Crozer Seminary from 1882 to 1902, opening the door for what must have been a considerable millenarian influence during the last years of the century. Stifler, who had served eight pastorates before being called to the seminary, was one of the most active millenarians of whom we have any record. He signed the call of the 1878 Bible and Prophetic Conference, acted as a convener of the 1887 conference on inspiration and also spoke there, helped to organize and then spoke at the first meeting of the Baptist Society for Bible Study in 1900, appeared regularly at the Niagara meetings during the 1890s, spoke at the Seaside Bible Conference, organized in 1893 at Asbury Park, New Jersey, by L. W. Munhall, and appeared in 1895 at the Bible and Prophetic Conference in Allegheny, Pennsylvania, and at the Old Point Comfort Bible Conference in Virginia. Whether through Stifler's influence or not, the long-time president of Crozer, Henry G. Weston, was partially drawn into the millenarian movement — at least to the point that he became a favored speaker at Moody's Northfield conference during the late 1890s and served as one of the editors of the dispensationalist *Scofield Reference Bible*.[3] Such slight contact can easily be exaggerated, and it would not deserve citation if there were not quite a number of other such connections apparent in the millenarian movement of the 1890s. In earlier Bible and Prophetic conferences and in the Niagara meetings, no one not completely committed to premillennial truth was ever intentionally invited to speak. But in the later conferences, conservatives — particularly conservative scholars in the seminaries — seem to have been sought for these programs. There is a good deal of presumptive evidence that the millenarians were seeking allies in their efforts to protect their denominations from the disastrous consequences of biblical criticism. Howard Osgood, during the last quarter of the nineteenth century one of the stalwarts of the Rochester Divinity School faculty, addressed the 1887 conference on inspiration and appeared again at the Seaside Bible Conference in 1893 in company with Munhall, Brookes, Moorehead, Bishop, and

3. Another Crozer professor, George D. B. Pepper, defended the inerrancy of the Bible in his *Outlines of Systematic Theology* (Philadelphia, 1873). Some discussion of these conservative Baptists is given in Norman H. Maring, "Baptists and Changing Views of the Bible, 1865–1918," *Foundations* 1 (July and October 1958).

Stifler.[4] Edgar Y. Mullins, president of the Southern Baptist Seminary, Louisville, from 1899 to 1928, spoke at another in the series of Bible and Prophetic conferences in Boston in 1901 on the subject, "Redemption: Past, Present and Future."[5] As we turn to the Presbyterians, we will see this informal alliance in more extended form. But before we leave the Baptists, another comment on the Southern Baptists seems necessary. Before being named to his Louisville position, Mullins had served pastorates in Baltimore and Boston, where he probably made the contacts that brought him the invitation to speak at the 1901 conference. But dispensational millenarianism was being spread among Southern Baptists by James R. Graves, long-time editor of the *Tennessee Baptist*. Graves wrote a millenarian book entitled *The Work of Christ in the Covenant of Redemption; Developed in Seven Dispensations* which was published by the Baptist Book House in 1883 and in which Graves gives no evidence of his sources but does teach Darbyite dispensationalism, including the secret rapture. Perhaps as a result of this book, Graves was invited to deliver a paper at the 1886 Bible and Prophetic Conference. In the pages of his weekly newspaper Graves was teaching the same kind of dispensationalism as early as 1870, and in 1874 he published a series of seven articles by B. G. Hewlett entitled, "The Advent Premillennial and the Reign of Christ Personal — Is It Old or New Theology?" Since the *Tennessee Baptist* was a respected and widely read newspaper, the effect of several decades of consistent millenarian proselyting must have been substantial.[6]

Presbyterianism unquestionably provided more leadership

4. The Seaside Conference proceedings were published as L. W. Munhall, ed., *Anti-Higher Criticism* (New York, 1894).

5. *Addresses of the International Prophetic Conference Held December 10–15, 1901* (Boston, [1901 ?]).

6. In the *Work of Christ* see especially pp. 391 ff. For reasons that were never clarified, Graves did not deliver his paper at the

1886 premillennial conference. Hewlett's series in the *Tennessee Baptist* began on 21 February 1874. T. A. Patterson, "The Theology of J. R. Graves" (unpublished Th.D. thesis, Southwestern Baptist Theological Seminary, 1944), fails to discuss Graves's millenarianism in relation to dispensationalism or to identify its source.

and converts to the millenarian movement than any other denomination. In every conference and publication these names
recur — James H. Brookes, William J. Erdman, H. M. Parsons, Samuel H. Kellogg, William G. Moorehead, Nathaniel
West. When this leadership was thinned by death and no
new Presbyterian millenarians stepped in to fill their places,
the character of the cause was changed and the vitality ebbed.
The United Presbyterian church seems to have contained
more millenarians in proportion to its membership than any
other denomination in the United States, with the possible
exception of the Reformed Episcopal. The seminary at Xenia
was heavily represented, with three millenarian presidents in
succession — William G. Moorehead (professor of New Testament 1873–99, president 1899–1912), Joseph Kyle (professor of systematic theology 1899–1912, president 1912–22),
and Melvin Grove Kyle (professor of biblical archeology
1908–22, president 1922–30). The third Bible and Prophetic
Conference, held in the very Presbyterian town of Allegheny,
Pennsylvania, seems to have been run largely by United Presbyterians. J. T. Cooper, professor at Allegheny Seminary,
spoke at both the Niagara conferences and at the 1878 conference. At least one-quarter of the Presbyterians who signed
the call for the 1878 conference were affiliated with United
Presbyterian churches, most of them coming from the area
served by the Allegheny and Xenia seminaries.

Greater interest and significance attach, however, to the
millenarians within the main body of Presbyterianism and
to their relationship with the church's chief seminary,
Princeton. At least nine Presbyterian millenarians, including
Brookes, Bishop, Duffield, and Kellogg, were trained at
Princeton, but they were never encouraged to embrace millenarianism by the Princeton faculty. The editor of the Chicago *Interior*, himself a Princeton graduate, wrote, "We once
heard the venerable Dr. Archibald Alexander remark that
an absorbing study of the unfulfilled prophecies [*sic*] was
somewhat dangerous ground for unsteady people to tread;
that it had unsettled some minds and wrecked others."[7] Con-

7. Chicago *Interior*, 20 March 1879, p. 4.

sistent with that position, the faculty at the seminary kept clear of any involvement in the millenarian movement. A survey of the book reviews in the *Presbyterian and Reformed Review* at the end of the nineteenth century, however, shows that Princeton criticism of the millenarians was frequently tempered with appreciation when the authors under review fell in line with the tenets of the Princeton Theology. Warfield, whose keen mind and pungent pen were utilized most ably in his comments upon contemporary religious life, wrote a brief, calm review of Nathaniel West's *Studies in Eschatology* in which he acknowledged that West possessed both the "light of learning" and the "fire of genius," but, with all that, West still did not convince him. A few years later, reviewing R. A. Torrey's *What the Bible Teaches*, Warfield again mixed criticism and praise, calling the book "a series of thoughtful Bible readings . . . an admirable example of an admirable method of teaching." But he concluded, "Mr. Torrey still teaches his Arminianizing theory of redemption, and his Keswick doctrine of the Baptism of the Spirit, as well as his burning, evangelical blood-theology." James H. Brookes's voluminous publications were regularly reviewed. *Chaff and Wheat*, a defense of verbal inspiration, was simply noted in 1892, but Talbot W. Chambers praised and recommended *God Spake All These Words*, yet another defense of inspiration, *The Mystery of Suffering*, and *The Christ.*[8]

This kind of evidence is hardly necessary to demonstrate that considerable common theological ground existed between the millenarian and the Princeton positions. The similarity of their conclusions about the nature of biblical authority has already been noted in chapter 5. That Brookes's Niagara creed affirmed the inspiration of the "original autographs" in the same year that that phrase became a part of the apologetic of the Princeton theologians demonstrates remarkable similarity of views if not direct influence. Both groups agreed in their world view as well, remaining sharply critical of

8. *Presbyterian and Reformed Review* 1 (1890) : 513–14; 10 (1899) : 562; 3 (1892) : 369; 6 (1895) : 573; 1 (1890) : 705; and 5 (1894) : 554.

American secular and religious institutions and affirming what we might call a pessimistic but what they would probably have preferred to call a realistic view of the future, although they obviously differed in their interpretations of prophecy. Both schools of thought drew upon a Calvinistic view of man and, although they denigrated man's abilities, they elevated the character of the redemption that could save him. Both emphasized a method with intellectual roots in the empirical tradition of the eighteenth century. They thought in terms of absolutes and possessed no comprehension of history as process. The dispensationalism affirmed by so many millenarians allowed its adherents to perpetuate rather than to confront this misunderstanding — allowed its adherents to postulate a series of epochs with different ground rules, while safely preserving their own age from any reinterpretation. Neither Princeton nor the millenarians understood or could tolerate the new idea of *Heilsgeschichte*. And, last, both conceived of God's acts as qualitatively different from man's acts and placed great emphasis upon differences between the natural and supernatural. In an era in which the distance between the two was being narrowed by man's achievements on the one hand and the critics' judgments on the other, these two apologists were commonly and rigorously maintaining the disjunction, arguing, for instance, that any attempt to understand the human side of the Bible was tantamount to desecrating it.

The book reviews in the *Presbyterian and Reformed Review* demonstrate that Princeton theologians were not ready to join Briggs's campaign for the excommunication of the millenarians but rather were willing to say a good word for them when they stood up for what Princeton considered the true gospel. An informal alliance (already partly explored in its Baptist context) seems to have developed between the millenarians and that side of Presbyterianism represented by Princeton Seminary. We have already noticed that in the 1887 inspiration conference in Philadelphia, the Rochester professor Howard Osgood shared the platform with the millenarians. He was joined by several other nonmillenarians as well, including Talbot W. Chambers, professor of New Testament literature at Princeton during 1891–92. Chambers and William Henry Green, professor of Old Testament literature at Princeton, spoke in 1893 at the Seaside Bible Conference arranged by L. W. Munhall. The millenarians visited Princeton as well. In the correspondence of A. T. Pierson there is a letter dated 16 January 1884, from A. A. Hodge, urging Pierson to try to attend some special services for seminary students at which he also expected A. J. Gordon to be present. W. J. Erdman sent his son to Princeton Seminary and saw him eventually become a professor of practical theology. Charles R. Erdman, a millenarian product of the Niagara conferences he often attended, thus became a living symbol of the alliance between the two movements.[9]

A final example of this kind of cooperation is revealed in the minutes of the Presbyterian General Assembly for 1893. As one of its principal items of business the General Assembly overruled the presbytery of New York and suspended Charles Augustus Briggs from the Presbyterian ministry. Immediately after that judgment a committee of eighty ministers and elders, apparently convinced that Briggs's condemnation had been possible only because the Presbyterian clergy and elders had accepted the Princeton doctrine of inerrancy as the equivalent of the confessional standard, produced a lengthy protest. This read, in part:

> The undersigned enter respectful and earnest protest against the action of this Assembly, which declares the inerrancy of the original autographs of Scripture to be the faith of the Church. We protest against this action.
> 1. Because it is insisting upon a certain theory of inspiration, when our Standards have hitherto only emphasized the fact of inspiration. So far as the original manuscript came from God, undoubtedly it was without error. But we have no means of determining how far God controlled the penmen in tran-

9. The A. T. Pierson and Charles R. Erdman papers are located in the Speer Library of Princeton Seminary.

scribing from documents in matters purely circumstantial. . . .

4. Because it is setting up an imaginary Bible as
a test of orthodoxy. If an inerrant original Bible is
vital to faith, we cannot escape the conclusion that
an inerrant present Bible is vital to faith.

5. Because it is disparaging the Bible we have,
and endangering its authority under the pressure of
a prevalent hostile criticism. It seems like flying for
shelter to an original autograph, when the Bible we
have in our hands to-day is our impregnable
defense.

Believing these present Scriptures to be "The very
Word of God" and "immediately inspired by God,"
"kept pure in all ages" and "our only infallible rule
of faith and practice," notwithstanding some appar
ent discrepancies in matters purely circumstantial,
we earnestly protest against the imposing of this
new interpretation of our Standards upon the
Church, to bind men's consciences by enforced subscription to its terms.

The General Assembly's answer to this challenge to the Princeton and millenarian understanding of the inspiration of the
Bible was to appoint a committee of five, who after brief
deliberation presented a report which the Assembly approved.
The committee, in effect, denied the charges of the protestants,
arguing that the Princeton view of inspiration only affirmed
the Westminster Confession and the Larger Catechism. They
concluded:

We can, therefore, say with the protestants, we
believe "these present Scriptures to be the very
Word of God," and "immediately inspired by God,"
"kept pure in all ages," and "our only infallible
rule of faith and practice;" while if errors were
found in the original autographs they could not
have proceeded from "God, who is truth itself, the
author thereof."

The members of the committee were Ethelbert D. Warfield,
brother of B. B. Warfield, president of Lafayette College,
named the next year to the board of directors of the Princeton
Seminary; James T. Leftwich, a minister from Baltimore;

W. A. Eudaly, a ruling elder from Cincinnati; Hiram W. Congdon, New York minister and millenarian, respected leader of the Niagara conference; and — James H. Brookes.[10]

There is a good deal of evidence, then, pointing to a developing cordiality and cooperation between millenarians and defenders of the Princeton type of conservatism within both the Baptists and the Presbyterian denominations. There is very little evidence of millenarian beliefs among the scholars who were drawn into this alliance and nothing like an amalgamation of the two groups took place. But though not entirely compatible, a working agreement did seem to grow up between these very different kinds of Christians. Two more illustrations of this alliance remain to be discussed, both of them deserving extensive description and analysis. *The Fundamentals*, the ten volumes published from 1910 to 1915 and usually said to mark the beginning of the Fundamentalist controversy, will be treated in chapter 8. The Northfield conference will be discussed in the rest of this chapter.

DURING THE LAST two decades of the nineteenth century the unordained Dwight L. Moody was the most influential "clergyman" in America. With almost no formal education and only the simplest theological notions, Moody still managed to win the friendship and admiration of men as diverse as William Rainey Harper and James H. Brookes. From 1880 until his death Moody brought speakers to Northfield, Massachusetts, for summer conference sessions that attracted men of all persuasions and changed the character of American Protestantism. As a result of Moody's efforts a new kind of pietistic holiness was brought from England to this continent, the Bible institute movement began to gather momentum, and the missionary program of the evangelicals reached its crest in the Student Volunteer Movement. With Moody as ally and convert, and with the Northfield conference as a sounding board for their views, the millenarians had an unparalleled

10. *Minutes of the General Assembly of the Presbyterian Church*, 16 (1893) : pp. 163–69. Brookes and Congdon had also been members of the committee of fifteen which had presented the unfavorable report on Briggs.

opportunity to impress their own view of this world and the
next upon evangelical Christianity. During the late nineties
the movement reached a level of influence and power that
marks that era as the meridian of millenarianism.[11]

Moody was always willing to experiment and was open to
influence and suggestion from those whom he felt he could
trust. His theology was very much the product of the forces
prevailing in late nineteenth-century evangelicalism — among
which was, of course, millenarianism. While still known only
locally for his Sunday school work in Chicago, Moody met
and fell out with J. N. Darby. The visit of Harry Moorhouse,
with his week-long series of Bible readings on John 3:16, was
a great influence on Moody's style and content, and the
writings of C. H. Mackintosh, Darby's popularizer, were apparently even more significant. Moody wrote about them:

> Some time since I had my attention called to
> C. H. M.'s Notes, and was so much pleased and at
> the same time profited by the way they opened up
> Scripture truths, that I secured at once all the writ-
> ings of the same author, and if they could not be
> replaced, would rather part with my entire library,
> excepting my Bible, than with these writings. They
> have been to me a very key to the Scriptures.[12]

Moody was too independent and eclectic to tie himself completely to Plymouth Brethren theology, but there can be no
question that it had significant influence upon him. As early
as 1877 Moody had become a millenarian and was teaching,
in his own rough style, that Christians ought to be ready
to welcome Christ's second advent at any moment.

> Now I can't find any place in the Bible where it tells
> me to wait for signs of the coming of the millen-
> nium, as the return of the Jews, and such like; but
> it tells me to look for the coming of the Lord; to
> watch for it; to be ready at midnight to meet him,

11. Rather than compress
Moody's career into a much-too-
brief sketch, readers are referred
to the recent, much-needed critical study of the revivalist by
James Findlay (*Dwight L.*

*Moody: American Evangelist,
1837–1899* [Chicago, 1969]).
12. Quoted from a book adver-
tisement in *Watchword and Truth*
22 (1900) : 255.

like those five wise virgins. The trump of God may
be sounded, for any thing we know, before I finish
this sermon; at any rate we are told that he will
come as a thief in the night, and at an hour when
many look not for him.[13]

When Moody convened the first Northfield conference on
1 September 1880, he had chosen a group of speakers who
were almost all veteran leaders of the millenarian conferences
discussed in the last chapter — A. J. Gordon, George Needham, the Presbyterian evangelist Edward P. Hammond (who
is not known to have been a millenarian) and George F. Pentecost.[14] Pentecost (1842–1920), a Baptist minister who had
been quite friendly with A. J. Gordon during a Boston pastorate, had been persuaded by Moody to leave his settled ministry
for evangelism, in which he was moderately successful until
the turn of the century. Pentecost had signed the call for the
1878 premillennial conference and was active as a millenarian
up to 1918.[15] During the second year of the conference
(1881), when the theme was Bible study, Gordon, Needham,
and Pentecost were joined by James H. Brookes, E. P. Goodwin, and D. W. Whittle. Whittle (1840–1901), an evangelist
and hymn writer, was a close associate of Moody's and a familiar leader in the Niagara conferences from their inception
as well as lending his support to both the 1878 and 1886 Bible
and Prophetic conferences.

The series of conferences was interrupted during the next
few years while Moody was in Britain conducting revival
meetings, but was resumed in 1885. Except for temperance
speakers and a young English cricket hero, J. E. K. Studd, all
the speakers were millenarians — Gordon, Munhall, A. T.

13. W. H. Daniels, *Moody: His
Words, Work, and Workers*
(New York, 1877), pp. 472 ff.;
see also pp. 467 ff.
14. *Northfield Echoes* is the best
source of information about the
conference programs and, unless
otherwise noted, material is
taken from that periodical; see
especially A. T. Pierson, "The

Story of the Northfield Conferences," ibid., 1 (June 1894):1–13;
and A. T. Pierson, *Forward
Movements of the Last Half Century* (New York, 1900).
15. Phineas C. Headley,
George F. Pentecost (Boston,
1880). Pentecost spoke at a
Philadelphia premillennial conference in 1918.

Pierson, and W. W. Clark. By 1886 the influence of the millenarians had become so strong that they were referred to as the "usual war horses" in the list of speakers, and the topic for the week was dispensational truth, especially teaching concerning the second coming of Christ. Joining the "war horses" were Nathaniel West, W. J. Erdman, H. M. Parsons, W. E. Blackstone, and Marcus Rainsford, an Anglican millenarian who had spoken at the 1878 Mildmay Second Advent conference. By 1886 the leaders of the millenarian movement had practically taken over the Northfield conference and transformed it into another of their familiar premillennial gatherings.

Surprisingly, however, the next year the conference appears to have been arranged quite differently, with fewer millenarians present, and by 1888 their presence had been completely exorcised. This drought continued until 1893 when Whittle, Needham, and A. C. Dixon appeared as speakers. This number was increased in 1894 (Pierson, Gordon, and James M. Gray, as well as Needham, Whittle, and Dixon), and millenarians continued as the largest single group represented at Northfield from that time until several years after Moody's death in 1899. We can only speculate about the causes of this vacillation. Moody may simply have wished to bring in some new acquaintances. He did not reject millenarianism or object to the presence of millenarians — one or two of them were always invited even during the period 1888 to 1892. We may have some clue to the increasing number of millenarians after 1892 in the fact that Moody asked A. J. Gordon to take his place as director of the conference in 1892 and 1893.

Whatever the reasons, millenarians were represented and numerically dominant in most of the Northfield conferences, giving them a nationally prominent platform from which to teach and an extraordinary opportunity to establish themselves as prominent, reputable Protestant leaders. They also spoke in association with nonmillenarian conservatives such as Henry C. Mabie, secretary of the American Baptist Missionary Union, and Henry G. Weston, president of Crozer

Seminary, or John Balcom Shaw, pastor of the West End Presbyterian Church, New York City, and John Willis Baer, assistant secretary of the Presbyterian Board of Home Missions and president of Occidental College from 1906 to 1916. This, of course, helped to strengthen the associations between the millenarians and the conservatives within the Baptist and Presbyterian denominations. Not all of the speakers selected by Moody were considered safely orthodox by the millenarians, and they sometimes became alarmed that Moody was on the brink of selling out to Modernism. When Moody invited George Adam Smith, professor of Old Testament at Free Church College, Glasgow, a man feared for his acceptance of higher criticism, the *Watchword and Truth* began its editorial condemnation of Moody by quoting Paul's words in Galatians, "Though we, or an angel from heaven, preach any other gospel unto you than that which we have preached unto you, let him be accursed." Even Moody could go too far.[16]

Moody used the Northfield conferences to introduce British clergymen whom he had met on his evangelistic tours to American audiences. On one occasion the millenarians objected to one of these British speakers strenuously enough to caucus and then send a representative to Moody to protest against the new heresy this man was teaching.[17] The date was probably 1891, the man was the Reverend Frederick B. Meyer (1847–1929), a well-known Baptist minister whom Moody had met in York in 1872. Meyer's "heresy" was a doctrine of personal sanctification associated with the Keswick conferences in England. Moody managed to pacify the disgruntled millenarian leaders, and Meyer and other spokesmen for Keswick holiness ultimately convinced them that this was no heresy but an essential part of the Christian gospel. Thus Northfield served as an influence upon as well as a vehicle for millenarian teaching.

A chief concern among those, such as James Inglis and

16. *Watchword and Truth* 21 (August 1899). A similar response appeared in *Our Hope* 5 (1899) : 427.

17. William M. Runyan, *Dr. Gray at Moody Bible Institute* (New York, 1935), p. 5 ff.

George C. Needham, who in 1868 initiated the pre-Niagara conferences was "the ancient heresy of a sentimental higher life." Needham stated that "a fancied perfection was taught through fanciful interpretations, and the deceitful handling of God's Word to maintain such teaching, led Mr. Inglis . . . to call together the brethren." [18]

This antagonism toward the revival of perfectionism within American Protestantism helps to explain why the millenarian movement did not appeal to many Methodists or to the members of the Nazarene and Pentecostal groups which began to flourish later in the century. Through Charles G. Finney and Asa Mahan the Oberlin perfectionism influenced the reformed tradition in the United States, but it was opposed by the more conservative elements within the Presbyterian church and by the millenarians as well.[19] But the millenarians did not neglect the doctrine of the Holy Spirit or the need for holy living. The Niagara creed, it will be recalled, stressed in Article 11 that the Holy Spirit was an immediate personal influence in the lives of every believer and in Article 12 that every Christian was called "so to live in the Spirit that we should not fulfill the lusts of the flesh." [20] But even while affirming that belief, the Niagara creed warned that "the flesh being still in us to the end of our earthly pilgrimage needs to be kept constantly in subjection to Christ, or it will surely manifest its presence to the dishonor of His name." The millenarians evidently feared the antinomian tendencies which they felt were present within the holiness revival of the late nineteenth century.

For the millenarian, however, the traditional doctrine of the role of the Holy Spirit was hardly a suitable expression of his view of the spiritual world. The Spirit was at work within the Church, the Christian had traditionally affirmed, and with this statement the millenarian would not have quarreled. But the millenarians did not expect the Church to triumph in this world, and many of them felt that the Church was apos-

18. *Watchword* 13 (1891) : 60.
19. For an excellent discussion of the Oberlin perfectionism and the perfectionist movement

as a whole, see B. B. Warfield, *Perfectionism* (New York, 1931).
20. See Appendix A for the full text of the Niagara creed.

tate, adulterous, and ruined. This kind of attitude toward the Church naturally involved the millenarian in some reassessment of the Spirit's role in the world. This can be seen, apparently, in the consistent emphasis upon the Holy Spirit as a person and not a force, noted already in the Niagara creed. Churches for these millenarian believers (and, of course, for many nonmillenarians as well) were reduced to loose associations of individuals, and the Spirit's work was similarly seen as person-to-person activity. F. M. Ellis, a Baltimore Baptist minister and one of the speakers at the millenarian Bible conference on the Holy Spirit held in Baltimore in 1890, concluded in discussing the Spirit's role in the Church, "Our best service towards the spiritualization of the church will be found, I am persuaded, in our becoming personally more spiritual."[21] For the historian this personal spirituality rings with associations from the mystical tradition of the Church; and in that tradition the quest of the believer for sinless perfection and the problem of antinomianism has never been absent. Thus, the millenarians, though developing in part out of a desire to escape from the antinomian tendencies within the holiness revival of the 1850s, found themselves drawn back into the movement for personal sanctification.

The ambiguity of the millenarian position on the doctrine of sanctification is perfectly reflected in the history of the Keswick doctrine, for the Keswick movement originated in the Oberlin perfectionism that the millenarians had felt it necessary to condemn. A group of American perfectionists, visiting England after their success in the revivals of the late fifties and sixties in the United States, began to hold conferences, first privately at Langley Park, Norfolk, in 1873, and at Broadlands, Romsey, Hampshire, in 1874, and then publicly at Oxford, 29 August to 7 September 1874, where the conference was called the Oxford Union Meeting for the Promotion of Scriptural Holiness, and at Brighton, 29 May to 7 June 1875. Asa Mahan, the former president of Oberlin College, who had retired to England, participated in these

21. *Watchword* 13 (1891) : 153.

meetings, but the most significant leaders were Mr. and Mrs. William E. Boardman and Mr. and Mrs. Robert Pearsall Smith, all American Presbyterians. Women played a prominent part in the holiness revival. Both of these wives were well known through their books, especially Mrs. Hannah Whitall Smith, who was probably more influential than her husband. The Brighton meeting attracted eight thousand persons and marked the climax of this phase of the movement. R. P. Smith seems to have suffered some kind of nervous breakdown during which he may have said or done something scandalous. The periodicals are full of innuendoes about Smith and no clear report of his activities, save that he retired from active life very much like an invalid and never spoke again at holiness meetings, though his wife maintained her activities with continued success.[22]

The Keswick phase of the movement began when the vicar of Keswick, T. D. Harford-Battersby, impressed by the holiness teaching at Brighton, planned a similar conference in his Cumberland parish. Keswick soon became the center of British holiness teaching, but that teaching was modified by the Anglican clergy who dominated there. Gradually the emphasis upon the eradication of sin, the aspect of American holiness that the millenarians had found objectionable, dropped away and the Keswick teachers substituted an emphasis upon the power of the Spirit to lead the believer away from evil toward righteousness. The Keswick teachers were, as well, premillennialists.[23] Thus, when Moody began to bring the Keswick teachers to the Northfield conference, the holiness doctrines had undergone a transformation that made them acceptable to American millenarians. The millenarian

22. The London *Christian Observer* 75:830 ff., 916 ff., and 76:60 ff.; Julia M'Nair Wright, "Christian Conferences in London," *Presbyterian*, 28 August, 4 September, and 11 September 1875; see Warfield, *Perfectionism*, for an extensive bibliography, and ibid., 2:505–8 for the most satisfactory account of R. P. Smith's physical or moral collapse.

23. Walter B. Sloan, *These Sixty Years, the Story of the Keswick Convention* (London, 1935); L. Ashby, *Keswick and Its Message* (London, 1933); Timothy L. Smith, *Called unto Holiness* (Kansas City, 1963), chap. 1, is quite helpful.

"old guard" were not, apparently, aware of the shift in emphasis which Keswick had introduced and opposed what they took to be the same old Oberlin perfectionism. Moody's confidence and their own acquaintance with the message and the men who preached it soon reassured them, however, and the Keswick doctrines were heartily endorsed by most of the millenarians. F. B. Meyer came to Northfield for the first time in 1891 when Moody had selected "holiness" as the theme for the August conference. He returned to Northfield in 1894, 1896, 1899, 1900, and 1902. In 1895 the Keswick views were preached by Andrew Murray, Dutch Reformed minister from South Africa, and H. W. Webb-Peploe, prebendary of Saint Paul's Cathedral. Sydney A. Selwyn of Bournemouth spoke in 1896 and 1899, G. H. C. Macgregor spoke in 1897 and 1898, and G. Campbell Morgan was a regular preacher in the years following 1897.

With doctrinal objections removed, the holiness teaching of the Keswick movement rooted firmly in millenarian soil and had the effect of broadening the character of the millenarian movement in accentuation of the trend begun in the Niagara conferences.[24] An American Keswick movement was founded in the United States in 1913 with summer conferences being held in Princeton, New Jersey, and Stony Brook, Long Island, until the establishment of a permanent campground at Keswick, New Jersey, in 1923. The editor of the *Sunday School Times*, Charles G. Trumbull, experienced conversion to Keswick sanctification in 1910 and played an active role in the establishment of the conferences and also publicized "the victorious life," as it came to be called in the United States, in the pages of the *Sunday School Times*. Other leaders were C. I. Scofield; Robert Speer, the young missionary advocate; David Baron, a Jewish convert to Christianity who had spoken at Northfield in 1890; and W. H. Griffith Thomas, an English Anglican who had come to America in 1910 to teach at Wycliffe College, Toronto. In the American

24. F. B. Meyer's articles began appearing in the pages of *Truth* in 1893. D. M. Stearns and G. C. Needham, leading millenarians, spoke at the 1895 English Keswick conference.

Keswick conferences the holiness teachings took precedence over the millenarian emphasis, but both were present.[25]

A second area in which Moody contributed to the changing character of the millenarian movement was the founding of Bible institutes. Bible institutes form one of the most important bridges between the millenarian and Fundamentalist movements, and millenarianism has been taught in the twentieth century principally by Bible institute instructors and in Bible institute classrooms. During the late nineteenth century many evangelicals were convinced that zealous laymen could function effectively in home and foreign missions with only a minimum of practical training and Bible knowledge. Opportunities for evangelists and the prospects of almost unlimited expansion of foreign missions impressed many Christian leaders, and their own pietistic and biblicistic faith allowed them to assume that advanced academic degrees and rigorous intellectual training might only open these prospective workers to corruption from the apostate scholars then appearing in such alarming numbers. Moody, who himself was an example of the successful lay leader, referred to this type of trainee as a "gapman"; someone who could stand between the ordained minister and ordinary layman.

There was some interest in turning the Niagara conference into such a training school. Although nothing came of the suggestion, Brookes announced that the 1882 Believers' Meeting had had such success that an expansion of that ministry was being considered:

> Indeed, so deep has been the impression made by the meeting, that steps have already been taken to

25. Warfield, *Perfectionism*, provides an adequate account and bibliography for American Keswick. The most significant volume is *Victory in Christ: A Report of the Princeton Conference of 1916* (Philadelphia, 1916), the first American Keswick conference proceedings. Another active advocate of Keswick views was Albert B. Simpson (1844–1919), a Presbyterian minister who left that denomination for independent evangelism and eventually founded the Christian and Missionary Alliance in New York City, preaching what he called the fourfold gospel, emphasizing Christ as savior, sanctifier, healer, and coming king (A. E. Thompson, *The Life of A. B. Simpson* [Brooklyn, 1920]).

establish in connection with subsequent meetings a
Summer School for the training of young men, who
have neither means nor time to attend College and
Seminary. There are hundreds of these scattered
throughout the country, longing to have expounded
unto them the way of God more perfectly; and they
would receive more instruction out of the Scriptures
in one month at such a school, than in three years
at most of the Theological institutions.[26]

Although that school never materialized, millenarians did
work toward the founding of such an institution in Chicago
during the 1880s and eventually saw their efforts culminate
in the school known after Moody's death as Moody Bible
Institute. W. J. Erdman and W. G. Moorehead cooperated
with Emma Dryer to initiate some pilot sessions of this school,
Moorehead teaching some classes in 1883–84 and 1884–85.
Moody came to Chicago to lend his support in 1886, but personal rivalries and Moody's absenteeism contributed to extensive delays so that the school did not open full-time until
October 1889, with R. A. Torrey serving as superintendent.
All of these men were active millenarians, as was Miss Dryer.[27]
At the same time, A. J. Gordon founded a school especially
to train missionaries for the Congo, a school which never
rivaled Moody Bible Institute, but which trained small numbers of students every year. The faculty, mostly part-time,
were all millenarians — James M. Gray, J. M. Stifler, Robert
Cameron, and A. J. Gordon himself.[28] Northwestern Bible
Training School in Minneapolis was begun just after the turn
of the century by A. J. Frost, a Baptist who had spoken at the
1886 prophetic conference, and William Bell Riley, a Baptist just beginning a long career in the millenarian movement. The Bible Institute of Los Angeles, under the direction

26. *Truth* 8 (1882) : 387.
27. James Findlay, "Moody,
'Gapmen,' and the Gospel,"
Church History 31 (September
1962) ; Charles A. Blanchard
dedicated a millenarian work to
Emma Dryer, "the friend who
first opened my mind to the

Dispensational Teaching of the
Word of God" (*Light on Last
Days* [Chicago, 1913]).
28. E. B. Gordon, *Adoniram J.
Gordon*, and Gordon's paper,
Watchword, carry accounts of the
school's founding and operation.

of millenarian Thomas C. Horton, was founded in 1907 and quickly became the equal in influence of Moody Bible Institute. The Toronto Bible Training School, the Philadelphia Bible Institute, and many others joined the growing ranks of such institutions. After the turn of the century most of the millenarians without pastoral charge found their base of operations in one of these schools, or like W. B. Riley, managed to handle both tasks simultaneously. Fundamentalism owed its survival to the Bible institutes, and the institutes were the product of the millenarian leadership.

In a third instance Moody was instrumental in shaping the millenarian movement — in this case by amplifying its missionary zeal and ambition through the Student Volunteer Movement. The Northfield conference developed out of a single session for adults into a series of meetings for adults, students, women, and Christian workers. The first student conference was held in 1886 and marked the beginning of the Student Volunteer Movement within the YMCA. One hundred of the students present at that meeting dedicated themselves to serve as foreign missionaries, and within a few years thousands had taken the same pledge, thus initiating the greatest demonstration of missionary interest ever known in the United States. The SVM was not dominated by the millenarians, but they did play a crucial and unexamined role in the conferences and in the missionary revival as a whole.

No subject tangential to the millenarian cause received fuller and more exhaustive treatment in their literature than missions. No defense or attack upon premillennialism was felt to be complete unless the author explained how the millenarian view would (depending upon his position) destroy or greatly strengthen the missionary program.[29] Throughout the nineteenth century, within Great Britain and America, the

29. See for example, "The Influence of Prophetical Truth on Missionary Exertions," *Investigator* 1 (1831):117–24; "Millenarianism neither Indifferent nor Opposed to Christian Missions," *American Millenarian* 2 (1843):92 ff.; "The Second Advent the Missionary's Story," *Quarterly Journal of Prophecy* 18 (1866):289 ff.

constant refrain of their antagonists was, "You millenarians don't expect to succeed; you don't think that the gospel will eventually convert the heathen world to Christianity." This charge was correct, of course. But the millenarians did not, therefore, accept the conclusion that they had "cut the nerve of foreign missions" — had lost the vision of bringing the gospel to the heathen. What nonmillenarians everlastingly failed to realize was that millenarianism carried with it a new philosophy of missions. The outlines of this philosophy can be sketched by summarizing a typical millenarian mission address.

Speaking on the topic "The Present Age and Development of Anti-Christ" at the 1878 Bible and Prophetic Conference, Henry M. Parsons showed that, according to Acts 15:14, God had visited the Gentiles "to take out of them a people," not to convert them all. The parable of the wheat and tares simply repeated the message as did other Scripture references to which he directed his listeners' attention. The Word of God declared that evil would survive to the end of the age. What kind of Christian disagreed with God's word? he argued. If, indeed, it was intended that the gospel so purify the world and work in sinners' hearts that all men would be saved, then so far the gospel had not fulfilled biblical expectations. "If this dispensation is for the conversion of the whole world to Christ, then, for more than 1,800 years, any one can see, it has been a stupendous failure." But that was certainly not so, Parsons responded. The gospel had accomplished its mission; the men whom God had intended to save had indeed been redeemed. But if God had not failed, man had.

> Instead of dispersing the church in its representa-
> tives to the end of the earth, to preach the Gospel
> to every creature — that the seed of Christ might be
> speedily gathered — we have been massing the best
> forces upon a few favored spots, to convert all the
> people, without success, hitherto, in a single case.
> Conversion of men, by the instruments he is pleased
> to use, is God's work. And He has commanded us to
> evangelize the world that He may do it on whom
> he pleases.[30]

30. West, *Premillennial Essays*, pp. 210–11.

What the millenarians had in mind might be called a doctrine of free access to Christian teachings. The millenarian missionary challenge was conceived in terms of "dispersing" information rather than Christianizing the whole world, and it was in that sense that they understood the word "evangelization." They did not expect that their preaching would produce mass conversions. Nonmillenarians accused them of pessimism, but they continually denied that they were pessimistic, arguing, with a good deal of credibility, that pessimism was hardly the word to describe a view of the world supported alike by scriptural prediction and contemporary events. The millenarians did not accept what they took to be the impossibly grandiose hopes of some missions' advocates, but they felt that they deserved to be described as realists rather than pessimists for their skepticism. We cannot ignore the shadowy and somber aspects of our present age, they argued, but we are not discouraged by them either, for we recognize in those very shadows the outlines of events predicted by the apostles and prophets. How can we be pessimistic while we are watching God work in the world?

Significantly, the philosophy of missions incorporated in the SVM motto, "the evangelization of the world in this generation," seems modeled after that of the millenarians. John R. Mott, though no millenarian, defined the task of the SVM in words that ring with millenarian associations.

> To consider negatively the meaning of the evangelization of the world in this generation may serve to prevent some misconceptions. It does not mean the conversion of the world within the generation. Our part consists in bringing the Gospel to bear on unsaved men. The results are with the men whom we would reach and with the Spirit of God. We have no warrant for believing that all who have the Gospel preached unto them will accept it. On the other hand, however, we have a right to expect that the faithful preaching of the Gospel will be attended with conversions. . . . We are not responsible for the results of our work, however, but for our fidelity and thoroughness.[31]

31. John R. Mott, *The Evangelization of the World in This Generation* (New York, 1900), p. 7.

This similarity in outlook is not surprising, since the SVM originated in conferences completely dominated by millenarian speakers, particularly A. T. Pierson and A. J. Gordon. Joining these two in 1886 were Brookes, West, Moorehead, Whittle, and W. W. Clark, and in 1887 Pentecost and W. W. Clark. During later years the representation of millenarian speakers was much smaller and quite irregular.

Millenarians did not dominate or control the SVM, nor would it be possible to prove that their philosophy of missions was adopted by the SVM. There were no more sincere advocates of foreign missionary enterprise than the millenarians, however, and in this enterprise they found themselves within the mainstream of contemporary evangelical Protestantism. Their leaders were influential and their ideas resembled those adopted by the SVM, if they were not in fact their source. In championing missionary work they could ally themselves with the best men in America's colleges and fill them with a vision which has seemed since that day to represent a culmination in American idealism and zeal, however much we may feel obliged to qualify our judgments about its wisdom.[32] There is no way of knowing how many missionary volunteers left America as millenarians or became millenarian converts in the field, but there seems little doubt that millenarians were better represented in mission fields than within the American churches. Independent "faith missions," such as the China Inland Mission and the African Inland Mission, were generally committed to the millenarian cause, and the many missionaries trained in Bible schools and institutes were almost all millenarians.[33]

NORTHFIELD thus illustrates a phase of the millenarian movement which has been too little understood. Although not convincing the nation of the truth of its position, and not even

32. For one illustration of millenarian influence upon ׳SVM leaders, see Howard Taylor, *By Faith: Henry W. Frost and the China Inland Mission* (Philadelphia, 1938).

33. The United States branch of the China Inland Mission was founded almost entirely by persons associated with the Niagara conferences where missionary emphasis meetings were held annually after 1885 (ibid.).

winning a majority within the two denominations where their reception was warmest, the millenarians nevertheless reached a position of relative success and influence by the end of the nineteenth century. They were treated with respect by conservatives within Baptist and Presbyterian seminaries and denominational boards. They led the way in the creation of a new kind of school, the Bible institute, without as yet alienating or frightening most seminary officials. They spoke out against weakening the doctrinal standards and guarded against theological drift. And they aggressively pursued the work of evangelism, particularly in foreign missions.

One man's personification of this alliance provides a last illustration with which to conclude this chapter. William Whiting Borden, heir to a millionaire's fortune, dedicated his life to service in the China Inland Mission. Borden was a graduate of Yale and of Princeton Seminary, and was taken around the world by Walter Erdman, a brother of Charles R. Erdman and the son of W. J. Erdman. He was much influenced by R. A. Torrey. A Student Volunteer, he was elected to the board of the Moody Bible Institute and the China Inland Mission before he had graduated from seminary. He attended the Edinburgh Missionary Conference in 1910 as a delegate for the CIM. He was ordained September 1912 in Moody Church, Chicago. But on his way to the mission field, Borden died in Cairo in 1913. In his will he left bequests to the China Inland Mission, the National Bible Institute of New York City, Moody Bible Institute, and Moody Church.[34] He epitomized an American ideal — a rich man's son totally consecrated to the service of the unfortunate in foreign lands. And that American ideal was also a millenarian ideal. Borden of Yale was both an American and a millenarian hero. In life he symbolized America's acceptance of the millenarian, but in death he represented the fleeting nature of that acceptance and to us seems to prophesy a tragic end for this promising alliance.

34. Charles R. Erdman, "William Whiting Borden: An Ideal Missionary Volunteer," *Missionary Review of the World* 36 (August 1913): 567–77.

The Fundamentals

LYMAN STEWART, by his own admission, was a shy and retiring man. Yet he was convinced that something must be done to reassert the truth of the Christian faith and to strengthen those Christians who were being seduced by biblical criticism and contemporary unbelief. He had determined to devote his wealth especially to the publication and free distribution of Christian evangelistic and apologetic literature. It was his aim, as he frequently reiterated, "to have any means transmitted into living gospel truth."[1] During a Sunday in August 1909, as he sat listening to a sermon by the Reverend A. C. Dixon, Lyman Stewart realized that he had found the man who could help him initiate this project. And so *The Fundamentals* was born. Six years later, Lyman Stewart recalled their first meeting in a letter addressed to A. C. Dixon:

> Now that we are closing up the final details of
> The Fundamentals, my thoughts have reverted to
> you very frequently, and especially to that Sunday
> afternoon when, in our [Baptist] Temple Auditorium
> [in Los Angeles], you were replying to something
> that one of those infidel professors in Chicago University
> had published, and during which lecture I
> was very definitely impressed to ask for an interview
> with you. As I have thought about that since, it
> seems as though the Lord must have given me
> courage to ask for the interview, as I naturally have
> a great shrinking from meeting strangers, and this
> matter which I had to present to you I had never
> mentioned to a single soul, not even to my own

1. Lyman Stewart correspondence, 18 November 1910, Lyman Stewart Papers, Bible Institute of Los Angeles. I would like to express my appreciation for the special helpfulness of BIOLA librarian Arnold Ehlert.

wife. So you were the first that heard it and when you remarked, "It is of the Lord; let us pray," I was very deeply impressed.[2]

A few months after this meeting in February, 1910, the first volume of *The Fundamentals* was published, followed from 1910 to 1915 by eleven others — three million copies in all.[3] This series is regularly referred to as the epitome of Fundamentalist belief, and the commencement of the vigorous campaign to discredit Modernism which eventually culminated in the controversy of the 1920s. As we shall see, these volumes can better be understood in the context of the late nineteenth than of the twentieth century. *The Fundamentals* affords the best and most auspicious example of that alliance between millenarians and conservatives described in the last chapter. At the same time that these volumes were being published, the united front was breaking down and the divisive spirit of Fundamentalism was emerging — a story we will trace in chapter 9. But as the millenarians were falling out with each other over theological details and many supporters were beginning to desert their ranks, Lyman Stewart and A. C. Dixon collaborated to raise this monument to conservative evangelicalism.

ON THE COVER and title page of every volume of *The Fundamentals* it was stated that each copy was being sent out with the "Compliments of Two Christian Laymen." The two who thus shunned publicity, Lyman and Milton Stewart, were seldom separated from each other in business or in benevolence and appear from their correspondence to have been especially attached to each other. Born in Pennsylvania, they were involved in early oil speculation and wildcatting near Titusville but, at least in Lyman Stewart's case, did not make a success of it. Practically bankrupt, Lyman made his way to Los Angeles, where both he and Milton made a dazzling

2. Lyman Stewart to A. C. Dixon, 29 July 1915, Dixon Papers, XI-6, Southern Baptist Historical Commission Library.

3. Thomas E. Stephens to H. C. A. Dixon, Dixon Papers, XI-6; and Lyman Stewart to Charles C. Cook, 28 February 1910, Stewart Papers.

success of their oil investments, eventually becoming the chief stockholders in the Union Oil Company, Lyman serving as its president.[4]

The early years of the twentieth century were not placid ones for the Union Oil Company. Lyman Stewart found himself unable to obtain badly needed capital and was threatened by Standard Oil interests, which he customarily referred to as "the octopus." Though he had become a millionaire, he seems to have wished to get out of the business entirely and in 1908 wrote that he was "pledged to never make another investment for profit."[5] Although he does not seem to have been able to accomplish this disentanglement from business and probably underestimated his own attachment to oil, there can be no doubt that Christian benevolence was as much a vocation for the Stewarts as their business concerns. In 1911 Lyman wrote to Milton, "The Lord certainly has something a great deal better for both of us than to have us spend our time and thought dealing with business affairs."[6]

Their great wealth naturally made the Stewarts targets for fund-raisers of all types but, in Lyman's case at least, very few of these requests were met with anything but a token gift. The Stewarts had firm convictions about their benevolences and planned their charitable ventures with the same entrepreneurial command that marked their business activities. Although both brothers contributed to each Stewart charitable enterprise, each initiated his own programs and invited the other to contribute. Milton was especially interested in mission work in China, and Lyman devoted most of his attention to educational and publishing ventures which offered support to the Christian faith and particularly to the understanding of the Bible. Already in 1909 he was supporting the work of T. C. Horton at the Bible Institute of Los Angeles, a work which continued to be his favorite, and the

4. Stewart Papers, *passim*, and "The Stewarts as Christian Stewards, the Story of Milton and Lyman Stewart," *Missionary Review of the World* 47 (August 1924) : 595–602.

5. Stewart Papers, 29 July 1908, and *passim*.

6. Lyman Stewart to Milton Stewart, 19 May 1911, Stewart Papers.

Bible department of Occidental College.[7] He also contributed substantially to, if he did not indeed completely plan for, the republication of W. E. Blackstone's *Jesus Is Coming*, the most popular of the many millenarian tracts of its type. Very much in the manner in which *The Fundamentals* was later to be distributed, Stewart drew up a list of English-speaking missionaries, theological students, and professors, and paid for the distribution of free copies of Blackstone's dispensationalist book.[8] He also contributed one thousand dollars toward the publication of the *Scofield Reference Bible*. The year before this Bible was published and two years before the appearance of the first volume of *The Fundamentals*, Stewart appealed to Scofield to write a book of "warning and testimony to the English-speaking ministers, theological teachers and students." Although not directly stated, it was implied in Stewart's letter that he would pay for the distribution of such a work.[9] Although Lyman Stewart may have made a secret of his desire to publish *The Fundamentals*, as he remarked to A. C. Dixon, the pattern of Stewart's benevolences had been evolved before the Los Angeles meeting.

At first glance Lyman Stewart's theological commitment appears to reflect only a staunch belief in traditional dogmas. In connection with his support of the Bible department of

7. Lyman Stewart was certainly the most important single donor to the Bible Institute and was constantly attending to its affairs. His contribution to Occidental College involved an annual donation to provide salaries for members of the Bible department and books for the library. Many letters between Occidental's president, John Willis Baer, and Lyman Stewart exist in the Stewart Papers.

8. Stewart had made plans to distribute a book on Christ's second advent by December 1906, but had not yet chosen the work. *Jesus Is Coming* was selected in 1907, and Lyman Stewart took responsibility for gathering testimonials to the influence of the book which were included in the presentation edition (Lyman Stewart to W. E. Blackstone, 27 December 1906; 14 October 1907; and 7 January, 15 February, and 25 November 1908, Stewart Papers). At least 691,000 copies of this book were eventually printed, and it was translated into no less than thirty-one languages (William E. Blackstone, *Jesus Is Coming* [1st ed., ? ; 2d ed., New York, 1886; and presentation ed., New York, 1908]).

9. Lyman Stewart to C. I. Scofield, 21 July 1908, Stewart Papers.

Occidental College, Stewart once suggested that a declaration of doctrine be included in the college constitution. This statement undoubtedly reflected his own beliefs; it included affirmation of the following points:

1. The verbal inspiration of the Bible "as originally given"
2. The deity of Christ
3. The vicarious death of Jesus
4. The personality of the Holy Spirit
5. The necessity of a personal infilling of the Spirit for victorious Christian living
6. The personal return of Christ
7. The urgency of speedy evangelization of the world [10]

When faced with this kind of declaration, historians of Fundamentalism have too often erroneously assumed that they were reading only a conservative restatement of doctrines traditionally accepted by the church. We have already attempted to show that such a judgment would be incorrect if applied to the Niagara creed or to the Princeton Theology. Quite clearly Lyman Stewart's statement of faith can make even less claim to represent classical Protestant orthodoxy. As is true of most creeds, this one was fashioned as an apologetic weapon and reflects the stress being placed upon Christian dogma at certain critical points. Thus, the first three articles mirror one troubled Christian's attempt to reaffirm doctrines being questioned by Liberal theologians. The last four articles, however, reflect not the attacks of the Modernists but the favorite themes of the millenarian movement. Points four and five seem to reflect the Keswick doctrines of personal holiness, the sixth the premillennial advent of Christ, and point seven the missionary concerns discussed in the last chapter. The declaration is also, quite obviously, the work of an untrained layman and not a professional theologian. Stewart expressed his concerns naively and carelessly. On another occasion, when more fully discussing his views on inspiration, he argued that biblical statements were made "for all peoples and for all time, and Jewish idiomatic usage

10. Lyman Stewart to J. W. Baer, 7 February 1907, Stewart Papers.

could not possibly have entered into them. All Scripture statements of fact are absolute, and to undertake to square them . . . with the traditions of men, is to make them void." [11] But though his own beliefs did not represent a Christian consensus and were often expressed so naively as to be incapable of defense even by his friends, Stewart continued to press them upon those seeking his financial support.

Stewart was, furthermore, a firm advocate of Darbyite dispensationalism. Writing in 1908 in connection with an appointment to the Bible department of Occidental College, he stated that he then believed "that a man who does not have a grasp of dispensational truth cannot possibly rightly divide 'the word of truth.' " [12] In spite of his California residence, Stewart seems to have been a regular visitor at both Niagara and Northfield conferences.[13] He attributed to James H. Brookes, long-time leader of the Niagara conference, his rescue from "this devilish thing called higher criticism." [14]

Although he had become a dispensationalist, Stewart maintained membership in the Immanuel Presbyterian Church of Los Angeles. He was, indeed, a very active Presbyterian layman, and was courted by missions board executives, especially Robert Speer.[15] But beginning about 1910 he began to withdraw his support from denominational agencies and to advise his friends to do the same. His complaints about the Presbyterian church included, as might be expected, his fears of the increasing doctrinal laxity found in the denomination's schools and seminaries, but involved, as well, his conviction

11. Lyman Stewart to T. C. Horton, 4 May 1911, Stewart Papers.

12. Lyman Stewart to J. W. Baer, 8 October 1908, Stewart Papers.

13. Lyman Stewart to George S. Fisher, 30 June 1911, Stewart Papers, where Stewart mentioned attending Northfield. One of the editors of *The Fundamentals*, Louis Meyer, stated that the idea for *The Fundamentals* first occurred to Stewart while attending the Niagara conference ("The Fundamentals," *King's Business* [December 1912], p. 333).

14. Lyman Stewart to C. I. Scofield, 15 April 1911, Stewart Papers.

15. Lyman Stewart to Robert Speer, 21 July 1908, Stewart Papers.

that ministers and missionaries were no longer receiving an adequate grounding in the Bible.[16]

THE MAN to whom Lyman Stewart had entrusted the publication of *The Fundamentals* had built a ministerial career devoted to evangelism and characterized by militant and polemical attacks upon forces of evil and unbelief. Born in Shelby, North Carolina, in 1854, the Reverend Amzi Clarence Dixon served Baptist pastorates in Baltimore from 1882 to 1890, in Brooklyn from 1890 to 1901, and in Boston from 1901 to 1906, and was, when he met Stewart, the pastor of Moody Church in Chicago. Throughout his ministerial career he moved away from strict denominational allegiance and "churchly" attitudes toward the type of tabernacle environment associated with many of the great evangelists of his day, especially A. T. Pierson and D. L. Moody. He terminated his pastorates in Baltimore and Brooklyn when his congregations were unable to agree with his plans for new church buildings which emphasized evangelistic functionalism at the cost of the trappings of Victorian charm. Wherever he served his ministry involved him in controversy, whether it was an attack on Robert Ingersoll (which resulted in a libel suit), Mary Baker Eddy and Christian Science, or William R. Harper and the University of Chicago.[17] Dixon appeared regularly as a speaker at millenarian meetings such as the Niagara, Northfield, Seaside, and Old Point Comfort conferences and organized conferences himself, including the Bible Conference on the Holy Spirit held in Baltimore in 1890 and the Baptist Conference for Bible Study held in his Brooklyn church in 1900.[18]

16. Lyman Stewart to Milton Stewart, 26 October 1910; Lyman Stewart to Louis Meyer, 24 March 1911; and Lyman Stewart to Mrs. T. C. Rounds, 23 February 1911, Stewart Papers.
17. Helen C. A. Dixon, *A. C. Dixon* (New York, 1931), *passim* and the A. C. Dixon Papers.

18. Ibid.; *Northfield Echoes* 1 (1894) : 1–13; *Bible Student and Teacher* 1 (1904) : 512–13; Dixon, *The Person and Ministry of the Holy Spirit*; and *Watchword and Truth* 22 (November 1900) : 321. He seems to have been a dispensationalist.

As a result of their meeting in August 1909, Stewart had agreed to put up a fund of three hundred thousand dollars for the publication of *The Fundamentals*. Dixon had returned to Chicago to choose a committee of editors and to organize the publishing of the volumes. Up to this point Lyman Stewart does not seem to have consulted his brother about this project, but he soon wrote him requesting that Milton consider supporting the work. When Milton consented Lyman wrote that he was "very much pleased and relieved to have you say in reference to the 'Testimony,' 'I will do something, perhaps to the extent of a third or more, to aid in carrying out the plan, which may appeal to me more strongly as I examine it more thoroughly.'"[19] Feeling that his brother might be encouraged to become more enthusiastic about this project, Lyman described what he felt to be the importance and scope of this "Testimony." Lyman realized that many of the ministers to whom the booklets would be sent were really unworthy of their vocation. He wrote:

> Of course there are a great many "wolves in sheep's clothing" among such a multitude, but there are also among them "the salt of the earth." These are the men from whom the present generation of the Anglo-Saxon people, as well as the large portion of the heathen world, are, in a large measure, to receive their spiritual instruction, and hence the great importance of getting them, as far as possible, into line for true service. The spiritual welfare of the present generation requires it; the safety of foreign mission work demands it. It is a work that will count for both time and eternity. . . . The best and most loyal Bible teachers in the world are supposed to be enlisted in the preparation of this "Testimony," and . . . these articles will doubtless be the masterpieces of the writers."[20]

Milton obviously did contribute to *The Fundamentals* but seems to have taken little further interest. Some years later

19. Thomas E. Stephens to H. C. A. Dixon, Dixon Papers, XI–6, and Lyman Stewart to Milton Stewart 26 October 1909, Stewart Papers.

20. Lyman Stewart to Milton Stewart, 26 October 1909, Stewart Papers.

Lyman thanked a friend, who was caring for his ailing brother, for conveying some comment of Milton's concerning *The Fundamentals*. He wrote, "Your reference to his interest in 'The Fundamentals' is very gratifying to me, for I think in all his correspondence he never even referred to it, and I had not known whether he was satisfied or not."[21] Lyman himself, though deeply concerned with the venture, does not seem to have exercised much, if any, control over selection of material. He occasionally commented about an article or remarked about future volumes, but he does not appear to have known what name had been chosen for the series or when the volumes were scheduled to appear. Over this side of the enterprise Dixon seems to have been given complete control.[22]

Dixon chose a committee equally divided between lay and clerical members. The three laymen, Henry P. Crowell, Thomas S. Smith, and D. W. Potter, had for several years been attending a Saturday night prayer meeting in Moody Church "asking God to indicate clearly how the flood-tide of modern infidelity might be met, and Christian believers strengthened to resist it."[23] The three clergymen were Reuben A. Torrey, Louis Meyer, and Elmore Harris. Torrey by this time had left Moody Bible Institute to become a full-time evangelist, and his success in that field gave him some claim to be considered the successor of Moody himself. Louis Meyer (?–1913) in 1909 was working with the Presbyterian Board of Home Missions in Chicago but resigned that connection in 1911 to work independently. He was himself a Jewish Christian and seems to have conducted his own ministry among the Jews of Chicago.[24] Elmore Harris (1854–1911), a Baptist minister from Brantford, Ontario, was in 1909

21. Lyman Stewart to J. M. Critchlow, 14 April 1911, Stewart Papers.

22. Lyman Stewart to Charles C. Cook, 28 February 1910, Stewart Papers, where Stewart indicates, by calling the publication "Testimony," that he does not know, within a few days of the publication of volume 1, what title had been chosen.

Lyman Stewart to A. C. Dixon, 29 July 1915, Dixon Papers, where Stewart gives Dixon credit for the success of the work.

23. Dixon, *A. C. Dixon*, p. 181.

24. Lyman Stewart to Mrs. T. C. Rounds, 23 February 1911, Stewart Papers; and Lyman Stewart to A. C. Dixon, 29 July 1915, Dixon Papers.

serving as the president of the Toronto Bible Training School. All these clergymen were millenarians and, quite probably, like Dixon and Stewart, dispensationalists.[25]

Unfortunately, there is little evidence to indicate the outlook and procedures adopted by this committee in preparing the copy for *The Fundamentals*. Scattered comments made in Stewart's correspondence would seem to support the conclusion that no general prospectus for the series of volumes was ever drawn up. As late as March 1911, Lyman wrote to his brother Milton that "thus far the articles have been more especially adapted to men of the highest culture, and that a series of articles adapted to the more ordinary preacher and teacher should follow."[26] He also noted that a volume concerning evangelism was being planned but would be held up until other volumes had created the proper climate for its reception. How Dixon proceeded with the selection of material must remain only a conjecture. When in 1910, after the publication of five volumes, Dixon left Chicago for the pastorate of Spurgeon's London Tabernacle, Stewart noted that it was planned "to have the articles for publication mimeographed and sent to every member of the committee for criticism and for his vote before being accepted."[27]

Regardless of our ignorance of procedures it is obvious that the enormous task of gathering the editorial material, compiling a mailing list, printing the volumes, and addressing the envelopes was accomplished with great efficiency and speed. The first volume appeared about February 1910, with two more following it in 1910, three in 1911, and three in 1912. The twelfth volume appeared in the spring of 1915.

25. Torrey was one of the conveners of the dispensationalist 1914 Philadelphia Prophetic Conference (*Light on Prophecy* [New York, 1918], p. 9). Lyman Stewart wrote to Louis Meyer in such a way as to imply that Meyer understood and accepted dispensational teaching (Lyman Stewart to Louis Meyer, 25 November 1910, Stewart Papers). Elmore Harris served as one of the editors of the *Scofield Reference Bible* and also participated in the Niagara Bible Conference (*Watchword and Truth* 20 [September 1898]).

26. Lyman Stewart to Milton Stewart, 3 March 1911, Stewart Papers.

27. Lyman Stewart to George S. Fisher, 30 June 1911, Stewart Papers.

The first volume was mailed out to one hundred seventy-five thousand recipients and each successive printing was increased in size until three hundred thousand copies of volume 3 were prepared, though this seems to have been a bit ambitious and the average printing amounted to about two hundred fifty thousand copies. Altogether, three million volumes were distributed at a total expenditure of approximately two hundred thousand dollars — a little more than six cents per copy. Over half of the expense was incurred in postage and handling.[28]

Insofar as *The Fundamentals* represented the fulfillment of a life-long ambition for Lyman Stewart, it was a success. Stewart read the mail that poured into the Testimony Publishing Company office with great enthusiasm (two hundred thousand letters were eventually received) and wrote to his brother, "I regard it as one of the greatest privileges of my life to have a part in it." [29] The denominational press did not react with much excitement to the publication of the volumes, however, perhaps because the editors assumed that all their ministers had received their own free copies and could judge the work for themselves. The *Princeton Theological Review* commented that "the ablest of our conservative scholars have been secured for this enterprise. We do not see how it can fail to do much good, and we wish for it great success." [30] The *Theological Quarterly* of the Missouri Synod Lutheran church called *The Fundamentals* one of "the most grateful surprises which this year's book market has brought us," and praised in particular the article in volume 2 on justification by faith.[31] The Southern Baptist *Review and Expositor* called

28. Louis Meyer, "The Fundamentals," *King's Business* (December 1912), p. 333; Lyman Stewart to Milton Stewart, 14 October, 1910, Stewart Papers; Thomas E. Stephens to H. C. A. Dixon, Dixon Papers, XI-6. Although three hundred thousand dollars had been established in a trust for *The Fundamentals*, only two hundred thousand dollars was actually spent.

29. Lyman Stewart to Milton Stewart, 18 June 1910, Stewart Papers; Thomas E. Stephens to H. C. A. Dixon, Dixon Papers, XI-6; and Lyman Stewart to Milton Stewart, 20 March 1911, Stewart Papers.

30. *Princeton Theological Review* 9 (1911) : 131. The review is signed by William B. Greene, Jr.

31. *Theological Quarterly* 15 (1911) : 50–53. Comment was also made in the Missouri Synod German language publication

The Fundamentals "a notable undertaking," and the *Methodist Review* was sufficiently impressed with physician Howard Kelly's personal testimony in volume 1 to reprint the entire text.[32]

But most of the scholarly journals seem to have ignored the whole enterprise. Whether or not this indicates their antipathy toward the project, it seems to raise the question of the total effect and impact made by *The Fundamentals*. There seems to be little question that the publication of this "testimony," as Lyman Stewart called it, produced scarcely a ripple in the scholarly world and had little impact upon biblical studies and theology.

SIXTY-FOUR AUTHORS were eventually chosen to appear in *The Fundamentals*. Anyone familiar with the millenarian movement would find many well-known names in the tables of contents — George S. Bishop, a Niagara founder; W. J. Erdman and his son, Charles; H. W. Frost, founder of the North American branch of the China Inland Mission; A. C. Gaebelein, editor of the millenarian periodical *Our Hope*; James M. Gray, by that time dean of Moody Bible Institute; W. G. Moorehead; L. W. Munhall; A. T. Pierson; C. I. Scofield; R. A. Torrey; and C. G. Trumbull. At least half the American authors were millenarians. The English Keswick conference was represented by H. C. G. Moule, bishop of Durham; H. W. Webb-Peploe; G. Campbell Morgan; and W. H. Griffith Thomas. Stewart had anticipated that these men would represent "the best and most loyal Bible teachers in the world," but true to contemporary prejudices and Stewart's own bias, the "world" was limited to the Anglo-Saxon community. The American authors represented the same denominational and geographical distribution found in the millenarian movement.[33]

Lehre und Wehre 56 (May 1910) : 224, and "Die 'Two Christian Laymen,' " *Lehre und Wehre* 59 (January 1913) : 36.

32. *Review and Expositor* 8 (1911) : 157–58. *Methodist Review* 92 (1910) : 491–94. A long and most thoughtful review appeared in the Swedenborgian *New-Church Review* 17 (1910) : 475–80.

33. Lyman Stewart to Milton Stewart, 26 October 1909, Stewart Papers. Forty-one authors were

In company with this veteran millenarian regiment, however, were many nonmillenarians who added greatly to the general aura of respectability surrounding the project. Many of these men had previously cooperated with the millenarians. For example, Dixon added some men to the committee supervising the publication of *The Fundamentals*, not all of whom were committed to the millenarian cause: Melvin G. Kyle, professor at Xenia Seminary; Charles R. Erdman; Delacan L. Pierson, son of A. T. Pierson; L. W. Munhall; T. C. Horton, superintendent of the Bible Institute of Los Angeles; Henry C. Mabie, the Baptist missions executive; and John Balcom Shaw, conservative New York Presbyterian. Neither Mabie nor Shaw, both of whom had spoken at Northfield during the 1890s, are known to have been millenarians. And both Erdman and Pierson, though children of the millenarian movement, had come to fill respectable and responsible positions outside millenarian circles. In addition, E. Y. Mullins, by then president of the Southern Baptist Seminary at Louisville; Franklin Johnson of the Chicago Divinity School; George Frederick Wright, the Oberlin geologist; George L. Robinson, an archeologist from McCormick Seminary; and Benjamin B. Warfield of Princeton Seminary wrote articles for the series. The British contributors undoubtedly also enhanced the prestige of *The Fundamentals*. As a group they hardly overmatched the American contributors, but some of them, such as James Orr, professor of theology at the United Free Church College in Glasgow, did possess a reputation for scholarship.

chosen from the United States, six from Canada, eleven from England, four from Scotland, one from Ireland, and one from Germany. United States authors generally came from the northeastern part of the country, principally from the larger cities. Over 50 percent of the United States authors resided and worked in the New York City, Philadelphia, Boston, and Chicago areas. Only five were from the South and five from west of the Mississippi. Among United States authors fifteen belonged to the Presbyterian church, eleven were Baptists, three were Dutch Reformed, and three were Congregationalists. The Protestant Episcopal, Lutheran, Methodist, and Disciples denominations were virtually unrepresented.

Simply by reading the tables of contents for these twelve volumes one can see the evidence for this alliance and in Dixon find the agent who was responsible for searching out the contributors from his own wide acquaintance. But the whole presentation reflects a kind of theatricality or artificiality which makes one wonder whether these same men, if gathered in one room, would have agreed with one another. Fortunately, we need not fall back upon supposition in this case. Both groups of men did meet, very often in the same room, and did — for a time at least — work harmoniously toward the ends for which *The Fundamentals* was created. The American Bible League, founded in 1903, worked through the organization of local branches and regional conferences and through its periodical, the *Bible Student and Teacher*, to reassert the preeminence of the Bible in the church and in the nation. In this organization we can see in operation the kind of alliance for which *The Fundamentals* offers only putative evidence. What adds greater significance to this example of millenarian-conservative cooperation is that the ABL was organized by the conservatives. Heretofore we have discovered examples of millenarian groups reaching out for conservative aid — as in the Northfield or Seaside conferences. But the ABL was organized by conservatives, and when it sought to expand its membership the men who most aided and occasionally dominated its operation were the millenarians.

When organized in 1903 the ABL was primarily a Presbyterian organization. The *Bible Student and Teacher*, its periodical, was taken over from the Presbyterian Theological Seminary at Columbia, South Carolina, and its contributors had been primarily Princeton Seminary professors. This imbalance was recognized by the officers of the league. In 1908 they announced a campaign to recruit Baptist members for the league and sent out several thousand free copies to Baptist ministers. The board of directors of the league in 1907 included among its twenty-one members Willis J. Beecher of Auburn Seminary; Henry A. Buttz, president of Drew Seminary; J. W. McGarvey, president of the College of the

Bible, Lexington, Kentucky; Principal McLaren of Knox College, Toronto; E. Y. Mullins, president of Louisville Seminary; Francis L. Patton, president of Princeton Seminary; and George F. Wright of Oberlin. Only a few millenarians, such as C. I. Scofield, were at that time members of the board. The organizing of local branches and the holding of local conferences comprised the most vigorous expression of league activities. The Boston branch held a conference in the Park Street Congregational Church, 6–8 December 1904, on the topic of biblical criticism, and the New York branch conducted similar ones 3–5 May 1904, on "The Bible in Its Present Day Relations" and 16–18 May 1905, on the theme "The Bible the Inspired Word of God." At these conferences conservatives such as Patton and R. D. Wilson from Princeton, Howard Osgood from Rochester, F. G. Wright of Oberlin, and Luther Townsend from Boston University shared the platform with millenarians such as Dixon and George F. Pentecost, but the millenarians formed a small minority at these conferences. The Chicago and Toronto branches of the league held conferences in 1906 and 1908 with very similar distribution of speakers. Elmore Harris, president of the Toronto Bible Institute and a millenarian, was chairman of the Toronto branch, and millenarians Dixon, John R. Straton, James M. Gray, and other members of the faculty at Moody Bible Institute were members of the Chicago branch. The millenarian Northwestern Bible Training School in Minneapolis, run by W. B. Riley and A. J. Frost, adopted the *Bible Student and Teacher* as its official school periodical in 1906, adding a few extra pages to deal with local news. The Los Angeles branch of the league was permanently housed in the Bible Institute of Los Angeles, and its first conference in 1908 was dominated by institute millenarians such as T. C. Horton, W. E. Blackstone, George Soltau, and R. A. Hadden. A survey of the pages of the *Bible Student and Teacher* during the last half of 1909 reveals conservatives Mabie, Wright, Patton, and Warfield appearing beside millenarians Gray, Griffith Thomas, and Munhall, and a number of British conservatives and millenarians completing the picture — John

Urquhart, Bishop J. C. Ryle, James Orr, and Bishop Moule. During 1911 and 1912 a great decline of fortunes overcame the league. Only seven issues of the *Bible Student and Teacher* appeared in sixteen months. The managing secretary complained of physical collapse and the treasury seems to have been empty. In 1913 the league changed the name of its periodical to the *Bible Champion* and continued to publish throughout the 1920s, but other activities of the league almost ceased.[34]

The supposition that Dixon and *The Fundamentals* committee became acquainted with the work of some of their authors through the ABL is supported by the fact that several articles printed in *The Fundamentals* had earlier appeared in the league's publication. In fact, the editor of the *Bible Student and Teacher*, Daniel Gregory, in reviewing volume 1 of *The Fundamentals*, took credit in the name of the league for having first published three of the best articles.[35] During the summer of 1910, feeling a bit more bitter about the situation, Gregory accused the editorial board of *The Fundamentals* of plagiarism. He was, Gregory said, willing to allow material to be reprinted, "but we do not think that the case just referred to would be adjudged by any fair-minded person to belong to this class."[36] Apparently Gregory had written before he checked his facts, for in the next issue of the *Bible Student and Teacher* he had to print an abject apology along with a letter from Dixon explaining that *The Fundamentals* committee had been in direct touch with the authors of their material. "If the matter was reproduced," Dixon stated, "it was done by the authors, and not by the editor."[37]

THE DEFENSE of Christian doctrine dominated *The Fundamentals*, and the defense of the Bible surpassed any other doctrinal issue. The ninety articles published in these volumes

---

34. All data on the American Bible League is taken from *Bible Student and Teacher*.

35. Ibid., 12 (May 1910) : 348. The articles referred to were by James Orr, Dyson Hague, and Howard Kelly.

36. Ibid., 13 (August–September 1910) : 150.

37. Ibid., 13 (November 1910) : 262.

divide quite evenly into a group of twenty-nine articles devoted to safeguarding the Bible, another group of thirty-one articles providing an apologetic for doctrines other than the Bible, and a third group of thirty articles devoted to personal testimonies, attacks upon variant forms of belief, discussions of the relationship of science and religion, and appeals for missions and evangelism. The whole series seems to be fabricated like a wheel — its central hub composed of articles related to the Bible, surrounded by general doctrinal articles arranged like spokes leading to the rim where the more practical or peripheral concerns were handled. The twenty-nine contributions devoted to the Bible seem to be divided in the same manner. Seven might be classified as panegyrics and two others discussed archeological confirmation of biblical statements. But fifteen authors either directly attacked higher criticism or contested the critics' interpretation of specific passages. Five articles were taken up with discussions of the doctrine of inspiration.

These five articles on inspiration show a clear relationship to the tradition of biblical authority discussed in chapter 5. All five were written by veteran millenarians. Three of them — those by Bishop, Pierson, and Moorehead — had been presented to the biblical inspiration conference conducted by A. T. Pierson in Philadelphia in 1887 and were simply reprinted in *The Fundamentals*. The other two articles, written by James M. Gray and L. W. Munhall specially for the series, quote from a similar and significant group of authorities.[38] Gray referred to Princeton professors Francis L. Patton, Charles Hodge, and John DeWitt and millenarians Louis Gaussen, Nathaniel West, and James H. Brookes. Munhall quoted Warfield extensively and also referred to A. A. Hodge, Louis Gaussen, and the British scholars Westcott and Burgon. Both referred deferentially and approvingly to the 1893 Presbyterian General Assembly statement which endorsed the Princeton position on inerrancy. But what these millenarians approved in the Princeton doctrine of inspiration, apparently, was the final conservative result rather than

38. The articles are found in volumes 3 and 7.

the method utilized in reaching that position, for none of these five articles followed Warfield and Hodge in their exclusive dependence upon external authority. The position argued in the five articles is almost identical to that being utilized in the early nineteenth century. Gray, for instance, argued:

> The character of its contents, the unity of its parts, the fulfillment of its prophecies, the miracles wrought in its attestation, the effects it has accomplished in the lives of nations and of men, all these go to show that it is divine, and if so, that it may be believed in what it says about itself.[39]

The Fundamentals shows that the problem of biblical inerrancy had not become any less crucial to the millenarians of the twentieth century than it had been to those of the nineteenth, nor had they managed to devise any stronger or more adequate doctrine of inspiration with which to defend it.

The second group of thirty-one articles, defending Christian doctrines other than the Bible, included four general apologetics for Christianity, two arguments for the existence of God, and seven articles dealing with beliefs about Christ — his deity, virgin birth, and resurrection from the dead. These thirteen articles rank among the most judicious and well argued in the entire collection. The only devoted to the Church, by Anglican bishop J. C. Ryle, took a low-church position, in effect proclaiming that the Church and the convert were synonymous. Two articles devoted to the Holy Spirit, reflecting some Keswick influence, reinforced this attitude by ignoring the traditional role of the Spirit in the Church and discussing the relationship of the individual to the Spirit — a position which involved a doctrine of personal sanctification. The fifteen articles discussing the Christian life, almost all of which occur in the later volumes, were also oriented entirely toward personal salvation, personal consecration, and the personal premillennial return of Christ. It is a measure of the irenic and cooperative spirit of Dixon and his committee that only two articles specifically devoted to the premillennial advent were published and that their authors,

39. James M. Gray, in *The Fundamentals*, 3:17.

Charles R. Erdman and John McNicol, were both considered moderate millenarians.

The third group of thirty articles was distributed among a series of five personal testimonies, seven articles attacking heretical faiths, a group of appeals for missions and evangelism, five discussions of science and Christian faith, and a number of miscellaneous pieces. The personal testimonies appear as the last article in each of the first five volumes and must have been intended to give substance to the series subtitle, "A Testimony to the Truth." This approach was abandoned when Dixon left the editorship in 1910, but in its place appeared a series of articles attacking the Millennial Dawn movement, Mormonism, Christian Science, Spiritualism, Roman Catholicism (two articles), and Socialism. The question of missions and evangelism was considered so important that all of volume 12 was given over to it. Science, particularly evolution, received in contrast scant attention, three articles being devoted to that subject and another to the general theme of "Science and the Christian Faith."

Thus a rough sense of the plan of this series emerges. Among the fundamentals to be defended the Bible easily claimed first place. The attention paid to science was minimal and was concentrated more upon biblical criticism than evolution. The editors of *The Fundamentals* evidently chose to emphasize the major truths early in the series, dealing with specific criticisms in later volumes. Throughout its pages the experiential rather than academic approach was stressed. The tone was predominantly practical, apologetic, and pastoral.

To ASSESS the influence of *The Fundamentals* is a most difficult problem. We know that several hundred thousand letters were received by the editors, but most of these were only changes of address or simple expressions of thanks.[40] *The Fundamentals* plainly failed in its primary purpose — checking the spread of Modernism. Although the series is often

40. Thomas E. Stephens to   H. C. A. Dixon, Dixon Papers, XI-6.

viewed as the first shot in the Fundamentalist controversy, there is little evidence of this in the pamphlets themselves. It is true that many participants in the controversy of the twenties looked back upon the publication of *The Fundamentals* as the origin of their crusade, but this must have been much more evident in retrospect. Although these volumes defended most of the same truths, their moderate style contrasts strongly with the stridency of later years. *The Fundamentals* might better be described as a typical product of that progressive era. The authors represented there belonged, at least in their own eyes, in the front rank of those defending the American way. As in World War I, an Anglo-American alliance had been formed — in this case to block the waves of criticism that threatened to destroy biblical faith and to weaken the great missionary task of evangelizing the world in that generation. The millenarianism represented among many of its editors and contributors is scarcely perceptible; the Keswick doctrine of personal holiness is only mildly stressed; and premillenialism is advocated with the best possible manners. In *The Fundamentals* we see the last flowering of a millenarian-conservative alliance dedicated at all costs to the defense of the cardinal doctrines of nineteenth-century American evangelicalism.

9

The Crisis
within Millenarianism
1895–1914

AT THE MOMENT of its greatest success and near triumph the millenarian movement ironically fell victim to an irreparable loss of leadership and a crisis of internal dissension that eventually turned hopes to ashes. An alliance of conservatives and millenarians was apparently achieving considerable success in stemming the flood of critical views and holding the churches to more specific and rigid statements of faith, such as the Presbyterian General Assembly declaration of 1893; but at the same time, the men who had led the millenarian movement for a generation began to die, bequeathing leadership to others whose abilities were not equal to the crisis into which they quickly blundered.

As we have seen in previous chapters, a small, stable group of men dominated late nineteenth-century Bible and prophetic conferences. As the accompanying table illustrates, these men were close contemporaries, most of them ranging from thirty-five to forty-five years of age in 1875 when the Niagara conference was beginning. All remained active in the millenarian movement until the last decade of the century and then, beginning with A. J. Gordon in 1895, the great majority of them died within ten years. By 1911 only W. J. Erdman, George S. Bishop, William G. Moorehead, and the very much younger Robert Cameron and L. W. Munhall remained alive to recall the early days of Niagara. That the two foremost leaders of the movement, Gordon and Brookes, should be

Life Span of the Millenarian Leadership

	Born	Died	Age, 1875	Age, 1900
Wm. R. Nicholson	1822	1901	53	78
Nathaniel West	1826	1906	49	74
Henry M. Parsons	1828	1913	47	72
James H. Brookes	1830	1897	45	ob.
Wm. J. Erdman	1833	1923	42	67
Benjamin F. Jacobs	1834	1902	41	66
Wm. G. Moorehead	1836	1914	37	64
Adoniram J. Gordon	1836	1895	37	ob.
Maurice Baldwin	1836	1904	37	64
George S. Bishop	1836	1914	37	64
Adoniram J. Frost	1837	—	38	63
Arthur T. Pierson	1837	1911	38	63
Samuel H. Kellogg	1839	1899	36	ob.
George C. Needham	1840	1902	35	60
Daniel W. Whittle	1840	1901	35	60
Wm. E. Blackstone	1841	1935	34	59
George F. Pentecost	1842	1920	33	58
Robert Cameron	ca. 1845–50	ca. 1922	25–30	50–55
Leander W. Munhall	1843	1934	32	57
Cyrus I. Scofield	1843	1921	—	57
Isaac M. Haldeman	1845	1933	—	55
James M. Gray	1851	1935	—	49
Elmore Harris	1854	1911	—	46
Amzi C. Dixon	1854	1925	—	46
Reuben A. Torrey	1856	1928	—	44
Henry W. Frost	1858	—	—	42
Wm. B. Riley	1861	1942	—	39
Arno C. Gaebelein	1861	1945	—	39
Wm. H. Griffith Thomas	1861	1924	—	39
Charles G. Trumbull	1872	1941	—	23

the first to pass away certainly added to the difficulties of the remaining millenarians.

A few years before his death Brookes complained that "it is a sad fact that pre-millennialists, notwithstanding their knowledge of the truth, are going to pieces."[1] That controversy did not break out within the Niagara leadership before Brookes's death seems due only to the reverence in which

1. *Watchword and Truth* 24 (1902) : 302, quoted from *Truth* 21 (April, 1895).

he was held by his friends. Perfect agreement has never been the rule among theologians, but the millenarians put a special premium upon unity. Since their position was grounded upon the literal interpretation of an inerrant revelation, they felt that they ought to be able to reach nearly unanimous agreement concerning the outlines of biblical prophecy. But this was further from realization at the end of Brookes's life than in 1875. We have seen that Niagara leaders had found it necessary to oppose certain aspects of Adventist teaching and had proscribed the annihilationists as early as 1878. But in later years, both in Britain and America, a school of interpretation usually referred to as Anglo-Israelism had begun teaching that the Anglo-Saxon peoples were the ten lost tribes of Israel; and another group began to spread the doctrine that some specially fortunate believers (144,000 of them) would escape the terrors of the great tribulation predicted in Mark 13. But the most serious crisis among American millenarians involved the acceptance of that crucial point in Darby's eschatology, the any-moment coming or secret rapture.

The catalyst in this controversy was Robert Cameron, a Canadian Baptist who had become a member of the executive committee of the Niagara group in the early 1880s. Cameron was troubled in 1884 by frequent reference in Niagara addresses to the possibility of Christ's imminent return — "before the morning dawned, before the meeting closed, and even before the speaker had completed his address."[2] Taking his problem to Nathaniel West, respected among all the Niagara leaders for his theological acuity, Cameron made enough of a case that West promised to give the matter his most serious attention and publicly refute that view if it proved to be unscriptural. The results of that review began to appear in the nineties when West attacked the theory of the secret rapture in a series of pamphlets and articles. In 1893 he put his position very succinctly: "The Darby-Doctrine has nothing new in it that is true and noth-

2. Cameron, *Scriptural Truth*, p. 144.

ing true in it that is new."[3] West's action was both courageous and potentially devastating. The leaders of the Niagara conference began to take sides, thus dividing the testimony of this influential agency, and — which was worse — many became convinced that they had been mistaken and that the Niagara conference had been teaching error for twenty years. In addition to West and Cameron, at least W. J. Erdman, James M. Stifler, William G. Moorehead, and Henry W. Frost changed their minds during the next few years.[4]

Brookes knew about this dissaffection and discussed the problem with his Niagara colleagues, but he never budged in his belief that the second advent might come before his life ended. His firm conviction was not at all academic, moreover, for Brookes felt the strongest aversion to death. He had suffered intensely through the deaths of two young daughters and had preached about death as a hideous ogre and the king of terrors.[5] Cameron wrote an article in 1895 showing that the apostles had been taught to look for intermediate events between the ascension and the second advent. Brookes, surprisingly, had published that article in *Truth*; but when Cameron visited him for a day during the summer of 1895, he asked Cameron to agree not to bring up the subject of the second coming. Cameron described their discussion several years later:

> About three o'clock in the afternoon, when sitting out on the verandah, he suddenly turned towards me and said: "I have read over again this morning, very carefully, that article of yours on the Lord's coming, and I confess to you that it seems to me absolutely unanswerable. The apostles did not expect the Lord to come in their day, but can't you leave me the hope, after all these years have passed away, that I may live to see my Lord come, and escape the clutches of that awful enemy, death." The depth of emotion with which this was said, the

3. Nathaniel West, *The Apostle Paul and the "Any Moment" Theory* (Philadelphia, 1893), p. 34. See also West's contribution in *Watchword and Truth* 19 (February 1897).

4. Cameron, *Scriptural Truth*, p. 148.

5. *Our Hope* 7 (1900) : 189–93, reprinted from *Truth*.

candor with which this change of conviction was expressed, the greatness of the man who spoke, and the reverence of my heart towards him overcame me to tears. I did not wish even to seem to break my promise, I felt more like being taught than teaching, more like hearing than speaking, and I only muttered in broken accents something like the following "Oh Dr. Brookes that is quite another matter — some will surely be alive and escape death at the coming of the Lord." [6]

Within two years Brookes faced his awful enemy and the millenarian movement lost the one man who seemed capable of calming the storm.

THE NIAGARA GROUP met as usual after Brookes's death, although the conference site was moved away from Niagara-on-the-Lake. That Brookes's influence was essential soon became evident, however, and talk of disbanding the conference began to be heard. After the 1900 conference held at Asbury Park, New Jersey, Robert Cameron complained of "an evident absence of fervor and depth of conviction which marked the teaching of former years." He was puzzled about the explanation of this decline. "Is it the calm before the storm; or is it a lapse from the first warm fervor of a great spiritual movement and life; or is it the gradual withdrawing of the Holy Spirit from the Christian assemblies preparatory to the Apostasy, the Antichrist and the Advent?" [7] He did not allude to the doctrinal disagreements then troubling the group, but called for an informal conference of Niagara leaders to help diagnose and solve the problem. Two months later he again referred to the subject and this time strongly implied that Niagara was suffering from divided leadership.

> As to the private meeting of the Teachers, we still feel that as the *end* is evidently *drawing near*, a meeting of the men most deeply taught of God ought to be held to consider, amongst other things (1)

6. *Watchword and Truth* 24 (1902) : 302.   7. Ibid., 22 (1900) : 227.

What we are specially to watch as evidences of the
near and speedy coming of the Lord; (2) What aspects of truth need now specially to be emphasized;
(3) What forms of apostasy need most carefully to
be guarded against; (4) What can be done to unify
and to make more harmonious the teachings of
those who are now to the front as defenders of the
faith and exponents of prophetic truth.[8]

This meeting did take place in Brooklyn, 14 November 1900,
as part of the Baptist Society for Bible Study meeting held
in the Hanson Place Baptist Church. This meeting proved
successful enough to prompt the scheduling of another similar meeting in February 1901, which lasted for three days.
Unfortunately, no record survives to reveal the names of
participants or the subjects which they discussed in these two
private sessions. W. J. Erdman presided at the November
meeting, which was conducted quietly and peacefully. In
February "very great divergencies of opinion on prophetic
themes were manifested at the beginning of the meeting,"
but "unanimity of thought and feeling on many points was
reached at the end."[9] One point on which everyone seemed
to agree was the need for more Bible and prophetic conferences, and plans for regular annual summer and winter meetings were announced as imminent. In spite of this apparent
surge of interest, however, the convening committee of the
Niagara conference announced in May 1901 that they had,
regretfully, decided to hold no further meetings. Thus, amid
the barely suppressed rumblings of controversy, Niagara
expired.[10]

Some millenarians were unwilling to let the testimony die
and immediately began pushing plans for a worthy successor
to Niagara — "a permanent annual conference to promul-
gate prophetic truth."[11] Most of those who signed the call
were formerly active in the Niagara group, which makes one
wonder why the Niagara conveners had found it necessary
to disband their work. But the summer passed and no conference was announced. Finally, in December 1901, in Bos-

8. Ibid., p. 292.
9. Ibid., 23 (1901) : 34.
10. Ibid., p. 150.
11. Ibid., p. 151.

ton, a Bible and prophetic conference was organized which gave unified expression to millenarian goals. The conference was held in Gordon's church, the Clarendon Street Baptist Church, and Baptists were prominent in the conference arrangements. A. C. Dixon served as chairman, J. D. Herr was corresponding secretary, and Cameron actively publicized the meetings. Millenarians from both sides of the any-moment dispute were represented. The pretribulationists, those who looked for the coming of Christ at any moment and therefore before the great tribulation, were represented by Scofield, Munhall, and Gray; the posttribulationists, those who were convinced that the Church would pass through the tribulation, included Cameron, Moorehead, and Erdman. There were, in addition, British speakers such as Sholto D. C. Douglas and Henry Varley, and some new faces, including Edgar Y. Mullins, president of the Southern Baptist Seminary in Louisville, and William W. Niles, bishop of New Hampshire for the Protestant Episcopal church.[12]

But such union meetings, in which contending factions simply ignore their differences for the sake of appearances, seldom fool the public and scarcely ever solve anything. Within a few weeks of the Boston conference the strife flamed up more hotly than ever and premillennialism was torn apart. The leaders of the Darbyite or pretribulationist party were Arno C. Gaebelein and Cyrus I. Scofield. Gaebelein (1861–1945), a German immigrant who arrived in the United States

12. *Addresses of the International Prophetic Conference Held December 10–15, 1901* (Boston, 1901?). In several places in the New Testament and particularly in Mark 13:19 ff., a time of troubles is predicted before the coming of the Son of man. This period of natural calamities and astronomical omens was expected by the millenarians to occur in the immediate future. The debate within millenarianism focused upon the church's relationship to that tribulation. Those who were called the posttribulationists believed that Christ would not return until after the great tribulation. The pretribulationists, who were nearly all dispensationalists, argued, as had J. N. Darby, that the coming of Christ for his church was a secret coming not commented upon in the prophecies; the church would be taken out of the world before the tribulation. They argued that the coming of the Son of man referred to in Mark 13 should be interpreted only as the public and open return of Christ in judgment.

in 1879 and became a minister in the German conference of the Methodist church, only became a millenarian in 1887. He attended but probably never spoke at the Niagara conferences. Brookes, however, seems to have been impressed with him and, after putting him through an oral examination to be sure that he was not tinged with German rationalism, recommended him and his work in the pages of *Truth*. Gaebelein's work, during the nineties, was a ministry of evangelism among the Jews of New York's East Side. He learned Yiddish well enough to be accused of attempting to pass as a Gentile and preached to large audiences of Jewish men on Saturday afternoons with considerable success. He began publishing a Yiddish monthly paper and, in 1894, established an English periodical called *Our Hope* to publicize his work, proclaim the imminent second advent, and alert Gentiles to the remarkable Zionist awakening among the Jewish population. Ernst F. Stroeter, a professor at Denver University, and W. J. Erdman, both Niagara leaders, worked with Erdman on *Our Hope*. Because of the influence of Niagara and the writings of the Plymouth Brethren, to whose theology he became a virtual convert, Gaebelein moved away from his Methodist affiliations until in 1899 he decided to cut himself off from their apostasy and conduct his work entirely on faith. He was forced to organize support for his work, naturally, and this process of itinerant preaching in support of his mission gradually transformed the whole character of his ministry. His preaching and conference engagements became the ends rather than the means, his Jewish mission occupied less and less of his time, and Gaebelein began to play the role of the millenarian impressario.[13]

The any-moment coming controversy was evident in the pages of *Our Hope* as early as 1898 when W. J. Erdman, writing about Saint Paul at Thessalonica, took a strong posttribulationist position: "It is therefore conclusive that Paul neither taught an immediate coming of the Lord either 'for' or 'with' His saints, nor that he changed his mind."[14] Al-

13. A. C. Gaebelein, *Half a Century* (New York, 1930).

14. *Our Hope* 5 (1898–99) : 19.

though at this point Erdman was serving in effect as a contributing editor to *Our Hope*, Gaebelein quickly challenged his position, but his gentle and considerate style reflected his respect for Erdman and his willingness to discuss the issue as a matter of legitimate investigation.[15] But this style did not long survive. Gaebelein reacted to the tensions of 1900 by publishing a special December issue of *Our Hope* entirely devoted to Christ's premillennial advent. He urged his readers to order this issue in bulk to distribute to millenarians who did not know of *Our Hope* or to give away to Christians who might be won to that cause. The special number contained articles written by Gaebelein, Scofield, and Erdman, and reprinted something from *Truth* by James H. Brookes. Scofield's article, entitled "May the Lord Come at Any Time," was strongly pretribulationist. Although his article did not touch on the controversy, Erdman was never invited to write for *Our Hope* again. In February 1901, Gaebelein made his point bluntly: "No one can continue to give out a true, scriptural, *edifying* testimony of the coming of the Lord who believes that certain events must come to pass before the Lord comes or that the church will pass through the tribulation."[16] Gaebelein had, in effect, excommunicated the posttribulationists and had begun to treat them as defectors from the grand old party.

The controversy apparently involved more than theology, for both Cameron and Gaebelein were running periodicals which claimed to be in apostolic succession from Brookes and Gordon. A large part of the furor revolved around the right to wear the prophets' mantles. Technically there were no grounds for dispute. Cameron had stepped into Gordon's editorial position in 1895 with scarcely a break in cadence. During the last two years of Brookes's life, when the great

15. Ibid., pp. 156–62. Gaebelein took an unusual position in this article, arguing that Paul's knowledge of the secret rapture came to him as the result of "a new and direct revelation."

16. Ibid., 7 (1901) : 262. Erdman claimed that he received such severe treatment from his former friends that he was forced to publish a pamphlet privately in order to defend himself. I am indebted to his son, Mr. Frederick Erdman, for the gift of a copy of this booklet.

man was ailing and scarcely able to continue editing *Truth*, Cameron had negotiated with him about merging their two papers. Nothing came of that, but when Brookes died Cameron bought the magazine from the publisher, Fleming H. Revell. Cameron could not have possibly carried out the editorial policies of both men in the same paper since Gordon had been a historicist and Brookes a Darbyite dispensationalist. It is true, however, that both men had looked for the imminent advent of Christ. Gaebelein chose to ignore whatever legal rights Cameron might have had to support his claims to succession and emphasized (with something less than complete candor) that he represented the beliefs of both Brookes and Gordon.[17]

Both editors suppressed this rivalry during the nineteenth century and spoke kindly of each other's papers on occasion. As late as July 1901, Cameron was still attempting to play the role of the pacifier, commending not only *Our Hope* but the two British Darbyite millenarian periodicals of that day, *Morning Star* and *Things to Come*. Then in May 1902, Cameron began an eight-part series entitled, "To the Friends of Prophetic Truth," which so antagonized and alienated the pretribulationists that the breach was never healed.[18] In a rambling autobiographical style Cameron proceeded month by month to explain how he had come first to accept and then later to reject the Darbyite doctrine of the secret rapture. He marshaled the usual arguments and made no new points until in July he stated, almost in passing, that both Gordon and Brookes at the end of their lives had "modified their views" about the second coming. Then, in August Cameron turned historian and attempted to trace the origin

17. *Watchword and Truth, passim*, and *Our Hope*. The negotiations for merger took place in the summer of 1895 during the interview already quoted. Gaebelein claimed that *Watchword and Truth* was an entirely new publication.

18. The first installment was largely autobiographical and has little interest in this context, but Cameron related such a striking and significant view of his religious development that this part of the series is reprinted in Appendix B. His brief retrospect provides an almost complete summary of the argument of this book concerning the development of nineteenth-century millenarianism.

of the pretribulationist position to the fanatical utterances of the illuminati in Edward Irving's London church. On the basis of Tregelles's poorly grounded supposition, Cameron had been led to read Robert Baxter's *Narrative*, where he became convinced he had found the source of the unscriptural doctrine against which he was contesting. In the heat of the controversy Cameron drew this noose remorselessly tight. "Now I have this much to say in all kindness." And he proceeded to list his conclusions. The pretribulationists were accepting a doctrine first taught by a heretic, supported by lying spirits.

> Do you think it wise to exalt into "a test of fellowship" a doctrine so recently enunciated, that does not have a single passage of Scripture beyond the question of a doubt upon which to rest its feet, that had such a questionable origin, from the lips of a heretic, and supported by the testimony of demons, and that was enforced by him and by them, *then*, as it is by many *now*, as the only means by which a sleeping church could be aroused to activity? [19]

This harsh and quite pointless argument aroused *Our Hope* to retaliate in kind — "surely every spiritual believer will at once recognize who is back of all this, *who* is thus attacking those who are waiting for His Son." [20]

Across the Atlantic, British millenarians responded to the sounds of controversy. Ethelbert W. Bullinger, editor of *Things to Come*, had hoped that this issue had lost its controversial appeal, "but there seems to be a recrudescence of the view on the part of some, who suddenly feel it to be their duty to act as monitors." [21] Cameron actually held a conference in London with pretribulationists Sir Robert Anderson, Richard C. Morgan, and Dr. Robert McKilliam, who was associated with the Plymouth Brethren and edited the *Morning Star*. When they could not settle their differences, they

19. *Watchword and Truth* 24 (1902) : 238.
20. Quoted from ibid., p. 293. One of the regular contributors to *Our Hope*, F. C. Jennings, wrote a pamphlet entitled *Is It Due to Demoniac Delusion?* (*Our Hope* 11 [1904]:575).
21. *Things to Come* 3 (February 1897) : 86.

agreed not to attack one another, but even this arrangement soon broke down.[22] A third British millenarian periodical gave the controversy its most comprehensive and able discussion. William Kelly, editor of the *Bible Treasury*, former associate of Darby and editor of his papers, pointed out the fallacies in Cameron's argument and asked plaintively why, if one disagrees with a man's doctrine, is it necessary to attribute it to a malignant source?[23]

THROUGHOUT the episodes of this rather nasty schism among the millenarians one is haunted by a feeling of *déjà vu*. Many readers will have realized that this turn-of-the-century dispute closely resembled the Darby-Newton quarrel of the 1840s. Cameron was quite aware of the parallel and consciously relied upon the arguments utilized by Newton in that previous attack upon the any-moment coming. It appears that Darbyite eschatology was taught in America without opposition for several decades, and that only in the 1880s did opposition to his teachings begin to spring up. When men like Cameron and West began to be troubled about the scriptural authority for the any-moment coming, they soon discovered a whole armory of apologetic literature attacking that belief. Millenarian teaching, as we have seen, was not accepted as a complete corpus but developed organically throughout the century. The first interest in the pre- or postmillennial appearance of Christ and the debate over the condition of the world at his appearance quickly became a matter of settled conviction among millenarians and, in fact, created their movement. Next in development, the interpretation of the Apocalypse seized the attention of commentators, until futurism gained the ascendancy over the historicist position. Although Darby and Newton had contested the issues in the 1840s, this pre- or posttribulationist aspect of millenarian doctrine did not become a point of controversy in America until the 1880s and then simmered under control until the

22. Cameron, *Scriptural Truth*, pp. 139–43. Cameron did not give a date for this encounter.

23. *Bible Treasury* 4 (1903) : 314–20.

outbreak of hostilities between *Watchword and Truth* and *Our Hope* during the last years of the nineteenth century.

Both pre- and posttribulationist champions exist within American Fundamentalism more than half a century after that paper war, but it would be irrelevant to this study to try to adjudicate their respective claims. What is significant is the fact that the Gaebelein-Scofield party emerged from the struggle far stronger than its opposition. As we shall see, the posttribulationists lost control of the millenarian movement and failed even to maintain what strength they had mustered in 1900. As death stripped their ranks, few new recruits filled the gaps. This can be explained partly by the superior organizational and editorial skill of the pretribulationists, and would be attributed in large part by the pretribulationists themselves to their better grasp of Scripture and the consequent blessing of God upon their party. But their superior skill in exegesis and argument is not at all obvious and their organization was very largely imitative of previous millenarian practice. Some other factor seems necessary to explain the relative success of the Darbyite dispensationalists at the beginning of the twentieth century. Gaebelein provided one clue when he remarked in an account of the controversy, "The results of this deplorable disunity soon came to the front. A few of the affected teachers did not want to commit themselves on either side of the question and decided to give the teaching on the return of the Lord a less prominent place. After a short time they became altogether silent." [24] But perhaps more important was the continually reiterated argument of the pretribulationists that the hope of Chirst's return had to be an imminent hope or it was not hope at all. If one believes that a period of tribulation must first take place before the coming of Christ, they said, then he cannot look forward to the second advent but must wait only for greater suffering. Regardless of the question of scriptural justification for one point of view over the other, the pretribulationist position was certainly more likely to appeal to that portion

24. *Moody Monthly* 43 (1943) : 278.

of American Christendom which was attracted by the millenarian message.[25]

ARNO C. GAEBELEIN, ambitious and conscientious, provided the spark for the millenarian movement during the first two decades of the twentieth century. Rather than withdrawing to lick his wounds, Gaebelein led his followers in a vigorous campaign of expansion. While Cameron was defensively seeking to construct a united front for both post- and pretribulationist millenarians, Gaebelein cut off his former allies, such as W. J. Erdman, and planned an aggressive pretribulationist campaign. In February 1901 he rented the Park Street Church in Boston and held a three-day conference for his supporters in what must have been considered the stronghold of the posttribulationists. He followed this foray into enemy territory with a similar conference in May in New York City. Before the summer was over he had planned and conducted a well-attended summer conference at Sea Cliff, Long Island, which he announced as the successor to Niagara. By 1902 Gaebelein was almost constantly holding conferences somewhat in the United States. He repeated the Boston conference in February 1902, and eventually met there every

25. During this controversy the pretribulationists were faithfully maintaining the theological positions of J. N. Darby. As we have seen, not everyone holding those views necessarily derived them from him, and many whose eschatology was indistinguishable from Darby's hotly denied any relationship to his thought. Nevertheless, it is certainly legitimate to point out that one party in American millenarianism — beginning with James Inglis and James H. Brookes and continuing through C. I. Scofield and Arno C. Gaebelein to later twentieth-century defenders such as Lewis Sperry Chafer — has consistently maintained the Darbyite dispensational theology. The posttribulationists rejected the most important of Darby's positions, and it seems only logical that they should no longer be classed as dispensationalists. Pretribulationist apologists have taken this position, as have some historians of the controversy. Regardless of the logic of this argument, however, it should be pointed out that a posttribulationist such as Robert Cameron viewed the controversy as an intradispensational struggle and saw no reason for feeling that he had forfeited the right to call himself a dispensationalist. See, for example, *Watchword and Truth*, 23 (1901):102, and 18 (1896):258.

month. During March he visited Atlantic City, New Jersey, and Macon and Savannah, Georgia. From June through August 1902, he conducted two other summer conferences in addition to the second Sea Cliff conference. C. I. Scofield spoke at many of these conferences, as well as a roster of other speakers who appeared quite regularly — James M. Gray, Henry M. Parsons, F. C. Jennings, John James, and George L. Alrich.

At the Sea Cliff conference in 1901, Scofield first discussed with Gaebelein his plan to write an annotated version of the Bible.

> One night, about the middle of that week, Dr. Scofield suggested, after the evening service, that we take a stroll along the shore. It was a beautiful night. Our walk along the shore of the sound lasted until midnight. For the first time he mentioned the plan of producing a Reference Bible, and outlined the method he had in mind. He said he had thought of it for many years and had spoken to others about it, but had not received much encouragement. The scheme came to him in the early days of his ministry in Dallas, and later, during the balmy days of the Niagara Conferences he had submitted his desire to a number of brethren, who all approved of it, but nothing came of it. He expressed the hope that the new beginning and this new testimony in Sea Cliff might open the way to bring about the publication of such a Bible with references and copious footnotes.[26]

The Bible which Scofield discussed with Gaebelein that night is perhaps the most influential single publication in millenarian and Fundamentalist historiography. The *Scofield Reference Bible* combined an attractive format of typography, paragraphing, notes, and cross references with the theology of Darbyite dispensationalism. The book has thus been subtly but powerfully influential in spreading those views among hundreds of thousands who have regularly read that Bible and who often have been unaware of the distinction between the ancient text and the Scofield interpretation.

26. *Moody Monthly* 43 (1943) : 278.

Scofield (1843–1921) was raised in Tennessee and fought under Lee in the Civil War. He was admitted to the Kansas bar and served in the Kansas legislature before he was converted in Saint Louis in 1879. Turning away from the law and politics, he determined upon a ministerial career and became a disciple of James H. Brookes. Scofield once wrote, "During the last twenty years of his life Dr. Brookes was perhaps my most intimate friend, and to him I am indebted more than to all other men in the world for the establishment of my faith."[27] In 1882 he became the pastor of the First Congregational Church in Dallas, Texas, and then of Moody Church, Northfield, Massachusetts. He was chiefly responsible for the founding of Dallas Seminary in 1924, where his reputation and teachings are still upheld. During the controversy over the any-moment coming, Scofield remained a strong advocate of pretribulationism, but he showed much more willingness than Gaebelein to remain in good relations with the posttribulation party. He spoke, for example, at the 1901 Bible and Prophetic conference. He was continually associated with Gaebelein during the first years of the century and seems to have been his intimate friend.[28]

Scofield did not definitely decide to embark upon his project until at least 1902. Gaebelein, who never seems to have lacked funds for his projects, put Scofield in touch with several of his supporters, Alwyn Ball, Jr., John T. Pirie, and Francis E. Fitch, all of whom contributed toward Scofield's expenses during the next few years while he worked on the manuscript.[29] By the summer of 1908 he had completed his first draft, and he held a series of conferences to discuss the work. He wrote to Lyman Stewart that the first of these week-long conferences had been held at Grove City College in western Pennsylvania with William G. Moorehead, Charles R. Erdman, and W. J. Erdman. "We went minutely over the Four Gospels, & my work thereon, adding, clarifying, modifying," he wrote.

27. Quoted by Lyman Stewart in a letter to George S. Fisher, 5 May, 1911, Stewart Papers.

28. C. G. Trumbull, *Life Story* of C. I. Scofield (New York, 1920).

29. A. C. Gaebelein, "The Story of the Scofield Reference Bible," *Moody Monthly* 43 (1943) : 278.

The second conference was scheduled for the last week in August, also in Grove City, and the third in Princeton, New Jersey, and Scofield planned to have "different groups of brethren of different denominations" present.[30] On the title page of the *Scofield Reference Bible* seven "consulting editors" were named: Henry G. Weston, James M. Gray, W. J. Erdman, A. T. Pierson, W. G. Moorehead, Elmore Harris, and A. C. Gaebelein. Just what role these consulting editors played in the project has been the subject of some confusion. Apparently Scofield only meant to acknowledge their assistance, though some have speculated that he hoped to gain support for his publication from both sides of the millenarian movement with this device. At any rate it is clear that the *Scofield Reference Bible* was uncompromisingly Darbyite dispensationalist in doctrine and taught the any-moment coming and the secret rapture of the church. Although he consulted posttribulationist scholars, their views about the time of the advent were not reflected in his work.

Scofield wrote in the preface to the *Reference Bible*, "The editor disclaims originality." This apology was also his boast. To be original was not the mark of good millenarian exegesis. But Scofield also meant to acknowledge that he had done very little more than put his predecessors' work into a most ingenious and assimilable form. Scofield never demonstrated great ability as a biblical scholar, apologist, or organizer, but in the calendar of Fundamentalist saints no name is better known or more revered.

ON THE EVE of the First World War, in February 1914, another in the long series of Bible and prophecy conferences was held at Moody Bible Institute. But unlike its immediate predecessor of 1901, this conference clearly and forcefully advocated the Darbyite pretribulationist position. The call for the conference, signed 1 December 1913, included the names of twelve prominent evangelical leaders, most of whom were pretribulationists. Three of the men listed did not fit this

30. Holographic letter, C. I. Scofield to Lyman Stewart, 7 August 1908, Stewart Papers.

pattern. John Timothy Stone, then serving as moderator of the Presbyterian General Assembly, was a prominent Chicago Presbyterian conservative but had not been known as an active millenarian. Edgar Y. Mullins had spoken at the 1901 Bible and Prophetic Conference, but his address there had not revealed any strong millenarian convictions. William G. Moorehead, of course, had played a leading role in the millenarian movement since the early days of Niagara, but was known to have reversed himself concerning the any-moment coming. None of these men appeared at the conference itself, however. Moorehead died a few days after the conference closed, Mullins was simply never mentioned, and Stone found himself obliged to accept out-of-town invitations in connection with his duties as moderator of the General Assembly. The actual leadership of the conference was provided by James M. Gray, William B. Riley, Scofield, and Gaebelein.[31] At no previous conference was the emphasis upon the details of the Darbyite dispensationalist doctrines so explicit and dogmatic as at this gathering. Robert M. Russell, the president of Westminster College and moderator of the United Presbyterian church, lumped together in a single condemnation both the postmillennialist and the postribulationist. In an address entitled "Wrongly Dividing the Word of Truth," he discussed the most disputed biblical passage of the recent any-moment controversy, 2 Thessalonians 2, and gave it this striking interpretation:

> The Thessalonians had been comforted by Paul's message and were believers in the imminence of our Lord's return for the resurrection of the just and rapture of the waiting living. There had come into their hearts, however, the thought that perhaps the first stage of our Lord's second coming had taken place, that the great magnet of His glorious presence had swept above the earth and that they had failed to share in "the upward calling," and that "the day of the Lord" had thus arrived without their sharing in the glorious rapture which belonged

31. The conference proceedings were published as *Coming and Kingdom of Christ* (Chicago, 1914).

to the period of darkness before the dawn of His day.[32]

The Reverend George E. Guille, a teacher from Moody Bible Institute, told the conference, "The last member of that bride, may, from some remote island of the sea, be called out during this hour in which we are together, and, immediately, the next event in God's program will transpire. It will be . . . the descent of the Lord into the air, and the rapture of the saints to meet Him there."[33] In the last address of the conference, Reuben A. Torrey linked the second advent to the Keswick doctrine of holiness in the fashion that had become customary since the turn of the century, speaking on "The Lord's Second Coming a Motive for Personal Holiness."[34]

The contrast of the 1914 pretribulationist conference with its predecessor of 1901 illustrates the measure of success gained by this ambitious and energetic wing of the millenarian movement. The 1914 conference was as well attended and was marked by as much enthusiasm as most of the recent millenarian gatherings. And although its impact upon American society was scarcely perceptible, it was certainly no less effective than its immediate predecessors. The millenarians had suffered a serious schism, just at the moment when the church in America was facing possibly its most serious challenge. One part, the posttribulationist, had apparently dissolved as an effective agent in the fight against apostasy. But the other wing of the movement was vigorous and aggressive. Had any really serious loss been suffered? Had the millenarians triumphed over crisis?

IN THE TWENTY YEARS before World War I the millenarians reached the pinnacle of their national influence and were able to cooperate with other conservatives in the semblance of an alliance which apparently at least temporarily held Liberalism in check. During the same period, the grand old leaders of the millenarian movement were being taken in death and the strength of the movement was being dissipated in schismatic

32. Ibid., pp. 54–55.   34. Ibid., pp. 223 ff.
33. Ibid., p. 183.

strife. In our previous discussion these two strands of the narrative have been kept separate, but if we are to understand the history of millenarianism and its legacy to the Fundamentalist movement we must confront this paradox. How can one reconcile the success of the millenarians with their simultaneous loss of leadership and unity? Illogical though this situation might appear to be, historians have shown that many aspects of American intellectual life during these years reflected the same appearance of outward success and deeper symptoms of disintegration. Henry F. May has argued this thesis extensively and persuasively in *The End of American Innocence.* His comment upon the whole of American intellectual life is completely applicable to American millenarianism:

> We do not have to choose between the two pictures of prewar America: the end of Victorian calm and the beginning of cultural revolution. Both of these pictures are true. In the years we are going to examine, the few years just before the impact of war on America, we are uniquely able to look at both pictures at once. We can see the massive walls of nineteenth-century America still apparently intact, and then turn our spotlight on many different kinds of people cheerfully laying dynamite in the hidden cracks.[35]

Although belied by their popular reputation as fanatics, the millenarians played a central and not an eccentric role in nineteenth-century intellectual life and very frequently epitomized its strongest convictions. In the 1870s, when most of the American Protestant churchmen remained vaguely optimistic about the future of evangelical denominationalism, the millenarians were thought to be raucously out of tune. But as the century lengthened and Romanism, ritualism, and rationalism (the evangelical's particular unholy three Rs) swept to ever greater triumphs, the millenarian outlook began to appear increasingly realistic to American evangelical pastors and laymen. By the nineties there was very little to separate the world view — although there remained a good deal to separate the theology — of the millenarian from that of the nonmil-

35. (New York, 1959), p. xi.

lenarian conservative. Furthermore, the men who led the millenarian movement were successful urban pastors who won converts, inspired and trained missionary candidates, and raised money to finance this work both at home and in foreign fields. They were meeting the challenge of the late nineteenth century in the way that seemed most effective and meaningful to many if not most of the evangelical Protestants of that day. The reputation of these millenarian leaders — Brookes, Gordon, Pierson, Erdman, Moorehead — was sufficient to carry the credit of the millenarians for a few years. But movements cannot flourish on memories.

At the same time, Liberalism had been neither destroyed nor contained by the millenarian-conservative alliance of the 1890s. The valiant campaign of Princeton and Niagara in the Presbyterian church, for example, had done little to affect the training of ministers in that church. While conservatives spoke of "The Fallacies of Higher Criticism," and "Learned Doubt and the Living Word," the development of biblical criticism proceeded rapidly and its method proved convincing to an increasingly large portion of the intelligentsia within the church. By 1914 a whole generation of seminary students trained in the critical understanding of the Bible were teaching these views to their own congregations.

During the early years of the twentieth century there is a good deal of evidence that America was passing a watershed in her intellectual history. Millenarianism seemed to pass a similar watershed at the same time. The millenarian schism of 1901–2 has been discussed as an episode in the doctrinal development of the movement. Although the evidence is not so concrete, there are signs that this schism was symptomatic of a deeper difficulty. As we have noted, the victory of the pretribulationist party in this dispute could not be claimed in the name of biblical authority or millenarian tradition. Both sides had at least some claim to both, and the posttribulationist party consistently maintained that the question was not one of honoring the heroes of the millenarian tradition or of their own strong desire to participate in the triumphal second advent of Christ, but the question, What does the Bible say? The arguments and attitudes of the pretribulationist party lead one to suspect that the psychology of deliverance inherent in the any-moment coming was a more potent force in adding adherents to their party than was the logic of their biblical exegesis. The millenarian movement was built upon a literalistic interpretation of the Bible by a body of Christians who accepted that book as the inerrant revelation of God. Although their premillennialism was unacceptable to most nineteenth-century clergymen, millenarians — especially those associated with Niagara and Northfield — won grudging respect from conservatives within their own denominations because they advocated their position with skill and fervor and based their defense upon a common foundation of biblical infallibility. In the first decade of the twentieth century, biblical criticism, combined with other developments within science and intellectual life generally, effectively undermined that common nineteenth-century presupposition. In that same decade the millenarians were feuding and separating because they could not agree on how to interpret the text of the inerrant Scriptures. While the greater part of the Protestant theologians were abandoning the position as indefensible (and at the same time forsaking the source of whatever common ground they had shared with the millenarians), the millenarians were demonstrating the weakness of their own position and the pretribulationist majority was giving evidence of an aggressive sectarian spirit.

HAD THE MILLENARIANS triumphed over crisis? There is considerable evidence that the outward signs of millenarian success, as seen in their prominence in the Northfield conferences and their alliance with reputable conservative scholars, were due to the reputation of the older generation of millenarian champions who were fast passing away and to the millenarian championing of a biblical theology no longer adjudged reputable. The schism of 1901–2, instead of being viewed as a passing episode in an otherwise vital movement, seems indicative of corrosion at the theological heart of millenarianism. In contrast to its position in the late nineteenth century, millenarianism seemed unable to attract new leadership of the same standing, or even to hold those it had previously won. Five millenarian patriarchs fathered sons who might have been expected to follow in their fathers' footsteps — Gordon, Pierson, Moody Stifler, Erdman — but only Ernest B. Gordon and Delavan Pierson played even a limited role in the movement during the twentieth century. William R. Moody did not ever attempt to become an evangelist but devoted himself to the schools his father had established at Northfield. In 1901 when the Northfield conference, run now by William R. Moody, failed to emphasize the second advent and prophetic themes, questions were raised about the younger Moody's position. Robert Cameron recalled that D. L. Moody himself had put less emphasis upon millenarian doctrine during the last years of his life.

> It has been known also that Mr. [D. L.] Moody was very "shy" of any prophetic preaching at Northfield during the later years of his life, but speaking for ourselves, we never dreamed that this great segment of truth was to be ruled out of the teachings of Northfield. If this is the fixed policy of those now guiding that movement, we venture to predict that Northfield will soon become a modified reproduction of the great Chautauqua — "ichabod" will be written upon its portals, and its glory will be but a sacred memory. There was a time when Gordon, Brooks [sic] and others were heard with delight. Is that day gone by?[36]

Apparently it was. W. R. Moody remained an active Christian layman but not a millenarian.

The son and namesake of James M. Stifler, long-time professor at Crozer Seminary, followed his father into the ministry — but as a liberal and not a millenarian. Pastor of the First Baptist Church of Evanston, Illinois, the younger Stifler was known as one of the leaders among the liberals in the Northern Baptist Convention of 1922 and was an active member of the University of Chicago board of trustees. William J.

36. *Watchword and Truth* 23 (1901) : 293.

Erdman's son Charles was, as we have already noted, professor of practical theology at Princeton Seminary from 1905 to 1936. Although he remained a premillennialist, Erdman never identified himself with millenarian conferences or periodicals, although he publicly professed admiration for his father and his father's colleagues and recalled the Niagara conferences of his youth with fondness. Not all of the movement was in one direction. Charles G. Trumbull, who had inherited the liberal-leaning *Sunday School Times* from his father, turned that journal into a millenarian and Keswick holiness organ after a conversion experience in 1910. But his example was almost unique.

The movement away from millenarianism was also visible among those who had been associated with the movement but drifted away during the first decade of the new century. What explanation can be offered for the failure of the millenarians to maintain their influence in the Student Volunteer Movement in which they played such a crucial catalytic role? How is it that Robert Wilder and Robert Speer, two of the most energetic SVM leaders, both of whom were active in late nineteenth-century millenarian groups, dropped their interest and failed to support the grand old cause after the world war? Perhaps the most striking illustration of a millenarian deserter is Cornelius Woelfkin, whose career in the Baptist ministry was almost equally divided between the millenarians and the liberals. During the first half of his adult life he contributed articles regularly to *Watchword and Truth*, taught at the Gordon Bible and Missionary Training School, and acted as one of the sponsors for the Baptist Society for Bible Study conference on prophecy in 1900. But after serving as professor of homiletics at Rochester from 1906 to 1912 and then as pastor of the Fifth Avenue Church in New York City, Woelfkin abandoned his millenarian views and became one of the leaders of the liberal wing of the Northern Baptist Convention. In 1921 he wrote an article for the *Journal of Religion* entitled "The Religious Appeal of Premillenialism," in which, without saying anything at all about his own religious pilgrimage, he seemed to be speaking autobiographically:

The critical study of the Scriptures and their sources has brought into the field of vision the historic backgrounds and conditions out of which these Scriptures — including this doctrine — have grown. The apocalyptic writings current for two centuries B.C., but not included in the canon, threw their color if not their forms into Christian thought. In proportion to one's acquaintance with the sources of these writings as viewed against the background of modern knowledge, is the millenarian view completely outgrown. It can only maintain its hold and interest over belated minds which are still moving with the horizons of primitive knowledge, and hold their hopes by the canons of literal interpretation. For all who arrive at any knowledge revealed by science, discovered by historic methods and held by the lovers of facts and truth in all departments of research, the conceptions of the Kingdom of God shift their bases from the doctrine of premillennialism, and the religious appeal must be molded by something different from that one-time stimulating, but now archaic dream.[37]

If read as only one liberal's attack upon another man's faith, that statement would hardly arrest the eye, but when seen as a testimony of Woelfkin's own difficult intellectual journey, the phrases seem to ring not so much with the apostasy of one poor saint as with the failure of millenarianism.

A few cases of desertion and defection, some men's sons who chose paths other than those their fathers trod — this may not seem to make an overpowering case for the decline of the millenarian movement. But it ought to be remembered that virtually no one abandoned the movement during the Niagara conference period, and that even its opponents treated it with respect. Indeed, millenarianism survived and, in its strongly pretribulationist style, made a considerable impact upon American Protestantism during the 1920s. But the movement had changed — changed in both doctrine and strategy. That difference was so decided and prominent that a new name was coined for the movement — Fundamentalism.

37. "The Religious Appeal of Premillennialism," *Journal of Religion* 1 (1921) : 263.

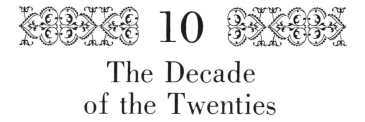

10

The Decade
of the Twenties

BOTH THE CHAMPIONS and the critics of the millenarians agreed that World War I greatly stimulated interest in the second advent of Christ and the interpretation of prophecy. During the closing months of the war, prophetic conferences gathered unprecedented numbers of convinced and potential millenarians. The Philadelphia Academy of Music, which could seat thirty-three hundred, was completely filled for some sessions of the conference held 28–30 May 1918. The news of the British capture of Jerusalem by General Allenby had stimulated several British conferences on prophecy and these, combined with the news about Jerusalem, prompted a committee made up largely of Philadelphia businessmen to organize this conference. Although the committee members were largely newcomers to the conference scene, the speakers were well known. The conference opened by invoking the memory of James H. Brookes.[1] Scofield, though not able to be present, sent a telegram of regret which was read to the audience. Charles G. Trumbull responded with a glowing tribute to Scofield which provides some indication of the unparalleled success of the *Scofield Reference Bible* and the status which that success had conferred upon its editor. Trumbull said, in part:

> God has given you a place in our hearts' love that it is difficult to describe and express. A great warmth of tenderness and affection springs up in

1. The conference proceedings were published as *Light on Prophecy* (New York, 1918). The first speaker, Harris H. Gregg, was introduced as the successor of J. H. Brookes.

our hearts as we think of you, and as we turn the
pages of the Reference Bible, and as we remember
you in prayer, asking God to more than make up to
you and to us the losses of this temporary
separation.[2]

The high point of the conference seems to have been the address of A. E. Thompson, who had been pastor of the American Church in Jerusalem until driven out of the city by the
Turks at the beginning of the war. Weaving together his own
recollections of the Holy City, the prophetic significance of
General Allenby's conquest, and denunciation of Germany,
he set the tone for the two succeeding addresses, "The Re-
gathering of Israel in Unbelief," by James M. Gray, and
"War on German Theology," by Cortland Myers.

Millenarian expectations concerning the future sometimes
came harrowingly close to the mark, and never more so than
when they were explaining God's prophetic plan for the Jews.
Throughout the nineteenth century, as we have seen, the
millenarians confidently predicted the return of the Jews to
Palestine "in unbelief" — that is, without recognizing Jesus
as their Messiah. Although confusion and controversy marked
the exegesis of some aspects of their theology, no millenarians
except the Millerites ever disputed the restoration of the Jews.
Millenarians watched in fascination the formation of Zionism
under Theodor Herzl and the meeting of the first Zionist congress in Basel in 1897, and millenarians correctly, almost in-
stinctively, grasped the significance of Allenby's capture of
Jerusalem and celebrated the event as the fulfillment of
prophecy. At the Philadelphia conference A. E. Thompson
gave this interpretation:

> The capture of Jerusalem is one of those events to
> which students of prophecy have been looking for-
> ward for many years. Even before Great Britain
> took possession of Egypt, there were keen-sighted
> seers who foresaw the day when God would use the
> Anglo-Saxon peoples to restore Jerusalem. When
> the war broke out, there were some of us who were
> convinced that it would never end until Turkish

2. Ibid., p. 34.

tyranny was for ever a thing of the past in the Holy City. When the city was captured, we felt very confident we could put one hand upon this great event which had stirred the heart of the whole Christian world, and, laying open our Bible at many places in the Prophets, say as confidently as Peter on the day of Pentecost, "This is that which was spoken by the prophets." [3]

Within a few months of the Philadelphia meeting, A. C. Gaebelein convened a similar conference in New York City. During 25–28 November 1918, large crowds attended sessions in Carnegie Hall, thankful for the end of the war, amazed at the providential coincidence in the timing of the conference and the armistice, and pondering the prophetic future in a world made safe for democracy. Reuben A. Torrey set the tone for the expectant audience when he told them, "Now that the armistice has come, the minds of people on both sides of the water are filled with all kinds of fantastic hopes and anticipations that are doomed to disappointments." Peace is a delusive hope in this world, Torrey told them, and the League of Nations can never achieve more than a temporary cessation in hostilities. Meanwhile, the present scene offered no really cheering aspect. "But as I hear the low rumblings of the thunder of the coming storm, as I go over to the East Side in New York, as I go across the river in Chicago, as I walk the streets of Milwaukee, as I go down the Los Angeles streets and see the soap box orators of the I.W.W., my heart is not heavy, not a bit. . . . The Lord is coming." [4]

The resurgence of millenarian interest during the world war, illustrated in these two conferences, distressed many liberals, particularly Shailer Mathews and Shirley Jackson Case of the University of Chicago Divinity School. Case devoted two books to the theme, first discussing the thesis that apocalyptic movements gain special prominence in crises such as the world war in *The Millennial Hope* (Chicago, 1918), and then attempting to show in *The Revelation of John*

3. Ibid., p. 144.
4. The conference proceedings were published as A. C. Gaebe- lein, ed., *Christ and Glory* (New York, 1919) ; the quotations come from pp. 21 and 33.

(Chicago, 1919) that the last book of the Bible could not possibly support the kind of exegesis common to millenarians, but was firmly tied to the sociopolitical problems of the Roman Empire in about 90 A.D. Mathews, then acting as the editor of *Biblical World*, published a cannonade of articles, the most vitriolic of which also came from Shirley Jackson Case. His article "The Premillennial Menace" appeared in the July 1918 issue immediately following the Philadelphia conference and may have been provoked, in part, by reports of that gathering. The *Biblical World*, like so much of the religious press at that time, was red-white-and-blue patriotic and bumptiously militant, not to say militaristic. In "The Premillennial menace," Case surpassed the standards being set in the journal and produced so distorted a portrait of the millenarians that one is tempted to believe he was being satirical. These men, Case argued, were subversive to the American war effort, "fundamentally antagonistic to our present national idea." "Premillenarianism is a serious menace to our democracy," it "throws up the sponge, . . . raises the white flag," is a "spiritual virus," and the "most helpless of all gospels." As if these epithets were not adequate, Case noted that the millenarians operated with a "thoroughness suspiciously Teutonic" and implied that they were financed by German secret agents. As the frosting on the cake, Case insisted that millenarians were indistinguishable from the Russellites and lent themselves to the same purposes as the IWW.[5] The Fundamentalists, apparently, never cornered the market on invective.

Although Mathews did not relent in his campaign against the millenarian threat, the contributions he published in later months practically disowned Case's diatribe and censured his attitude.[6] The millenarians were furious. W. H. Griffith Thomas, in his address to the New York Prophetic Conference replied:

5. *Biblical World* 51 (1918) : 16–23.

6. See, e.g., T. V. Parker, "Premillenarianism," ibid., 53 (1919) : 37–40.

Pacifism? Why, everyone knows that the Christians who believe in what we believe as represented by this Conference have been among the strongest and most determined advocates of this war from the very first. . . . And yet you know the other day a leading American told us this. I must be careful to give you his words. He called those who held the premillenial [*sic*] view [of] our Lord's coming "misguided," and he classes them with Millennial Dawnists, pro-Germans and Pacifists, and he says that in its practical bearings the view will smell the same by any name.[7]

This war-induced antagonism may have done much to set the tone for the disputes between Fundamentalists and Modernists in the next few months. Rancor had existed in previous decades, but the spirit of open hostility, so characteristic of the twenties, seemed to find food for its soul in the First World War.

David James Burrell, pastor of the prominent Marble Collegiate Church in New York City, not only offered his church for some sessions of the 1918 conference, but spoke himself. Seemingly a bit surprised to find himself addressing a millenarian conference, he did not retreat into platitudes, though protesting that he had no expertise in prophetic teachings. "Am I a pre-millenarian?" he asked, and answered his own question, "Am I good enough for such folks? Well, I declare I feel at home among you. I love the Lord's appearing." In his address Burrell took occasion to point out that the infidel had disappeared from the American scene and offered an explanation for that puzzling phenomenon:

> We used to have Ingersoll and Bradlaw, the last of the old guard, who stood like Goliath, shaking their spears like weavers' beams, and crying out against God Almighty. And there is something frightful in the thought of old time infidelity. But, gentlemen, it has gone out of vogue, and the only atheism and infidelity in the world today which has any fight left in it is within the professing Church. It is in

7. *Christ and Glory*, pp. 225–26; more comment of the same kind from Torrey can be found in ibid., pp. 29, 134, 136.

the pulpit, it is in the pews, where Christ is denied
and travestied and reduced to the meanest dimen-
sions of diminutive man; and where the Bible is
derided so that it is no longer even the best of
books, far from it, not true, only true in occasional
spots. The Word of God! All that inside of the
Church. . . . The only belligerent, aggressive, effective, destructive infidelity in the world today is
from the belly of the Trojan horse that has been
wheeled within our gates.[8]

These two 1918 prophetic conferences set the tone of the millenarian movement for the decade of the twenties. They were
consistently and typically millenarian, emphasizing the any-
moment coming with great force and frequency. In one of
Riley's addresses in New York he referred explicitly to the
controversy over that issue and indicated that he and his
fellow pretribulationists were still being annoyed by posttribulationist literature. Ford C. Ottman, at the same conference, gladly gave credit for his own exposition of Revelation
to F. W. Grant, the colleague and disciple of Darby. The
attacks upon the higher criticism were fierce but not out of
character for this kind of gathering. Evolution did, perhaps,
receive a few more slaps than had been customary, but, even
at that, it was almost overlooked. Evidently the millenarians
could count upon a broad and influential base of lay support,
though they remained very much a minority even in those
two cities where the attendance was so surprising.

The leadership for the twenties was, with a few exceptions,
already in evidence. The rising star was William Bell Riley,
whose ambition, energy, and pulpit presence were shown off
in both conferences. Riley (1861–1942) was born in Indiana,
raised in Kentucky, and trained for the ministry at Southern
Baptist Seminary in Louisville. After a few short pastorates
he accepted a call to the First Baptist Church of Minneapolis
in 1897 and remained in that position for the remainder of
his career. He played an important role in the founding and
became the president of the Northwestern Bible and Missionary Training School in 1902 and first published his mil-

8. Ibid., pp. 74, 72.

lenarian views in 1912. Exactly how and where he became converted to millenarianism, he never discussed. Although he made frequent reference to the patriarchs of millenarianism, Brookes and Gordon, there is no reason to believe that he ever knew them personally. In a sense, Riley represented the third generation from Niagara.[9] The other leaders had had longer experience — James M. Gray, the dean of Moody Bible Institute; Reuben A. Torrey, dean of the Bible Institute of Los Angeles; William M. Pettingill, dean of the Philadelphia School of the Bible; and W. H. Griffith Thomas, who would shortly leave his professorship at Wycliffe College for independent conference preaching. J. Wilbur Chapman, who appeared at both conferences, died within a few weeks of the New York meeting. Scofield, whose absence at Philadelphia has already been noted, never regained his health in sufficient measure to appear at other conferences, and died in 1921. A. C. Gaebelein, though active as the editor of *Our Hope* and as a preacher for two more decades, played very little role in the conferences that followed. A. C. Dixon, who was active in later conferences, had not participated in the 1918 meetings, since he was in London from 1911 to 1919 serving as pastor of the Metropolitan Tabernacle.

This group of leaders offers some significant contrasts with the men we have analyzed in previous generations. One is immediately struck by the fact that few of these leaders possessed any firm denominational ties and that most of them were affiliated with Bible institutes. If any denominational loyalty did manifest itself, it was only among Baptists. In fact, there were no Presbyterians among the 1918 conference speakers, in contrast to the domination of the movement by Presbyterians throughout the nineteenth century. In previous analyses of denominational loyalty we have noticed how the Protestant Episcopal interest in the millenarian movement seemed to disappear after the 1870s. After World War I the

9. Lloyd B. Hull, "A Rhetorical Study of the Preaching of William Bell Riley" (unpublished Ph.D. dissertation, Wayne State University, 1960) ; and Robert S. McBirnie, "Basic Issues in the Fundamentalism of William Bell Riley" (unpublished Ph.D. dissertation, State University of Iowa, 1952).

same thing seemed to be happening among the Presbyterians. Many hundreds of millenarian advocates existed within the Presbyterian denomination at that time, of course, but the fact that virtually none rose to the prominence of Brookes, Parsons, West, Moorehead, and Kellogg indicates that the character of millenarianism was changing significantly.

GENERALLY SPEAKING, denominational loyalties seemed much less important to twentieth-century millenarians than to their nineteenth-century predecessors. Among the Niagara group, it will be recalled, denominational affiliation, though deprecated and deemphasized, was ordinarily considered necessary. Robert Cameron, in the statement quoted in Appendix B, made it quite plain that his Baptist loyalties were purely formal and adventitious, but A. C. Gaebelein, when he was contemplating cutting himself loose from the Methodist church and operating without denominational affiliation, remembered that the older generation of Niagara leaders had generally counseled against it.[10] During this period of transition the millenarians' attitude toward the Church did not change; they continued to teach that the Church possessed only spiritual characteristics and could not be identified with any denominational or institutional structure.[11]

What then occurred to effect the change we have just noticed? Why did twentieth-century millenarians find it possible to drop denominational affiliations when the much admired patriarchs of the movement, though not theologically committed to them, felt they should not? Dissatisfaction with the denominations certainly grew stronger with the progress of Liberalism, but the really decisive factor seems to have been the development of nondenominational institutional structures which could function in the same manner as the denomination. Historians of religion in America have stressed the functional nature of the American denomination. Ameri-

10. Gaebelein, *Half a Century.* W. J. Erdman specifically warned him that if he left the Methodists he would never be heard of again.

11. See the 1918 addresses of F. C. Ottman and William Pettingill in *Christ and Glory.*

can loyalty to a particular denomination, never a really significant factor save in ethnic enclaves, has tended to decrease with the years. The millenarian movement was not exceptional in that regard. Similarly, American Protestants, millenarian or not, have been unwilling to identify their denomination with the true church. Nineteenth-century millenarians realized that they needed the denomination to maintain their influence and support their ministerial status. Darby, who was independently wealthy, was able to dismiss these considerations and operate outside "systems." George Müller, the orphan-master, and J. Hudson Taylor, the founder of the China Inland Mission, both of whom operated without denominational ties and largely without overt solicitation of funds, were greatly admired but not often imitated. If a nineteenth-century minister established a great reputation as an evangelist, he might break away from denominational ties, as did D. W. Whittle, George F. Pentecost, or D. L. Moody, but the denomination was generally necessary as a springboard to fame. The development of the Bible institute changed this situation and made it possible for the twentieth-century millenarian to drop denominational affiliation without cutting himself off from some base of operations.

No analysis of the structure of the Fundamentalist movement can proceed very far if the role of the Bible institute is ignored. A great deal of the confusion which has existed over the nature of the Fundamentalist movement could have been resolved by devoting more attention to this aspect of the problem. Fundamentalism was a part of both the intellectual and the social history of the United States — that is, its thought can be identified, analyzed, and placed in historical context. Its institutional structure possesses some of the same distinctiveness. By assuming that the faith of Fundamentalism simply reflected traditional Protestantism, scholars have lost one key to understanding; and by failing to examine the manner in which the Bible institutes provided a form of social structure for Fundamentalism, they have lost another.

The simplest way to explain the function of the Bible institute within the Fundamentalist movement is to compare its role to that of the headquarters of a denomination. In many cases, the educational task of the institute, though never derogated, formed only a small part of the school's total mission. Students would be drawn to a Bible institute because of its reputation as a center of piety and sound doctrine, as these concepts had been understood in the millenarian tradition. Perhaps the family of the student had heard of the school through its periodical or had heard one of its faculty preach at a Bible conference or in a series of special meetings in their local church. Possibly their own pastor graduated from the school. Since the 1930s radio has often been used by Bible institutes. When the student arrived at the school he would be grounded in the doctrine and philosophy of the movement and receive training in the practical application of his beliefs — possibly as a musician, preacher, church-school teacher, or "personal worker." The student might be drawn by the appeal from foreign missions and dedicate himself to service overseas, perhaps through a denominational board, but more probably in one of the many "faith" missions which, like the China Inland Mission, maintained close contacts with these schools. If the student returned to his home town and local church, he would be kept in touch with his old school much more actively than most college alumni and would be prepared to repeat the cycle with his own children. He would probably return to the school for conferences, which were often held with the regularity and ceremony usually associated with the annual meeting of a denomination.

Moody Bible Institute, certainly the most influential such school, has exhibited this pattern for most of the twentieth century. In addition to its educational facilities, MBI has maintained a monthly magazine, *Moody Monthly*, which compares in typography and format with such denominational periodicals as *Presbyterian Life*, and has operated both AM and FM radio stations, maintained an extension staff which supplies conference and local church engagements, conducted summer conferences at sites such as the Winona Lake conference grounds, and held annual Founder's Day conferences in February to celebrate the anniversary of Moody's birth.

Thousands of Christians in the Middle West have thus been drawn to Moody Bible Institute and have looked upon the group of leaders, friends and acquaintances they have met under its influence as their community of primary allegiance.

THE STRUCTURE just summarized received explicit statement and, for a brief time, corporate expression with the founding of the World's Christian Fundamentals Association at a conference held in Philadelphia, 25 May to 1 June 1919. During the 1918 Philadelphia prophetic conference plans had already been made to meet again the following year. In the summer of 1918, at R. A. Torrey's summer home at the Montrose, Pennsylvania, conference grounds, Riley and Torrey met with several other millenarians and changed the program of the conference from an emphasis upon prophecy to an emphasis upon the fundamentals of the faith.[12] These men were convinced that they had to restate the great truths of their faith, for, as they put it in the proceedings of the conference, "The Great Apostasy was spreading like a plague throughout Christendom." The response again was great; six thousand persons attended the session, coming from forty-two states of the Union and from Canada.[13] The program that they listened to seems like a latter-day version of *The Fundamentals*. Beginning with biblical inspiration, the speakers discussed the doctrines of God, Christ, Satan, sin, atonement, sanctification, grace, redemption, Church, second advent, prophecy, resurrection, and future punishment. The speakers were very largely familiar faces at such conferences — Riley (now quite clearly in command), Gray, Griffith Thomas, Torrey, Chafer, Pettingill, and Munhall. Two Presbyterians with familiar associations spoke: Joseph Kyle, then

---

12. Cole, citing Riley as his source (*History of Fundamentalism*, p. 298), listed the names of the participants as W. B. Riley, A. C. Dixon, John Campbell, William Evans, W. H. Griffith Thomas, R. M. Russell, H. Wyse Jones, and Charles Alexander;

Dixon, who was in England, cannot have been there, however (see Dixon, *A. C. Dixon*, pp. 238 ff.).

13. The conference proceedings were published as *God Hath Spoken* (Philadelphia, 1919); the quote is on page 7.

president of Xenia Seminary in succession to William G. Moorehead, and A. B. Winchester, pastor of Knox Presbyterian Church, Toronto, the successor to H. M. Parsons. Six Baptists spoke; among them were three millenarians who, along with Riley, played active roles in the controversy within the Baptist denomination during the next few years — Isaac M. Haldeman, J. C. Massee, and John Roach Straton. A. C. Dixon returned to the United States just after the conclusion of the conference.

The most significant aspect of the proceedings, however, was not the addresses but the resolutions of the five committees that had been set up as a part of the conference. James M. Gray was working to bring about standardization and creedal subscription in a group of correlated Bible schools — rather like an agency of Christian accreditation. A Committee on Correlation of Colleges, Seminaries, and Academies, led by Charles A. Blanchard, president of Wheaton College, limited itself to denouncing the perfidy of Modernist colleges. Charles G. Trumbull, the editor of the *Sunday School Times*, reported for a committee on religious periodicals that his members hoped to aid the WCFA by sending delegates to future conferences, giving wide publicity to all activities of the association and by publishing only those articles which were true to the faith. The Bible conference committee reported through Riley that the time had come to coordinate and expand the work of Bible conferences so that the WCFA might reach beyond the fifty to seventy-five large centers of American population.

> We feel . . . that in the interests of economy and efficiency, the time has come to more perfectly systematize this Bible study movement. We are persuaded that these assemblies can be so arranged in complete and adaptable circuits as that a company of speakers given such a circuit could cover within a month from ten to twenty centers without the loss of time on the part of any speaker and with the least possible expenditure in travel and entertainment.[14]

14. Ibid., p. 22.

There was also a committee to correlate foreign missionary societies which had representatives from the China Inland Mission, the Central American Mission, the South Africa General Mission, the Inland South America Missionary Union, the Woman's Missionary Union, the Sudan Interior Mission, and the Africa Inland Mission.

All these committees were intended to function permanently and were organized very much like denominational boards. In further imitation of denominationalism, the WCFA announced its adherence to a nine-point creed which included articles devoted to the verbally inspired and inerrant Bible and the personal premillennial, imminent return of Christ. In commenting upon the reports of its subcommittees, the conference executive committee stated, "While deploring the wave of skepticism that has wrecked many theological seminaries and so rendered them unfit places for the education of our ministry, we rejoice that in the Bible school God has again raised up a standard against the enemy." [15] They then suggested that they would soon be able to supply a list of approved Bible schools to which they urged the young to apply. In commenting upon the religious press, they complained that a plot was afoot to centralize denominational publications in such a way that the few periodicals which survived this process would be completely controlled by the Modernists. They charged that "the carefully conceived and thoroughly planned intention is to make these denominational magazines and papers the medium of modernism." [16] This appears to be a reference to the controversy then brewing among the Baptists over the threat posed by a new periodical called the *Baptist*, established in 1919 by the annual convention. They were similarly alarmed by the activities of the Federal Council of Churches, the Interchurch World Movement, and the Council on Organic Union. [17]

15. Ibid., p. 12. Members of the executive committee were Griffith Thomas, Riley, James M. Gray, Charles A. Blanchard, Charles G. Trumbull, William L. Pettingill, L. W. Munhall, Charles L. Huston, J. R. Schaffer, Orson R. Palmer, and J. Davis Adams.

16. Ibid., p. 14.

17. Loetscher, *Broadening Church*, pp. 100 ff.

We note with interest the determined endeavor to force the various evangelical denominations into a *federation* in which the "fundamentals of the faith" will play little or no conspicuous part. We believe that the accomplishment of such a religious corporation, at the cost of truth, would provide a flashing spectacle of apparent church success to be speedily succeeded by the most colossal failure that has characterized Christianity since the dark days when an ecclesiastical corporation (the Roman Catholic Church) controlled the religious thinking of the world. We voice our determined protest, and as members of the various evangelical denominations hereby declare our utter unwillingness to enter into any such federation movement. In the event of its formal adoption by our respective denominations, it is our fixed determination to find for ourselves a *new fellowship*.[18]

As a result of the 1919 World's Conference on Christian Fundamentals, the millenarian movement had changed its name. The millenarians had become Fundamentalists.[19] Whether they were the only ones with exclusive rights to the title remains to be seen, but there is no doubt that the movement which we have traced from its revival in the early nineteenth century had dropped one badge and picked up another without altering its basic character or drive. Riley himself, when looking back upon the founding of the World's Christian Fundamentals Association in 1922, stated that he and his colleagues "were among the natural and recognized successors, both in doctrinal views and educational endeavors, of Moody, Morehead [*sic*], Brooks [*sic*], Gordon and that whole generation of believing Bible students and teachers who had given birth to the conferences at Niagara and Northfield, and to the Bible Institutions at Boston and Chicago."[20] Furthermore, the 1919 conference had placed planks in a platform on which the millenarian-Fundamentalists would

18. *God Hath Spoken*, p. 15.
19. The word Fundamentalist was apparently coined by Curtis Lee Laws in an editorial in the *Watchman-Examiner*, 1 July 1920.
20. *Scriptural Inspiration* versus *Scientific Imagination* (Los Angeles, 1922), p. 8.

stand for the next thirty years. The leaders had reiterated the creedal basis of the movement with its characteristic biblical and millenarian articles, called for the exorcism of Modernism and all its associated demons (especially evolution), practically abandoned the educational institutions of the nineteenth century and placed their faith in the more recently founded Bible schools, denounced the unitive and cooperative spirit exemplified in the Federal Council of Churches, and threatened schism if this type of spiritual declension persisted. At the same time, they were buoyed up by the success of the 1918 and 1919 conferences to hope that a revival might yet sweep over the United States.

During the next few years, Riley, Dixon, Torrey, and other millenarians worked with all their might to foster this anticipated harvest. But the fig tree was barren — and cursed. The organization which had offered so much promise never materialized. Only the committee on conferences, behind Riley's towering energy and administrative efficiency, produced any results. They planned and held hundreds of local conferences which have left very little evidence of their existence, and annual conferences which were more fully reported. During the crucial years of the Fundamentalist controversy, the association was drawn into warfare against apostate educational institutions and the spread of evolution. But when that great enterprise fizzled out Riley resigned, and the organization lost its following and ceased to play any significant role.

WITH THE DECLINE of the World's Christian Fundamentals Association we have gone as far as seems necessary in tracing the roots of Fundamentalism. The history of the millenarian movement has been examined in sufficient detail to distinguish it from other forms of nineteenth-century Protestant Christianity, and the transformation of the millenarian into the Fundamentalist movement has been adequately documented.[21] We have traced one aspect of American religious life from

21. Louis Gasper has provided a guide to the character and activities of Fundamentalists since 1930 (*The Fundamentalist Movement* [Hague, 1963]).

origins in Britain in the early nineteenth century down to the 1920s and beyond, and have analyzed its distinctive theology and social organization. Previous histories of Fundamentalism have dealt in considerable detail with the events of the 1920s and paid very little attention to the preceding or succeeding years. When combined with the traditional reluctance to take a serious look at Fundamentalist theology, that method has produced an understandable confusion between the Fundamentalist movement and the Fundamentalist controversy. The traditional histories of Fundamentalism tend to deny that Fundamentalism has existed — to say nothing of the significance of its role — outside of the controversies in the twenties, and, in default of other criteria, have been forced to define Fundamentalism within the context of those confrontations. From the point of view of this book it would seem more accurate to describe the events of the twenties as an important but definitely not a definitive part of the movement. In fact, there are good reasons, as we shall see, for arguing that much of what has been described as typical of Fundamentalism has been aberrant when looked at within the context of its own theology and the history of the movement. In the past, incomplete analysis has produced distorted history. The danger in the present book, of course, is that the pendulum will swing in the other direction and that all the events of the 1920s will be interpreted through the history of the millenarian-Fundamentalist movement. Such a reductionist solution would produce an equally distorted history. Not everyone who called himself a Fundamentalist in the twenties was a millenarian, and not every event in the Fundamentalist controversy bears a direct relationship to the movement whose history we have been tracing. Dependence upon simple answers and theories of single causation led the Fundamentalists and their antagonists into the tragedy of that conflict, but will not lead the historian out. With this warning in mind, but without attempting to write yet another descriptive account of the Fundamentalist controversy, let us examine some of the significant events of the twenties to determine to what degree the millenarian-Fundamentalist was involved and to what degree that movement affected the history of those times.

Perhaps the second most celebrated event in the Fundamentalist controversy took place on 22 May 1922, when Harry Emerson Fosdick preached the sermon "Shall the Fundamentalists Win?" This sermon, soon the center of an ever widening circle of reaction and recrimination, was prompted by Fosdick's experience among the missionaries of China. Was this most significant aspect of the Fundamentalist controversy — the dispute over missions — related to the millenarians? Here the answer is unequivocally yes. The problems in China developed out of the organization of the Bible Union of China in August 1920, at a missionary conference held in Kuling. Most of the missionaries in China seem to have left their posts during the summer and retreated to the mountains or seashore resorts to escape the heat. In imitation of their British and American experience, many of these missionaries organized and attended conferences similar to the Keswick or Niagara conferences. In the early twentieth century the missionaries in China, and everywhere for that matter, were quite predictably and understandably more conservative than the Christians at home. A great many were millenarians. In view of the distance and the difficulty of communicating with the European and United States home bases, the relatively large proportion of conservatives represented on the field in comparison with home parishes, and the great conservatism of the native churches, there is some justification for seeing China's Christians as more characteristic of the theological climate of the late nineteenth century than of the 1920s. Into this situation stepped the agents of the Stewart Evangelistic Fund, whose capital had been furnished by Milton Stewart, millionaire stockholder in the Union Oil Company, millenarian philanthropist, and brother of Lyman Stewart, the originator and financial backer of *The Fundamentals*. Milton had tended to devote more of his resources to missionary projects than Lyman and had spent quite a lot of money in free literature distribution and mission-school building, par-

ticularly in Korea.[22] At the instigation of the Stewarts and
with their financial support, at least five eminent millenarian
leaders visited China during the period 1920–22 — W. H.
Griffith Thomas, C. G. Trumbull, Melvin G. Kyle, R. A.
Torrey, and A. C. Dixon.[23] These men had a double effect.
First, while in China they encouraged and supported those
missionaries who founded the Bible Union; and, second, when
they returned to the United States they attacked as apostates
and heretics the liberal missionaries whom they had met in
China. When first organized the Bible Union had only four
hundred members and its leadership was dominated by China
Inland Mission and Southern Presbyterian missionaries. At
this point it was feared that it might prove sectarian and
divisive, but within a year its character changed and its mili-
tancy moderated, owing to some criticism and the accession
of a different, more influential group of leaders. Even so, a
contemporary observer claimed that, "It is probable that a
large majority of the members of the Bible Union are premillennialists. Most of them are ardent premillennialists." [24]
Thus the threat of division among the Protestant missionaries
of China stemmed directly from millenarian influence. When
Thomas and Trumbull returned from their visit to China in
1920 they quickly raised the cry of Modernism on the mission
field, Thomas creating a famous incident by attacking the
Christian fidelity of some missionaries in China before the
Presbyterian Social Union of Philadelphia on 24 January
1921.[25] Not everyone troubled about Modernism in missions
was a millenarian, of course, but it is quite clear that some of
the earliest and most significant agents in the missionary
heresy hunt were millenarians.

WITHIN THE DENOMINATIONS the Fundamentalist controversy
was fought with varying intensity. The most widely reported

22. "The Stewarts as Christian
Stewards," *Missionary Review of
the World* 47 (August
1924) : 595–602; and the
Stewart Papers.
23. Dixon, *A. C. Dixon*; and

Paul Hutchinson, "The Conservative Reaction in China," *Journal
of Religion* 2 (July 1922) : 337–61.
24. Ibid., p. 352.
25. Loetscher, *Broadening
Church*, p. 104.

struggle occurred in the Presbyterian church and was tied directly to the millenarianism of the Fundamentalist movement. The conservative-millenarian alliance which we have discussed in previous chapters had succeeded in imposing its position upon that denomination in quite explicit fashion before the end of the nineteenth century. C. A. Briggs, Arthur Cushman McGiffert, and Henry Preserved Smith had been driven out of the Presbyterian ministry for their Liberalism, and the General Assembly had declared certain doctrines essential to the faith. This practice had begun in 1892 with the Portland Deliverance, which named the inerrancy of the Scriptures as an essential doctrine, was continued with a statement of four "fundamental doctrines" in 1899, and was consummated when the General Assembly in 1910 affirmed five points as essential.[26] The leadership in this campaign came from the representatives of the Princeton Theology, but the large number of millenarians within the Presbyterian church at that time completely supported the Princeton policy. So successful was this alliance of conservatives that they might have considered the battle won had they not had to compete outside as well as inside the General Assembly. Declarations of the General Assembly did not produce conviction in the minds of those determined to investigate the issues for themselves. Not all those who read the works of the Liberals were convinced, but enough younger ministers accepted their views to create a potentially explosive situation.

Thus, by the end of the world war the Presbyterian church had compromised its traditional tolerance of diversity by establishing the restrictive views of the Princeton Theology as the definitive standard of belief within the denomination. Although unable to prohibit the discussion of positions at variance with its own, the denomination had proved capable of defrocking those in its ministry who too publicly declared their differences with the Princeton views. In order to retain their control of the church, the conservatives had only to maintain their own defenses and attack the dissidents.

26. See, as well, the discussion of this five-point deliverance in the introduction.

Their failure to accomplish this is due more to the collapse
of their own party than to any new vehemence or strength
among the liberals. Harry Emerson Fosdick's sermon "Shall
the Fundamentalists Win?" touched off the dispute in the
twenties. The 1923 General Assembly, rejecting the majority
recommendation of their committee, adopted a motion which
expressed sorrow over Fosdick's sermon, called upon the
presbytery of New York to take action to bring the pulpit of
the First Presbyterian Church of New York City into line
with Presbyterian doctrine, and for the second time restated
the five points first declared essential to the faith in 1910.[27]
But this triumph on the old model was actually the last
victory for the conservatives. At the next General Assembly
the Permanent Judicial Commission took the Fosdick case
under consideration and declared that the root of the problem lay in the "anomalous situation" of the Baptist Fosdick,
who had not joined the Presbyterian church, serving for the
past five years as "guest" pastor.[28] The commission invited
Fosdick to join the denomination. Feeling unable to consent, he resigned from the ministry of the First Church, giving
the conservatives the form but not the substance of their de-
mands. Fosdick's views were never made the basis of discussion. In a second defeat during the 1924 General Assembly,
the Judicial Commission ruled against the legality of accepting an overture from the conservative Philadelphia presbytery
which would have compelled all denominational officials "to
affirm or reaffirm their faith in the Standards of the Church,
together with the historic interpretations as contained in the
doctrinal deliverances of the General Assembly, notably that
of 1910." The commission ruled that it was not legal for
the General Assembly alone to erect new standards of belief.
"The constitution of our Church clearly specifies the doctrinal
requirement for ministers and elders, and any change in
these must be by concurrent action of the Assembly and
Presbyteries."[29] This judgment threatened to reduce the

27. *Minutes of the General
Assembly of the Presbyterian
Church in the U.S.A.* (1923),
pp. 252–53.

28. Ibid. (1924), pp. 194–96.
29. Ibid., pp. 197, 198.

famous five-point declaration to an empty gesture. But in the next year conservative hopes were reignited by another judgment of the Permanent Judicial Commission relating to the licensing of candidates for the ministry. Two candidates for the ministry in the presbytery of New York refused to either affirm or deny belief in the virgin birth of Jesus, and conservatives in the presbytery protested their licensing to the General Assembly. The commission reported:

> The applicants, being each uncertain as to his belief and being unable to affirm his belief in the Virgin Birth of our Lord as set forth in the Gospels and declared in the Confession of Faith, the Presbytery erred in not deferring the licensing until the candidates were clear and positive, no matter how amiable, educated, or talented the candidates may have been.[30]

This ruling seemed to foreshadow a schism in the church. If the conservatives were to press belief in all particulars of the creed upon all candidates for the ministry, many Liberals felt that they would be forced to withdraw from the denomination. This is, of course, precisely what the old-line millenarians such as James H. Brookes had hoped would happen in their own day and exactly what J. Gresham Machen, one of the leaders of the extreme conservatives in the denomination and professor at Princeton Seminary, had called for in his 1923 manifesto, *Christianity and Liberalism.* Instead of schism, however, the General Assembly took action that moved the denomination away from exclusivism and strict subscription toward inclusivism and toleration of doctrinal diversity. The moderator of the 1925 General Assembly, Princeton professor Charles R. Erdman, immediately following the report of the Judicial Commission, moved the following resolution:

> That a Commission of Fifteen members be appointed to study the present spiritual condition of our Church and the causes making for unrest, and to report to the next General Assembly, to the end that the purity, peace, unity and progress of the Church may be assured.[31]

30. Ibid. (1925), p. 87. 31. Ibid., p. 88.

The Commission of Fifteen produced reports for both the 1926 and the 1927 General Assembly which, among other points, stressed the Presbyterian church's history of toleration and argued quite persuasively that "the Presbyterian system admits diversity of view where the core of truth is identical." [32] In discussing the powers of the General Assembly the commission stressed the limitations which its representative nature imposed upon it and argued that it did not have the right or power to determine which were the "essential and necessary" doctrines in which every minister must affirm faith. To put the matter as simply as possible, the commission affirmed the responsibility and authority of the presbyteries in their task of licensing and ordaining ministers and rejected the right of the General Assembly to make statements concerning necessary articles of faith which were interpretations of and not direct quotations from the Westminster Confession of faith. Thus the commission declared the General Assembly's often reiterated five-point deliverance void and reversed the Judicial Commission ruling of 1925. In effect, the denomination had taken a hard look at the alternatives of strict subscription and schism or broad churchmanship and a more general evangelical harmony — and had chosen the latter. The Presbyterians had decided that the Liberals belonged in the church, but the question remained, Would the extreme conservatives be willing to remain in this kind of church?

Before we look at the course of events which led some conservatives to answer no to that question, let us stop to analyze the meaning of this decisive commission report. The Princeton-millenarian alliance here suffered a signal, conclusive defeat in a denomination where it had earlier thought itself triumphant. That defeat cannot fairly be described as another triumph of denominational politicians over doctrinal purists, for, as we have seen, the Princeton and millenarian apologists had insisted upon defending their concept of the inspiration of Scripture in terms that had no parallel in the

32. The words of the Commission report are quoted in   Loetscher, *Broadening Church,* p. 131.

Westminster Confession, and with methods inherited from the eighteenth century. The Presbyterians were anxious to avoid the scandal involved in driving their most learned teachers out of the church and desperately longed to get on with their task, but they did not take peace at any price. In rejecting the five points the Presbyterians did not reject orthodoxy; they affirmed it, if by orthodoxy one means the acceptance of those beliefs and practices which lie closest to the heart of any movement.

But the real question of concern within the context of this book is, Why did the conservatives collapse? As we have already noted, the conservatives had gained control of the denomination in the late nineteenth century when these issues were first raised. They needed nothing more than a strong grip to perpetuate their power. The Commission of Fifteen, in fact, had quite a number of conservative members who, if they had so desired, might have obstructed the proceedings and disrupted the harmony of the final report. Three of them at least were millenarians or near-millenarians. Mark Matthews of Seattle had delivered an address on the premillennial coming of Christ at the 1918 Philadelphia prophetic conference. Charles R. Erdman, whom we have met often before in these pages, was a moderate millenarian. Robert E. Speer, who played such a prominent part in the American Keswick movement, sympathized with, if he did not actually teach, millenarian doctrines. These men were among some of the most influential conservatives in the church, and yet they not only accepted the report of the commission, they were largely responsible for writing it. Whether one views it as fortunate or unfortunate, it is apparent that the iron-hard, schism-before-compromise policy typical of the nineteenth-century millenarians had lost its appeal among some of the most able descendants of those patriarchs. The decade looked upon as the zenith of militant censoriousness actually witnessed a striking degree of compromise. Separation and schism did occur in the Presbyterian denomination, but those who left the church left behind them the more moderate and irenic members of their own movement. Like the troubles which beset the millenarians at the turn of the century, the controversy of the twenties represented a further attrition in the already weakened movement.

Even without the millenarians, the Presbyterian church would have faced a crisis in the twenties. Much of the difficulty the church faced, as we have seen, developed out of the complex nature of its denominational constitution and involved legal more than theological problems. But the five-point doctrinal deliverance was the product of Princeton-millenarian alliance and some millenarians were convinced that it was the last outpost in the defense of their faith. A small group of men drawn from the Princeton and millenarian positions found they could no longer remain in a Presbyterian church which had repudiated the basis of their faith. The schism actually did not occur until 1936, but its development can be traced over the preceding decade. What is significant about that schism in the context of this study is the manner in which the vestiges of the Princeton-millenarian alliance worked together in the 1927–36 protests and in the organizing of the new denomination after 1936. As we have already noted, the settlement devised by the Commission of Fifteen split the conservative forces in the denomination, the moderates abandoning their opposition to Liberalism. Within a few months of the commission's final report, a reorganization at Princeton Seminary was begun which ultimately turned the school away from the logical rigidity of the Princeton Theology and ended the domination of the school by the Hodge-Warfield faction. The seminary, although it remained one of the most conservative institutions in the denomination, became much more representative of the whole denomination. Four faculty members resigned in protest over this reorganization and (with others) founded Westminster Seminary in competition with the new Princeton and in imitation of the old. The leading rebel in this cause was J. Gresham Machen, the leader of the extreme conservatives within the denomination.[33]

33. Other Princeton faculty who resigned and joined the Westminster faculty were Oswald T. Allis, Cornelius Van Til, and Robert Dick Wilson.

Historians have uniformly given Machen the most considerate treatment. His consistency, intelligence, and good manners have exempted him from the condescension and vilification that have generally been the historiographical lot of Fundamentalist champions — presumably because those are the values historians believe they possess. Machen could be understood by other intellectuals, though they might not agree with him; he was known to have addressed letters to the editor of the New York *Times*. But when he stepped out of his role as the intellectual into that of the denominational politician, he proved hopelessly inept. He had no notion of the essence of politics — compromise. What he called faithful, militant witnessing for the truth was often nothing more than perverse obstinacy and a fatal lack of openness to the truth that might (however dimly) glow in some other heart. When crossed, Machen typically cut off the former friend or ally with an irreversible anathema and proceeded on his way uncompromised but more than ever the hermit saint. The medieval anchorites may have been honored in some Christian communities, but few were ever elected pope.

Machen honored the system of dogma which had been created at Princeton Seminary and found it to be equivalent to Christianity. He could not understand how conservatives, such as Charles R. Erdman, could play the role they did in the Presbyterian denomination. He once wrote about Erdman:

> Dr. Erdman does not indeed reject the doctrinal system of our church, but he is perfectly willing to make common cause with those who reject it, and he is perfectly willing on many occasions to keep it in the background. I, on the other hand, can never consent to keep it in the background. Christian doctrine, I hold, is not merely connected with the gospel, but it is identical with the gospel.[34]

Rather curiously, in the light of that argument, Machen did not see any difficulty in cooperating with the millenarians. In *Christianity and Liberalism* he offered them a qualified hand of friendship:

34. Ned B. Stonehouse, *J. Gresham Machen* (Grand Rapids, 1955), p. 376.

CHAPTER TEN

The recrudescence of "Chiliasm" or "premillennialism" in the modern Church causes us serious
concern; it is coupled, we think, with a false method
in interpreting Scripture which in the long run will
be productive of harm. Yet how great is our agreement with those who hold the premillennial view!
They share to the full our reverence for the authority of the Bible, and differ from us only in the
interpretation of the Bible; they share our ascription of diety to the Lord Jesus, and our super-
naturalistic conception both of the entrance of Jesus
into the world and of the consummation when He
shall come again. Certainly, then, from our point of
view, their error, serious though it may be, is not
deadly error; and Christian fellowship, with loyalty
not only to the Bible but to the great creeds of the
Church, can still unite us with them.[35]

This alliance with the millenarians seems to have troubled
some of the Princeton faculty who were working to reform
the seminary. President J. Ross Stevenson stated the problem as though it were a contest to win the seminary from the
millenarians for the Presbyterians: "Shall Princeton Seminary now, fretted by the interference of the General Assembly,
in rebellion against the Presbyterian Church as at present
organized and controlled . . . be permited to swing off to
the extreme right wing so as to become an interdenominational Seminary for Bible School-premillennial-secession
fundamentalism?"[36]

The founding of Westminster Seminary was only the first
step in the schism within the Presbyterian church. The dissi-
dent conservatives also formed a rival mission board through
which they encouraged other conservatives to channel their
gifts, holding out the hope that the missionaries accepted by
the new board would not be tainted by Liberalism. This was
viewed as tantamount to denominational treason by the main
body of Presbyterians and eventually the Machen party was
forced to withdraw. Machen expressed his relief in words

35. Machen, *Christianity and
Liberalism* (New York, 1924),
p. 49.

36. Quoted in Loetscher,
Broadening Church, p. 143.

[258]

that would soon ring hollow: "On Thursday, June 11, 1936, the hopes of many long years were realized. We became members, at last, of a true Presbyterian Church."[37] The small group of separatists, who called themselves the Presbyterian Church of America, were a combination of Princeton and millenarian Christians, a mixture which proved to be unexpectedly unstable. Within a few months Professor R. B. Kuiper, of Westminster, a member of the Christian Reformed church, itself a splinter group within the Reformed tradition, troubled the waters by writing about the manner in which the error of dispensationalism was being closely checked in ordination examinations for the new denomination. Kuiper observed, "The Presbyterian Church of America is not just another fundamentalist church."[38] By November the situation had deteriorated to such an extent that Machen had to call for unity and charity — something of a new role for him. He opposed any move to line up all the congregations of the church in either millenarian or antimillenarian factions.

> We have always abhorred with all our souls a "peace-and-work" program that covers up real doctrinal divergence. But then, you see, a peace and work program is very different when it is advocated over against Auburn Affirmationists from what it is when it is advocated over against brethren who bear in their bodies the marks of the Lord Jesus and have shown very plainly that they are not ashamed of Him.[39]

Denominational officials attempted to draw a line between millenarians, whom they were willing to tolerate, and Scofield dispensationalists, who were less acceptable, but this tactic only demonstrated that nearly all the millenarians within the denomination were Scofield dispensationalists.[40] By the summer of 1937 the Presbyterian Church of America was

37. *Presbyterian Guardian*, 22 June 1936.
38. Ibid., 12 September 1936. In response, the California presbytery of the new denomination protested, stating that their ministers were nearly all premillennialists (ibid., 14 November 1936).
39. Ibid.
40. Ibid., 28 November 1936.

CHAPTER TEN

split and the millenarians formed the Bible Presbyterian
Synod led by J. Oliver Buswell, president of Wheaton College, Allen MacRae, one of the professors at Westminster,
and Carl McIntire, at that time only a minister but later to
become one of the leaders of the antiecumenical and anti-
communist crusades of the 1940s and 1950s. The new millenarian group stated that they would adhere to the Westminster Confession except "in any particular in which the
premillennial teaching of the Scriptures may be held to be
obscured."[41]

Without question, then, millenarianism was an integral
part of the strife which troubled and eventually split the
Presbyterian denomination. But rather than acting in unity,
millenarians worked both for and against the denomination.
The Princeton-millenarian alliance, which we first noted in
the 1890s, continued to function as late as the 1930s. But
some conservatives and millenarians, in opposition to the philosophy and practice of the previous half century within both
camps, chose to stay within the denomination and to work
for its strengthening. Those who went out also represented
both sides of the alliance. They cooperated for a few months
until their previously unperceived incompatibility became
evident, and then they split into two distinct sects.

THE EXTENT of millenarian involvement in the Baptist denomination during its struggle in the 1920s can be summarized more easily, for the events virtually duplicate those
already analyzed among the Presbyterians. The denomination met for an annual convention, but this meeting was
much more loosely organized than the annual meeting of the
General Assembly and functioned much like the convention
of one of the political parties. In 1920 the conservative Baptists were enough alarmed by the progress of Liberalism within their denomination to call a Conference on Fundamentals of
Our Baptist Faith for the two days immediately preceding the
convening of the annual convention. The group which assembled for this conference also represented a continuation

41. Ibid., 26 June 1937.

[260]

of the conservative-millenarian alliance. At least six of the thirteen speakers at the conference were millenarians.[42] The format of the meetings resembled that utilized in the Dixon-Stewart pamphlet series, *The Fundamentals,* and the 1919 session of the World's Christian Fundamentals Association. The whole idea of holding a conference and publishing the proceedings was, as we have had many occasions to note, practically a reflex response to crisis by the millenarians. These preconvention conferences became an annual institution for Baptist Fundamentalists and those millenarian and nonmillenarian conservatives who participated in them called their organization the National Federation of Fundamentalists. Modernism among the missionaries and in the colleges and seminaries of the denomination was again the focus of accusation, as it had been among the Presbyterians. The campaign began with a survey of the graduates of Baptist schools in an effort to determine whether their faith had been detrimentally affected by their educational experience.[43] In the preconvention conference of 1920, W. B. Riley, speaking on the topic "Modernism in Baptist Schools," denounced Chicago Divinity School and Crozer Seminary for their apostasy and claimed that many colleges were turning out students who could write in their examination papers, "It comes as a shock to the faith of many Christians when they are compelled to face the fact that the Bible is not inerrant."[44] A denominational inquiry was set in motion, but the committee of nine — most of whom were Fundamentalists — brought in a calm and reasonable report which stated that only a slight fraction of the Baptist teachers were at all disloyal.[45] Members of the federation continued to badger and bully college administrators for some years, however. In November 1921 they wrote a letter to Baptist college presidents stating that

42. *Baptist Fundamentals* (Philadelphia, 1920). The six millenarians were J. C. Massee, Emory W. Hunt, J. W. Porter, A. C. Dixon, Cortland Myers, and W. B. Riley.

43. Robert A. Ashworth, "The Fundamentalist Movement among the Baptists," *Journal of Religion* 4 (1924) : 617–18.

44. *Baptist Fundamentals,* p. 177.

45. *Journal of Religion* 4 (1924) : 618–19.

the report of the committee could not allay suspicion and that the drift toward radicalism had gone too far. The colleges were charged with checking to see that all instructors accepted such Baptist beliefs as "the full inspiration of the Bible, the deity of the Lord Jesus Christ, the vicarious atonement, the bodily resurrection, the return of the Lord, and the spiritual nature . . . of the church."[46] The federation also agitated for a creedal statement against which they might measure suspected Modernists and for conservative control of denominational boards — in both of which moves they failed.

The more aggressive and contentious Baptists were disappointed at the results achieved by the federation and found its leaders too amicable and prone to compromise with the Modernists. In the 1922 Indianapolis convention these militants, led by W. B. Riley, J. R. Straton, and T. T. Shields, launched a competing organization called the Baptist Bible Union. During the following three years both groups worked within the Northern Baptist Convention, but found it more and more difficult to cooperate. As in the Presbyterian church, the fruits of this squabbling were becoming distressingly evident, and the venom in the charges of the BBU leaders began to bring a reaction among the men whom the extreme conservatives had to convince if their case were to succeed. In 1924 the two Fundamentalist factions could not agree about subscription to a creed, federation members refusing to support the BBU's exclusivist Declaration of Faith. The controversy over heresy on the mission field split the two groups even further. Straton became involved in sensational charges based upon evidence which was obtained under false pretenses and was not representative, and Riley became involved in a reckless scene on the convention floor in 1924.[47] J. C. Massee, the federation leader, was appointed to the 1924 committee of inquiry which largely exonerated the foreign missionaries and, from that time on, he supported the denominational program. In 1925 Massee resigned from

46. Ibid., p. 620.   47. Cole, *History of Fundamentalism*, pp. 85 ff.

the federation and was succeeded by the even more moderate Frank M. Goodchild. At the 1926 Washington convention the situation had been so far reversed that the attacks of the BBU were met largely by conservatives associated with the federation. Not only did the extremism of the BBU alienate conservatives from the federation, it even dismayed some of the BBU leaders, such as A. C. Dixon, the editor of *The Fundamentals,* who had been working quite closely with Riley since his return from England in 1919. In the summer of 1925 Dixon resigned from the BBU and published his letter of resignation in a number of Baptist newspapers:

> After prayerfully considering the whole situation as it now exists, I am convinced that the Baptist Bible Union of America has fulfilled its great mission, and ought, therefore, to be dissolved. It has raised the danger signal and thoroughly aroused the Baptist denomination to the perils of Modernism. It has made it easy for Fundamentalists to bear testimony to the truth within our churches, associations and conventions. This work from within ought to be continued with increased energy, and I believe that it can now be done more effectively without any other organization. This will be the consummation of the work so well accomplished by the Baptist Bible Union. I therefore resign my position as a member of the board of managers and my membership in the Baptist Bible Union of America, believing that God will lead the Fundamentalists to ultimate victory in our beloved denomination.[48]

Although not explicitly criticizing any actions of the BBU, Dixon's resignation statement seems more damning of the extreme conservatives than any denunciation from Modernists. If the radical party in Fundamentalism could not keep the loyalty of its Dixons, it was a bankrupt crusade.

As in the case of the Presbyterians, the division within the ranks of the Baptist Fundamentalists did not occur between millenarians and nonmillenarians, but between moderates and radicals of both camps. Among the members of the federation, both millenarians and nonmillenarians pulled back from

48. Quoted from Dixon Papers, XI–6.

the prospect of denominational anarchy and supported the church's program. The BBU also included nonmillenarians, but with this extreme Fundamentalist group the case for millenarian domination is much clearer than among the Presbyterians. Whether or not this was due to the absence of some strong conservative nonmillenarian leader or institution such as Machen and Princeton, it is clear that the BBU membership was largely premillenarian. When the organization was founded in 1922, Riley wrote a premillenarian creed for it but was forced to drop that particular emphasis by pressure from the South and from T. T. Shields. But though there was no creedal manifestation of this doctrine, BBU sentiment remained almost unanimously premillenarian.[49] And when schisms occurred in the Northern Baptist Convention with the organization of the General Association of Regular Baptists in 1932, the new Association continued to emphasize the millenarian sentiments of the BBU.

ONLY ONE OTHER denomination suffered from extensive controversy in this period — the Disciples of Christ. In this case, millenarian beliefs did not contribute to the dispute. In fact, it has proved impossible to find more than a handful of Disciples represented in millenarian activities. The denomination seems to have been practically immune to millenarian ideas, possibly because of its strong anti-Calvinist theological stance. At any rate, millenarianism does not help explain the issues or outcome of the struggle in the Disciples denomination during the 1920s.

The Southern Baptist denomination was penetrated by millenarianism, but was scarcely troubled by the Fundamentalist controversy of the 1920s, since Liberalism had had very little impact upon the denomination to that date. Probably the most influential advocate of millenarian doctrines among nineteenth-century Southern Baptists was James R. Graves, whose *Tennessee Baptist* taught a Darbyite dispensational

49. Robert C. Delnay, "A History of the Baptist Bible Union" (unpublished Th.D. dissertation, Dallas Theological Seminary, 1963).

theology quite aggressively during the last quarter of the century. William O. Carver, professor of missions at the Southern Baptist Seminary in Louisville during the 1920s and as nearly a Modernist as one could find within that denomination, complained of the impact of Graves's teaching. He also thought the BBU, which worked among Southern as well as Northern Baptists, and Trumbull's *Sunday School Times* played a great role in spreading dispensational millenarianism in the South.[50]

The Southern Presbyterian church was similarly free from any extensive controversy during the 1920s because of the more conservative nature of its congregations, but many members of this denomination did become millenarians. During the 1930s and early 1940s, denominational officials became concerned with the influence of dispensational theology among their ministers and laymen, owing particularly to a series of articles written by Professor James E. Bear of Union Seminary, Richmond.[51] The General Assembly of the Southern church in 1944 heard a special committee, appointed to examine dispensational theology, report that that form of millenarianism was incompatible with their Confession of Faith.[52]

In attempting to integrate the study of millenarianism with the Fundamentalist controversy of the 1920s within the churches, we have discovered quite a bit of correlation. Three denominations suffered from major controversies, and in two of them — the Northern Baptists and the Northern Pres-

---

50. W. O. Carver, *Out of His Treasure* (Nashville, 1956), particularly pp. 76–78.

51. Most of these articles appeared in the *Presbyterian of the South* from 1938 to 1944. Another series of articles appeared in the *Union Seminary Review*, July 1938; October 1940; January and July 1941; and May 1944.

52. Many smaller sects could have been discussed. The Naza-

rene and Evangelical Mission Covenant denominations were divided between millenarians and nonmillenarians during the early part of the century (T. L. Smith, *Called unto Holiness* [Kansas City, 1963]; and Karl Olsson, *By One Spirit* [Chicago, 1962]). Other groups, such as the Plymouth Brethren, Christian and Missionary Alliance, and the Evangelical Free church, remained entirely millenarian.

byterians — millenarians contributed significantly to the crisis and were well represented among those who finally withdrew. Within the Disciples denomination, where a large-scale dispute also broke out, no appreciable amount of millenarianism can be identified. Within the South, millenarian ideas had begun to have an impact, but no serious controversy disturbed the churches. Among the Methodist and Episcopal denominations, both in the North and South, there was neither an active millenarian party nor serious contention.

THERE REMAINS one more significant aspect of the Fundamentalist controversy to discuss in relation to millenarianism. The crusade against evolution was without question the most notorious aspect of the Fundamentalist controversy. The Scopes trial in Dayton, Tennessee, probably attracted more interest than any other single event in that decade. Historians, who of course have a vested interest in freedom of inquiry, have found this attempt to muzzle academic freedom a most difficult subject to analyze impartially. But in such recent studies as Lawrence Levine's *Defender of the Faith*, a biography of William Jennings Bryan from 1915 to 1925, the appeal of the movement and the place that it filled in the twenties have become much clearer and more easily understood. Millenarians were deeply concerned with the increasing popularity of what they considered anti-Christian beliefs, and in the twenties, Darwinism became the special focus for their anxiety. Many millenarians joined the campaign to root this theory out of the public schools. Bryan was not a millenarian and never made an adequate theological defense of those doctrines that he did accept. But Riley, Dixon, Straton, Paul Rader, and Paul W. Rood — all anti-evolution champions — were dedicated millenarians. The participation of millenarians in this aspect of the controversy does not seem to have been essential to its initiation and development, however. As we have noted, the millenarians were most strongly represented in the eastern, midwestern, and far-western states. They were especially strong in the Boston, New York, and Philadelphia area of the East, and around

Chicago and Los Angeles. The antievolution campaign concentrated upon southern states for the most part and hardly
affected those areas where millenarian support might have
been counted upon most heavily. Furthermore, antagonism
toward evolution did not follow the same denominational
demarcations as millenarianism, but proved as appealing to
Methodists or Disciples as to Baptists or Presbyterians. There
does not seem to be any justification for arguing that millenarians were more ready than other conservative Christians
of the twenties to join the crusade against evolution. Even if
they had stood aloof, there would probably have been such
a protest movement. As Levine has shown, the reaction to
evolution was a typical expression of the America of the 1920s.

> The thirty-seven anti-evolution bills that were in-
> troduced into twenty state legislatures between 1921
> and 1929 were products of the American faith that
> legislative action can bring into being pure morals,
> right thinking, and patriotic action. They were
> drawn up by a generation that ratified the Eigh-
> teenth Amendment, legislated against vivisection,
> passed the Lusk laws to root out political heresy,
> and attempted to purge textbooks in all disciplines
> of anything even remotely smacking of dissent from
> the established order.[53]

Levine's comparison points out the greatest anomaly of
the Fundamentalist controversy. Antievolution and premillennialism appear to be the most characteristic beliefs of
Fundamentalists during the twenties. And yet the philosophy of William Jennings Bryan and the antievolution crusade
was incompatible with the assumptions on which millenarianism was built. The millenarian did not believe that legislative
action could produce pure morals or right thinking. He was
convinced that only the Spirit of God could furnish the
power by which these things could be accomplished. And
he was convinced even more deeply, moreover, that man's
thinking and acting were on an irretrievable downgrade

53. Lawrence Levine, *De-
fender of the Faith: William*
Jennings Bryan (New York,
1965), pp. 276–77.

which man was powerless to reverse and which was, indeed, one of the clearest signs of the imminence of the second advent. When a millenarian like Riley said such things as "If Christ delay, the defeat of Modernism is certain," he was falling into the most serious kind of millenarian contradiction.[54] There does not seem to be any way in which a consistent millenarian could have justified the attempt to force "creationism" upon the schools or, for that matter, "orthodoxy" upon the churches. To do so was to forsake one of the basic ingredients in the millenarian world view. Does this suggest why some conservative millenarians such as G. Campbell Morgan left the World's Christian Fundamentals Association when it had turned toward antievolutionary strategy, or why A. C. Dixon found he could not remain associated with the Baptist Bible Union?

The association of millenarian leaders with the antievolution crusade was a total failure in terms of its own goals. The teaching of evolution was not stopped. Within the context of millenarian history this tactic seems to represent a further example of the decadence of millenarianism during this century. During the nineteenth century, though not dominant, it had fought its theological battles on the same theoretical grounds as its opponents and received the respect a fair and honest opponent deserves. But during the twentieth century the group splintered over the attempt to interpret the Scriptures according to their crucial theory of literal exegesis. At the same time, the party of opposition rapidly discarded the assumptions and methods that it had shared with the millenarians and moved toward the liberal and critical understanding of the Bible and a wholly different conception of the nature of society and history.

The Fundamentalist controversy cannot be explained entirely through the millenarian movement, although millenarianism did play a large and quite unappreciated role there; but the controversy does illustrate quite poignantly the decline if not the collapse of this valiant nineteenth-century minority view. Millenarian leadership in the twenties did not

54. Cole, *History of Fundamentalism*, p. 303.

show the strength of character, deep grasp of and reverence for biblical truth, or intellectual acuity demonstrated by the late nineteenth-century leaders. The movement appears split and stricken, possibly because some of the men who became most popular could not direct their followers either as consistent conservatives or as moderate liberals.

 Appendixes

APPENDIX A

The 1878 Niagara Creed

So many in the latter times have departed from the faith, giving heed to seducing spirits, and doctrines of devils; so many have turned away their ears from the truth, and turned unto fables; so many are busily engaged in scattering broadcast the seeds of fatal error, directly affecting the honor of our Lord and the destiny of the soul, we are constrained by fidelity to Him to make the following declaration of our doctrinal belief, and to present it as the bond of union with those who wish to be connected with the Niagara Bible Conference.

I

We believe "that all Scripture is given by inspiration of God," by which we understand the whole of the book called the Bible; nor do we take the statement in the sense in which it is sometimes foolishly said that works of human genius are inspired, but in the sense that the Holy Ghost gave the very words of the sacred writings to holy men of old; and that His Divine inspiration is not in different degrees, but extends equally and fully to all parts of these writings, historical, poetical, doctrinal and prophetical, and to the smallest word, and inflection of a word, provided such word is found in the original manuscripts: 2 Tim. 3:16, 17; 2 Pet. 1:21; 1 Cor. 2:13; Mark 12:26, 36; 13:11; Acts 1:16; 2:4.

II

We believe that the Godhead eternally exists in three persons, the Father, the Son, and the Holy Spirit; and that these three are one God, having precisely the same nature, attributes and perfections, and worthy of precisely the same homage, confidence, and obedience: Mark 12:29; John 1:1–4; Matt. 28:19, 20; Acts 5:3, 4; 2 Cor. 13:14; Heb. 1:1–3; Rev. 1:4–6.

III

We believe that man, originally created in the image and after the likeness of God, fell from his high and holy estate by eating

This text is taken from a pamphlet entitled "The Fundamentals of the Faith as Expressed in the Articles of Belief of the Niagara Bible Conference" (Chicago: Great Commission Prayer League, n.d.). For a discussion of the creed, see chapter 6.

the forbidden fruit, and as the consequence of his disobedience the threatened penalty of death was then and there inflicted, so that his moral nature was not only grievously injured by the fall, but he totally lost all spiritual life, becoming dead in trespasses and sins, and subject to the power of the devil: Gen. 1:26; 2:17; John 5:40; 6:53; Eph. 2:1–3; 1 Tim. 5:6; 1 John 3:8.

IV

We believe that this spiritual death, or total corruption of human nature, has been transmitted to the entire race of man, the man Christ Jesus alone excepted; and hence that every child of Adam is born into the world with a nature which not only possesses no spark of Divine life, but is essentially and unchangeably bad, being in enmity against God, and incapable by any educational process whatever of subjection to His law: Gen. 6:5; Psa. 14:1–3; 51:5; Jer. 17:9; John 3:6; Rom. 5:12–19; 8:6, 7.

V

We believe that, owing to this universal depravity and death in sin, no one can enter the kingdom of God unless born again; and that no degree of reformation however great, no attainment in morality however high, no culture however attractive, no humanitarian and philanthropic schemes and societies however useful, no baptism or other ordinance however administered, can help the sinner to take even one step toward heaven; but a new nature imparted from above, a new life implanted by the Holy Ghost through the Word, is absolutely essential to salvation: Isa. 64:6; John 3:5, 18; Gal. 6:15; Phil. 3:4–9; Tit. 3:5; Jas. 1:18; 1 Pet. 1:23.

VI

We believe that our redemption has been accomplished solely by the blood of our Lord Jesus Christ, who was made to be sin, and made a curse, for us, dying in our room and stead; and that no repentance, no feeling, no faith, no good resolutions, no sincere efforts, no submission to the rules and regulations of any church, or of all the churches that have existed since the days of the Apostles, can add in the very least to the value of that precious blood, or to the merit of that finished work, wrought for us by Him who united in His person true and proper divinity with perfect and sinless humanity: Lev. 17:11;

Matt. 26:28; Rom. 5:6–9; 2 Cor. 5:21; Gal. 3:13; Eph. 1:7; 1 Pet. 1:18, 19.

VII

We believe that Christ, in the fulness of the blessings He has secured by His obedience unto death, is received by faith alone, and that the moment we trust in Him as our Saviour we pass out of death into everlasting life, being justified from all things, accepted before the Father according to the measure of His acceptance, loved as He is loved, and having His place and portion, as linked to Him, and one with Him forever: John 5:24; 17:23; Acts 13:39; Rom. 5:1; Eph. 2:4–6, 13; 1 John 4:17; 5:11, 12.

VIII

We believe that it is the privilege, not only of some, but of all who are born again by the Spirit through faith in Christ as revealed in the Scriptures, to be assured of their salvation from the very day they take Him to be their Saviour; and that this assurance is not founded upon any fancied discovery of their own worthiness, but wholly upon the testimony of God in His written Word, exciting within His children filial love, gratitude, and obedience: Luke 10:20; 12:32; John 6:47; Rom. 8:33–39; 2 Cor. 5:1, 6–8; 2 Tim. 1:12; 1 John 5:13.

IX

We believe that all the Scriptures from first to last center about our Lord Jesus Christ, in His person and work, in His first and second coming; and hence that no chapter even of the Old Testament is properly read or understood until it leads to Him; and moreover that all the Scriptures from first to last, including every chapter even of the Old Testament, were designed for our practical instruction: Luke 24:27, 44; John 5:39; Acts 17:2, 3; 18:28; 26:22, 23; 28:23; Rom. 15:4; 1 Cor. 10:11.

X

We believe that the Church is composed of all who are united by the Holy Spirit to the risen and ascended Son of God, that by the same Spirit we are all baptized into one body, whether we be Jews or Gentiles, and thus being members one of another, we are responsible to keep the unity of the Spirit in the bond of peace, rising above all sectarian prejudices and denominational bigotry, and loving one another with a pure heart fervently: Matt. 16:16–18; Acts 2:32–47; Rom. 12:5; 1 Cor. 12:12–27; Eph. 1:20–23; 4:3–10; Col. 3:14, 15.

XI

We believe that the Holy Spirit, not as an influence, but as a Divine Person, the source and power of all acceptable worship and service, is our abiding Comforter and Helper, that He never takes His departure from the Church, nor from the feeblest of the saints, but is ever present to testify of Christ, seeking to occupy us with Him, and not with ourselves nor with our experiences: John 7:38, 39; 14:16, 17; 15:26; 16:13, 14; Acts 1:8; Rom. 8:9; Phil. 3:3.

XII

We believe that we are called with a holy calling to walk, not after the flesh, but after the Spirit, and so to live in the Spirit that we should not fulfill the lusts of the flesh; but the flesh being still in us to the end of our earthly pilgrimage needs to be kept constantly in subjection to Christ, or it will surely manifest its presence to the dishonor of His name: Rom. 8:12, 13; 13:14; Gal. 5:16–25; Eph. 4:22–24; Col. 3:1–10; 1 Pet. 1:14–16; 1 John 3:5–9.

XIII

We believe that the souls of those who have trusted in the Lord Jesus Christ for salvation do at death immediately pass into His presence, and there remain in conscious bliss until the resurrection of the body at His coming, when soul and body reunited shall be associated with Him forever in the glory; but the souls of unbelievers remain after death in conscious misery until the final judgment of the great white throne at the close of the millennium, when soul and body reunited shall be cast into the lake of fire, not to be annihilated, but to be punished with everlasting destruction from the presence of the Lord, and from the glory of His power: Luke 16:19–26; 23:43; 2 Cor. 5:8; Phil. 1:23; 2 Thess. 1:7–9; Jude 6:7; Rev. 20:11–15.

XIV

We believe that the world will not be converted during the present dispensation, but is fast ripening for judgment, while there will be a fearful apostasy in the professing Christian body; and hence that the Lord Jesus will come in person to

[276]

introduce the millennial age, when Israel shall be restored to their own land, and the earth shall be full of the knowledge of the Lord; and that this personal and premillennial advent is the blessed hope set before us in the Gospel for which we should be constantly looking: Luke 12:35–40; 17:26–30; 18:8; Acts 15:14–17; 2 Thess. 2:3–8; 2 Tim. 3:1–5; Tit. 2:11–15.

APPENDIX B

Robert Cameron's Autobiographical Reflections

Dear brethren: —

This letter is in the form of a personal history and experience, in connection with doctrines respecting some things that we believe must speedily come to pass. Let it be frankly granted, to begin with, that no *one* man ought to assume that he alone knows and teaches the whole truth. It will probably require the united attainments of the whole church of God, from Pentecost to Parousia, to comprehend the whole truth of revelation. It is also fully conceded that brethren who have been led to conclusions different from those reached by the writer are just as scholarly and sincere and devout as himself — and just as fully committed to the quest of truth also. What is to follow is in response to the request of many brethren from many quarters — brethren who are determined above all things to know the mind of the Lord respecting all things, and to keep heart and life in obedience to his will.

In my early years, before I knew the Lord as my personal Saviour, I can only recall a vague conception concerning "the great judgment day" and of "the destruction of the world by fire," as was so commonly taught amongst the Presbyterians at that time. When, however, the Lord opened my eyes, to see some of the glories of my Saviour, I began to see that the coming of the Lord Jesus back to this earth was *the hope* set before his people rather than the coming of the day of general judgment. At this time the writings of the Bonars and of Robert Murray McCheyne, and of others like them, came into my hands and I found that they magnified the Advent of Christ and not the judgment of the world, and looked forward with longing *hope* and not with shrinking *fear*. Shortly afterwards, when in Woodstock and Toronto, Canada, during the years of my studies in Toronto University, I met with a number of godly people who had been connected with "the Brethren," so-called, in England. This introduced me to a new world, much to my own liking and also, to the writings of Darby, McIntosh, Bellett, Troter, Kelly, Müller and others. So unspeakably precious were the teachings

Robert Cameron, "To the Friends of Prophetic Truth," *Watchword and Truth* 24 (1902) : 134–36.

of these brethren concerning the person and work of Christ, and concerning the presence and power of the Holy Spirit, that I was ready to absorb and accept anything they taught without doubt or question. Indeed, I had from the beginning of my Christian life endorsed their teachings respecting the unity of the body of Christ, the utter unscripturalness of the present sectarian divisions of the church, and the importance of keeping "the unity of the Spirit in the bond of peace," *long before* I knew of their existence. I preached the gospel more than two years before I was a member of any church — was pastor of the church over which I was subsequently ordained by the "laying on of hands," six months before I was taken into its membership. All of this happened near my home, where everyone knew my father's family and where I was known from my earliest childhood. When I joined the church near Woodstock, it was after the following statements were openly made: "I believe you are wrong — that the whole of Christendom is wrong — in dividing up into sects. There ought to be no sects or divisions in the Christian church. In the days of the Apostles it was enough to be a believer, baptized in the name of the Lord, and walking in the truth, and it ought to be so now. But I find that while I have been protesting against these divisions, I have really been adding to them, for already those who have been following my teachings, have been called "Cameronians." There is nothing left, so far as I can see, but to unite with that body of Christians that seem to me nearest to the New Testament pattern. But, I wish it clearly understood, that I reserve to myself the right of loving and having fellowship, with every true Christian, of any, or every sect, or no sect, wherever I may find him. I also reserve to myself the right, just as soon as it is possible for me to be recognized as a Christian and nothing more, to step down and out, from the denomination with which I now unite." With this frank statement I was accepted, and I have never seen any good reason to change the views I then expressed. I am a Baptist minister by compulsion rather than by choice. How happy I would be could I have nothing but the blessed name of Christ to wear and to honor!

Now, amongst the many good things accepted from "Brethren teaching" were some that I have been compelled to reject because, to my mind, they do not harmonize with the teachings of the Scriptures. "To the law and the testimony," "What saith the Scripture?" These are our final source of authority and of truth.

The Teaching, which is distinctively a doctrine of the "Brethren" is, what is sometimes called, the secret rapture of the church, or, what will be better understood as the belief, that the Lord will come, and change the living and raise the sleeping saints, and take them to himself, *before the great tribulation.* This I accepted with enthusiasm, and taught with fervor, just as many godly men, the latchet of whose shoes I am unworthy to loose, are doing today. I, too, used to say that there must not be so much as the thickness of a sheet of tissue paper between my heart and the coming of the Lord. Often, oh, so often in my zeal, but not according to knowledge, have I appealed to the unsaved to trust Jesus now for the Lord might come before I had finished my sermon. In like manner I have often said that the hope is no hope, if there is a single event that *must* transpire before the Lord comes back for his own. I used to think that it gave me great comfort to believe and teach these things, although I confess that very often when teaching them, there would be a *twitch* at my heart, because some Scripture would flash across my mind that did not harmonize with what I was saying respecting the Lord's return.

However, I went on preaching them — went to England and met many godly men of the Brethren, and amongst them Mr. Müller, Mr. Newton and Mr. Darby. Mr. Müller and Mr. Darby were often met in America afterwards, and both were dearly loved. All of them, as it now seems to me found me so much in the glow of my first joy in seeing these truths about the speedy coming of the Lord, that not one of them introduced me to the sad divisions amongst them on this and other questions. I settled in New York and through the late Geo. C. Needham became intimately acquainted with the late James Inglis, who was the most princely man in his bearing, and the most child-like in his spirit of any man whom I have ever met. Until "that day" makes it known, no one can understand how much evangelical truth in America owes to the life and testimony of James Inglis. Strange to say, although we spent several hours together, nearly every week for three years, the question of whether the church would, or would not, pass through the tribulation, never came up for consideration. It was not until after his death, and after I myself had become fully convinced that the church would remain on the earth during the tribulation that I found in his writing, in "Waymarks in the Wilderness" very clear and strong teaching to the same effect.

Appendixes

Shortly after the death of Mr. Inglis, when I began to feel my own responsibility *more* and leaned on Mr. Inglis *less*, I began to face the doubts in my mind concerning the tribulation and the translation of the church. It only took a few weeks of Scripture study to upset all that I had believed and taught, and, of course, to give me great sorrow at heart that I had been emphasizing in my ministry, what now seemed to have no basis in the Scriptures. Charles Campbell, of hallowed memory, then lived and ministered in Philadelphia, and I wrote to him asking for an interview concerning a matter that was gravely exercising my mind. A time was appointed and I went on to Philadelphia. After tea, he took me to his study and said: "Now, brother, what is it that concerns you so much and that brings you here to speak with me?" I at once opened my heart to him, and while doing so, I noticed the blush of confusion over his face, and much uneasiness in his manner. When I had done, he answered, as nearly as I can remember, "That is a difficult question, and it has caused much discussion and many heart burnings amongst brethren. I believe that the church *will not* pass through the tribulation, but unless you will accept the teachings of a type it will be difficult for me to convince you of the correctness of my views." I answered, "I can never accept from the teachings of a type the direct teachings of Scripture." "Well then," he replied, "there is no use of going any farther, for while there are four Scriptures which *seem to me*, to teach the rapture of the church *before* the tribulation, I admit that they are equally capable of another interpretation." What those Scriptures are and the subsequent discussion, must be reserved for another issue.

Bibliography

1. The Historiography of Fundamentalism and Millenarianism

The fate of Fundamentalism in historiography has been worse than its lot in history. The standard histories of Fundamentalism describe little more than the controversies within the denominations and the antievolution crusade of the 1920s. Stewart G. Cole, *History of Fundamentalism* (New York, 1931), has remained the standard authority for that decade. Essentially, perhaps inescapably descriptive, Cole's book reflects careful scholarship and an absence of rancor, though he made no attempt to disguise his own personal antipathy to the movement. The first section of the book, concerning the background of Fundamentalism, though gratefully acknowledged as the original stimulus of my own interest in Fundamentalist origins, cannot be considered satisfactory. The major contribution of Cole's work remains his discussion of the disputes which disrupted the Baptist, Presbyterian, Disciples, Methodist, and Episcopal denominations during the twenties. He devoted relatively little space to the antievolution controversy.

In recent years Cole's book has been referred to less frequently than Norman Furniss, *The Fundamentalist Controversy, 1918–1931* (New Haven, 1954), although the latter is decidedly inferior to it in several respects. Furniss's work is marred by rather more inaccuracies than are consistent with scholarly standards (the worst example, at least nine factual errors on one page, p. 50), but even more disconcerting is the practice of allowing rhetorical momentum to override evidence, giving rise to false impressions and plain error. For example, Fundamentalists are described (p. 20) as men "few of whom had read widely in the scholarly treatises of the day," and (p. 23) as men who "were unprepared for a scholarly justification of their beliefs." Furniss presented no evidence or source citations which substantiated these assertions. This criticism points to the main weakness of the book. Furniss never forged a definition of the phenomenon that he wished to analyze. In the first page of the preface he denied that he intended to analyze the religious character of Fundamentalism but stated that he wished to limit himself to a "factual account [description] of men and events." However, he was not able to resist the temptation, as the phrases quoted above indicate. The reader can find a long series of unsupported operational definitions of Fundamentalism masquerading as descriptive statements. This lack of analytic rigor

[285]

is expressed in other ways as well, as when (p. 27) Furniss falls into the trap of quoting what he admits is simply conjecture by another scholar about the "sinister" connection between Fundamentalists and large industrial interests. It is simply libel to print such a statement as, "But whether or not, as Siegfried maintains, 'two hundred of the most bigotted [*sic*] millionaires in New England' gave financial support to the conservatives' campaign is a question remaining to be proved" (p. 28). Chapter 3 represents the most glaring example of poor method: "Vaguely defined fear," "violence in thought and language," "ignorance," and "egotism" are picked out as the defining and identifying characteristics of Fundamentalism without any discussion of the degree to which these traits were representative of the whole American people or the state of mind that existed in the twenties. The length of this critique would not be justified if it were not apparent that modern historians are uncritically preferring Furniss's weak and shoddy treatment of the controversy to the older but far more dependable work by Cole.

Three dissertations devoted to this period may be of interest to specialists: Everett L. Perry, "The Role of Socio-Economic Factors in the Rise and Development of American Fundamentalism" (Ph.D. dissertation, University of Chicago, 1959); Roland Nelson, "Fundamentalism and the Northern Baptist Convention" (Ph.D. dissertation, University of Chicago, 1964); and Caroll Edwin Harrington, "The Fundamentalist Movement in America, 1870–1920" (Ph.D. dissertation, University of California, Berkeley, 1959). None of these studies possesses unusual merit, and I have found Harrington's work, though quoted more widely than normal in the case of dissertations, to be largely untrustworthy. Louis Gasper, *The Fundamentalist Movement* (The Hague, 1963), gives a factual, almost pedantic account of some of the agencies, such as the American Council of Churches and the National Association of Evangelicals, which have provided the institutional structure for Fundamentalism since 1930.

In the field of religious history, adherents of a movement have usually been the first contributors to the historical literature describing it, but no Fundamentalists have written about the nineteenth- and early twentieth-century history of their movement. Fundamentalist leaders have thought a great deal about origins but, in their haste to relate the movement to the earliest sources of Christian community and doctrine, they have jumped

Bibliography

over their most immediate predecessors. Fundamentalists have not been so much attracted to the muted, qualified conclusions of historical scholarship as to the clear but abstract arguments characteristic of deductive philosophy. A case in point, J. I. Packer, *"Fundamentalism" and the Word of God* (Grand Rapids, 1958), begins as though it were proceeding with historical analysis only to slip off into abstract, nonhistorical definitions.

The one exception to this practice is a class of books written by nondispensational millenarians in opposition to dispensationalists: Oswald T. Allis, *Prophecy and the Church* (Philadelphia, 1945); George E. Ladd, *The Blessed Hope* (Grand Rapids, 1956); Diedrich H. Kromminga, *The Millennium in the Church* (Grand Rapids, 1945); George L. Murray, *Millennial Studies: A Search for Truth* (Grand Rapids, 1948). The burden of these works is essentially similar. The authors attempt to demonstrate that dispensational eschatology is not identical with millenarianism or acceptable as Christian dogma. These polemical works have stirred responses from dispensationalists, but they have not proved acceptable to historians because they fail to provide evidence for the often discerning hypotheses they suggest. Although he was neither a millenarian nor a Fundamentalist, a similar criticism can be directed at the extensive polemical writings of Crozer Seminary professor Elmer W. Powell; see, for example, "Plymouth Brethrenism," *Crozer Quarterly* 14 (Jan. 1939).

The pioneer work in the history of dispensationalism is C. Norman Kraus, *Dispensationalism in America* (Richmond, 1958), a book to which I am much indebted. Equally useful but virtually unknown is Daniel P. Fuller, "The Hermeneutics of Dispensationalism" (Th.D. dissertation, Northern Baptist Seminary, Chicago, 1957), a work which is much broader than its title would indicate. Suggestive but less reliable is Talmadge Wilson, "A History of Dispensationalism in the United States of America: The Nineteenth Century" (M.A. thesis, Pittsburgh Seminary, 1956). Arnold D. Ehlert, librarian at the Bible Institute of Los Angeles, has compiled a useful *Bibliographic History of Dispensationalism* (Grand Rapids, 1965).

Historical interest in millennialism and millenarianism has grown dramatically in the past decade, in part due to the impact of Norman R. C. Cohn, *The Pursuit of the Millennium: Revolu-*

tionary Messianism in Medieval and Reformation Europe and Its Bearing on Modern Totalitarian Movements (New York, 1957). Papers read at a symposium on millennialism held at the University of Chicago were published in Sylvia Thrupp, ed., *Millennial Dreams in Action* (The Hague, 1962). David E. Smith, "Millenarian Scholarship in America," *American Quarterly* 17 (1965): 535–49, summarized the state of the field in United States historiography. Useful older works include Ira V. Brown, "Watchers for the Second Coming: The Millenarian Tradition in America," *Mississippi Valley Historical Review* 39 (1952–53); Perry Miller, "The End of the World," chapter 10 in *Errand into the Wilderness* (New York, 1964); and the last chapter in Timothy L. Smith, *Revivalism and Social Reform* (New York, 1957). Ernest L. Tuveson, *Redeemer Nation: The Idea of America's Millennial Role* (Chicago, 1968) provides most helpful illustrations of the pervasiveness of millennial ideas in American literature, continuing an interest in millennialism begun in his *Millennium and Utopia: A Study in the Background of the Idea of Progress* (Berkeley, 1949). W. H. Rutgers, *Premillennialism in America* (Goes, Holland, 1930) is not very useful.

It only remains to mention LeRoy Edwin Froom, *The Prophetic Faith of Our Fathers* (Washington, D.C., 1946–54), 4 vols.; but no simple citation of this monumental work will suffice to give credit to the achievement of this scholar or to warn the unwary of the pitfalls into which he may fall by following Froom's guidance uncritically. *Prophetic Faith* is denominational history in the old style, which is to say it is a defense of Seventh-Day Adventist doctrines as the apostolic truth passed down through the centuries without interruption or depletion. Although never acting the part of the bigot or writing polemic, Froom nevertheless produced a strongly partisan history, championing openly the cause of historicist premillenarianism against allegorizers, millennialists, and futurist premillenarians. Furthermore, Froom has no concern with anything but history of dogma, and even dogma is narrowly construed. The result is that the work is useful as a reference work, astonishingly accurate in its references to particular men and events, but virtually without historical merit when Froom lifts his eyes above the level of the catalog of the British Museum. But for anyone inter-

Bibliography

ested in pursuing the study of millenarianism, Froom's volumes, which cover a period stretching from the Fathers down to the middle of the nineteenth century, provide invaluable bibliographic and reference service.

Relatively few manuscript collections have been discovered with direct relevance to this study. The most valuable, certainly, was the collection of letter books containing carbon copies of the correspondence of Lyman Stewart. These books are in the library of the Bible Institute of Los Angeles. The papers of Amzi C. Dixon can be seen in the library of the Southern Baptist Historical Commission, Nashville, Tennessee. The Dixon collection, though extensive, is composed primarily of printed material and was not found very useful. Although not of value for this book, it might be noted that the papers of John Franklyn Norris, the long-time Texas Fundamentalist leader, covering the period 1928–52 are also now housed in the Southern Baptist Historical Commission library. Some relatively fragmentary collections of personal papers of Charles R. Erdman and Arthur T. Pierson can be found in the Speer Library of Princeton Theological Seminary. The B. B. Warfield papers, though still in existence, have not been made available to scholars. A few of the papers of John Nelson Darby remain in the hands of Mr. Henry M. Sibthorpe, Redruth, Cornwall, who welcomes scholarly interest in them. The Darby letters are useful only in correcting omissions in the printed Darby correspondence, and there are relatively few Darby letters in the collection. It is more valuable for its materials relating to the evangelization of Canada, particularly the record of the work of Fred. W. and Robert T. Grant. Apparently, the letters and papers of Edward Irving, which were available at the time Mrs. Oliphant wrote her biography, have now perished. No Irving papers could be turned up during the research for this book.

There follows an annotated list of books which have been found useful in the writing of this history. Not every book cited in the footnotes has been cited here, and some not cited in the text of the book have been included here. My intention has been to provide those who may wish to pursue further the study of Fundamentalism and millenarianism with the benefit of my research in these fields. The list should not be considered as in any sense a complete bibliography of either subject.

BIBLIOGRAPHY

2. BRITISH MILLENARIANISM, 1800–1845

PERIODICALS

Achill Missionary Herald (Dublin). Edited by the Reverend Edward Nangle. 32 vols., 1837–69.

Christian Herald (Dublin). Edited by the Reverend Edward N. Hoare. 5 vols., 1830–35.

Investigator; or, Monthly Expositor and Register on Prophecy (London). Edited by Joshua W. Brooks. First series, 4 vols., 1831–35; new series, 1 vol., 1836.

Jewish Expositor (London). 16 vols., 1816–31. The organ of the London Society for Promoting Christianity among the Jews.

Jewish Repository (London). 2 vols., 1813–14. An early periodical of the London Society for Promoting Christianity among the Jews.

Morning Watch or Quarterly Journal on Prophecy, and Theological Review (London). Edited by John Tudor, 7 vols., 1829–33.

BOOKS

Anderson, William. *An Apology for Millennial Doctrine in the Form in Which It Was Entertained by the Primitive Church.* Glasgow, 1830.

———. *A Letter to the Author of Millenarianism Indefensible.* Glasgow, 1834.

Begg, James A. *A Connected View of Some of the Scriptural Evidence of the Redeemer's Speedy Personal Return.* Paisley, 1829.

Birks, Thomas R. *First Elements of Sacred Prophecy.* London, 1843. An attack on futurism.

———. *Memoir of the Rev. Edward Bickersteth, Late Rector of Watton, Herts.* 3d ed. London, 1852.

Brooks, Joshua W. *A Dictionary of Writers on Prophecy.* London, 1835. A mine of miscellaneous information; copies are often bound in files of Brooks's periodical, the *Investigator.*

———. *Lectures of Subjects Connected with Prophecy: Delivered at the Request of the Edinburgh Association for Promoting the Study of Prophecy.* Edinburgh, 1841.

Brown, John Aquila. *The Jew, the Master-key of the Apocalypse: In answer to Mr. F[rere].* London, 1827.

Burgh, William. *The Apocalypse Unfulfilled.* 2d ed. Dublin, 1833.

———. *Lectures on the Second Advent.* Dublin, 1832.

Cuninghame, William. *A Critical Examination of Some of the*

[290]

Bibliography

Fundamental Principles of the Rev. George Stanley Faber's Sacred Calendar of Prophecy. London, 1829.

————. *A Dissertation on the Seals and Trumpets of the Apocalypse, and the Prophetical Period of 1260 Years.* London, 1813.

————. *The Scheme of Prophetic Arrangement of the Rev. E. Irving and Mr. Frere.* London, 1826.

————. *Strictures on Certain Leading Positions and Interpretations of the Rev. Edward Irving's Lectures on the Apocalypse.* . . . Glasgow, 1831.

————. *A Summary View of the Scriptural Argument for the Second and Glorious Advent of Messiah before the Millennium.* Glasgow, 1828.

Dallas, Alexander R. C., ed. *Lift up Your Heads: Glimpses of Messiah's Glory: Being Lectures Delivered during Lent, 1848, at St. George's Bloomsbury.* London, 1848.

Dallas, (Mrs.) Alex. R. C. *Incidents in the Life and Ministry of the Rev. Alex. R. C. Dallas* . . . London, 1871. This book illustrates one problem in millenarian historiography: the author for undisclosed reasons suppressed any mention of Dallas's many millenarian activities.

Drummond, Henry. *A Defense of the Students of Prophecy in Answer to the Attack of the Rev. Dr. Hamilton of Strathblane.* London, 1828.

————. *Dialogues on Prophecy.* 3 vols. London, 1827–29. These volumes, though appearing to be parts of a single set, were published serially. The *second* preface was written after the publication of vol. 3 and inserted in vol. 1.

Faber, George Stanley. *A Dissertation on Prophecies* . . . *Relative to the 1260 Years* . . . *and Restoration of the Jews.* 2d ed. London, 1807.

————. *Eight Dissertations* . . . *on Prophetical Passages.* London, 1845.

————. *Remarks on the Effusion of the Fifth Apocalyptic Vial.* London, 1815.

————. *A Treatise on the Genius and Object of the Patriarchal, the Levitical, and the Christian Dispensations.* London, 1823.

Frere, James Hatley. *A Combined View of the Prophecies of Daniel, Esdras, and S. John Shewing That All Prophetic Writings Are Formed upon One Plan* . . . *with Critical Remarks upon* . . . *Mr. Faber and Mr. Cuninghame.* London, 1815.

————. *Eight Letters on the Prophecies Relating to the Last Times*. London, 1831.

————. *The Great Continental Revolution Marking the Expiration of the Times of the Gentiles*. London, 1848.

————. *The Harvest of the Earth prior to the Vintage of Wrath, Considered as Symbolical of the Evangelical Alliance*. London, 1846.

————. *On the General Structure of the Apocalypse*. London, 1826.

————. *Three Letters on the Prophecies*. London, 1833.

Gilfillian, George. *Life of the Rev. William Anderson*. London, 1873.

Halsted, T. D. *Our Missions . . . a History of the London Society for Promoting Christianity among the Jews*. London, 1866.

Herschell, Ridley H., ed. *"Far above Rubies": Memoir of Helen S. Herschell*. London, 1854.

Holmes, W. A. *The Time of the End: Being a Series of Lectures on Prophetical Chronology*. London, 1833.

Madden, S. *The Nature and Time of the Second Advent of Messiah Considered in Four Letters*. Dublin, 1829.

Maitland, Samuel R. *An Attempt to Elucidate the Prophecies concerning Anti-Christ with Remarks on Some Works of J. H. F[rere]*. London, 1853.

————. *An Enquiry into the Grounds on Which the Prophetic Period of Daniel and St. John Has Been Supposed to Consist of 1260 Years*. London, 1826. An early futurist tract which attacks the conclusions of Faber, Cuninghame, and Frere.

Marsh, Catharine M. *The Life of the Rev. William Marsh, D. D.* London, 1867.

Norris, H. H. *The Origin, Progress, and Existing Circumstances, of the London Society for Promoting Christianity amongst the Jews: An Historical Inquiry*. London, 1825. A work critical of the society.

Palmer, H. P. *Joseph Wolff, His Romantic Life and Travels*. Heath Cranton, 1935.

Papers Read before the Society for the Investigation of Prophecy. London, 1828.

Stirling, A. M. W. *The Ways of Yesterday . . . Chronicles of the Way Family from 1307–1885*. London, 1930. A work useful for details about the life of John Way, chief sponsor of the LSPCJ.

Bibliography

The book is catalogued under Pickering by the British Museum.

Story, Robert H. *Memoir of the Life of the Rev. Robert Story.* Cambridge, 1862. Useful for information relating to the Albury conferences.

Todd, James H. *Discourses on the Prophecies Relating to Antichrist in the Writings of Daniel and St. Paul.* Dublin, 1830. This and the following work were first delivered as Donnellan Lectures at Trinity College, Dublin.

———. *Six Discourses on the Prophecies Relating to Antichrist in the Apocalypse of St. John.* Dublin, 1846.

Waugh, John S. *Dissertations on the Prophecies of Sacred Scripture.* Annan, 1833. Waugh was a convert of Edward Irving.

Wolff, Joseph. *Missionary Journal and Memoir.* 2d ed. London, 1827.

———. *Travels and Adventures of the Rev. Joseph Wolff.* London, 1861.

3. BRITISH MILLENARIANISM AFTER 1845
PERIODICALS

Friend of Israel (Glasgow). 7 vols., 1851–57. Published by the Scottish Society for the Conversion of Israel.

Last Vials (Torquay). Edited by R. A. Purdon. 23 vols., 1846–72.

Prophetic Herald, and Churchman's Witness for Christ (Birkenhead). Edited by Joseph Baylee. 2 vols., 1845–47.

Quarterly Journal of Prophecy (London). Edited by Horatius Bonar. 25 vols., 1849–73.

Rainbow: A Magazine of Christian Literature, with Special Reference to the Revealed Future of the Church and the World (London). Edited by the Reverend Dr. William Leask. 24 vols., 1864–87. After 1873 the Reverend Leask was more concerned with the doctrines relating to the annihilation of the soul than with millenarianism.

Signs of Our Times (London). Edited by Michael P. Baxter. 9 vols., 1867–75. Continued as *Christian Herald and Signs of Our Times* (New York) beginning in October 1878.

Voice of Israel (London). Edited by Ridley Herschell. 2 vols., 1845–47.

BOOKS

Baxter, Michael P. *The Coming Battle, and the Appalling National Convulsions Foreshown in Prophecy Immediately to Occur during the Period 1861–67.* Philadelphia, 1860.

———. *Fifteen Predicted Events from 1892 until the End of this Age on April 11, 1901.* London, 1892.

———. *Louis Napoleon, the Destined Monarch of the World and Personal Antichrist.* Philadelphia, 1866.

[Baxter]. Wiseman, Nathaniel. *Michael Paget Baxter.* London, 1923. Wiseman was a pseudonym often used by Baxter. In this case he wrote his autobiography as biography in order to make his self-esteem more palatable to the reading public.

Cumming, John. *The End: Proximate Signs of the Close of this Dispensation.* London, 1855.

———. *The Great Consummation.* New York, 1854. The first and second parts of this trilogy of biblical commentaries were entitled *The Great Tribulation* (London, 1859) and *The Great Preparation* (New York, 1860).

Elliott, Edward Bishop. *Horae Apocalypticae.* 4 vols. 5th ed. London, 1857.

Govett, Robert. *The Saints' Rapture to the Presence of the Lord Jesus.* London, 1864.

Guinness, H. Grattan. *History Unveiling Prophecy.* New York, 1905.

Kelly, James. *The Apocalypse Interpreted.* London, 1849.

———. *Apocalyptic Interpretation; or, the Apocalypse Intelligible Not in Any History of the Past as Alleged by the Rev. E. B. Elliott . . . .* London, 1847.

———. *Fourth Series of Lectures on Subjects Connected with Prophecy.* 2d ed. London, 1847.

McCausland, Dominick. *The Times of the Gentiles.* Dublin, 1852.

Mildmay Second Advent Conference. *"Our God Shall Come": Addresses on the Second Coming of the Lord.* London, 1878.

———. *The Sure Word of Prophecy: Addresses on the Second Coming of the Lord.* London, 1879.

———. *"Things That Shall Come to Pass": Addresses on the Second Coming of the Lord.* London, 1886.

Pember, G. H. *The Great Prophecies.* London, 1881.

The Personal and Premillennial Coming of Our Lord and Saviour Jesus Christ. Edinburgh, 1888. Proceedings of the millenarian conference held in Free Assembly Hall, Edinburgh, 8–12 Oct. 1888.

Report of Three Days Meetings for Prayer, and for Addresses on the Subject of the Lord's Coming. London, [1866?].

Stevenson, John. *The Second Advent.* 2d ed. London, 1864.

[294]

Bibliography

4. THE PLYMOUTH BRETHREN
PRIMARY WORKS

Darby, John Nelson. *Collected Writings.* Edited by William Kelly. 34 vols. and index. 2d ed. London, 1967.

————. *The Letters of J. N. D.* 3 vols. 2d ed. London, n.d.

Gosse, Edmund. *Father and Son: A Study of Two Temperaments.* London, 1907. A poignant description of an unhappy childhood in a Brethren home.

Interesting Reminiscences of the Early History of "Brethren." Weston super Mare, n.d. A small pamphlet, but a primary source of considerable significance.

List of Gatherings in the United States and Canada, July, 1878. (For Brethren's Use Only). Vinton, Iowa, n.d. Useful in showing the growth and distribution of Brethren assemblies by 1878; intended only as an address book for traveling believers.

Mackintosh, C. H. *Papers on the Lord's Coming.* New York, n.d. C. H. M. was also the author of a whole series of influential biblical commentaries and religious tracts.

Madden, (Mrs.) Hamilton. *Memoir of the Late Right Rev. Robert Daly.* London, 1875. A source for the Powerscourt conferences.

Newman, Francis William. *Phases of Faith; or, Passages from the History of My Creed.* London, 1850. Autobiographical comments from an early disciple of J. N. Darby, who by 1850 had traveled far from Darby's teachings.

Newton, Benjamin Wills. *Five Letters on Events Predicted in Scripture as Antecedent to the Coming of the Lord.* 3d ed. London, 1877. Written in 1840, this attack upon the position of J. N. Darby was first published in an altered version in 1845, 2d ed. in 1847 as originally written, and 3d ed. also unaltered.

Newton, Benjamin Wills, and Borlase, H., *Answers to the Questions Considered at a Meeting Held in Plymouth on September 15, 1834, and the Following Days.* Preface by S. P. T[regelles]. 2d ed. Plymouth, 1847. A report of the proceedings of a conference held at the same time as the fourth Powerscourt conference.

Tregelles, Samuel P. *The Hope of Christ's Second Coming.* London, 1864. An important but apparently erroneous source for the origin of the doctrine of the "any-moment" coming.

BIBLIOGRAPHY

Wigram, George V. *Memorials of the Ministry of G. V. W.* 2d ed. London, 1881. Autobiographical materials of a relatively insignificant disciple of J. N. Darby. Contains some material relating to Canada and the United States.

Wingfield, Theodosia A. (Viscountess Powerscourt). *Letters and Papers.* Edited by R. Daly. London, 1838. Intended to illustrate the Viscountess's piety, the book has little historical significance.

SECONDARY WORKS

Bass, Clarence. *Backgrounds to Dispensationalism.* Grand Rapids, 1960. Of some value for Darby's theology.

Coad, F. Roy. *A History of thé Brethren Movement.* London, 1968.

Croskery, Thomas. "The Plymouth Brethren." *Princeton Review* 1 (1872), 48–77.

Fromow, George H., ed. *B. W. Newton and Dr. S. P. Tregelles.* London, n.d. Contains much primary material in extensive quotations.

Groves, Edward Kennaway. *George Müller and His Successors.* Bristol, 1906.

Ironside, Henry A. *A Historical Sketch of the Brethren Movement.* Grand Rapids, 1942.

King, Henry M. "The Plymouth Brethren." *Baptist Review* 3 (1881): 438–65.

Neatby, W. B. *History of the Plymouth Brethren.* London, 1901.

Pickering, Henry. *Chief Men among the Brethren.* London, n.d. A useful book of biographical sketches.

"Plymouth Brethren and Lay Preaching in Ireland." *London Quarterly Review* 27 (Oct. 1866): 1–37. An excellent review of nineteen mid-nineteenth-century books by or against Plymouth Brethren. Critical of Brethrenism.

Rowdon, Harold H. *The Origins of the Brethren, 1825–1850.* London, 1967. The best work in the field.

Ryrie, Charles C. *Dispensationalism Today.* Chicago, 1965. Written by a professor at Dallas Theological Seminary, where Darby's teachings are actively perpetuated and defended.

Stokes, G. T. "John Nelson Darby," *Contemporary Review* 48 (Oct. 1885).

Turner, W. G. *John Nelson Darby, a Biography.* London, 1926. Not of much value.

———. *William Kelly as I Knew Him.* London, 1936.

Bibliography

5. EDWARD IRVING AND THE IRVINGITES

Baxter, Robert. *Narrative of Facts Characterizing the Supernatural Manifestations in Members of Mr. Irving's Congregation and Other Individuals. . . .* 2d ed. London, 1833. An account by a disillusioned follower of the early days in Irving's congregation.

Bennett, William J. E. *The Church's Broken Unity.* London, 1867. Vol. 1 contains material about Irving.

Boase Collection, British Museum. An extensive collection of books and pamphlets relating to Irving, including a newspaper clipping book, BM #764, n. 19.

Carlyle, Thomas. *Reminiscences.* New York, 1881.

Drummond, Andrew Landale. *Edward Irving and His Circle.* London, 1934. A poor book, too much dependent on other secondary works.

Hazlitt, William. *The Spirit of the Age or Contemporary Portraits.* London, 1904. Contains an interesting and amusing essay on Irving.

Irving, Edward. *Babylon and Infidelity Foredoomed.* Glasgow, 1826. Contains a dedication to J. Hatley Frere in thanks for his teaching and counseling in prophecy. Originally the treatise was a sermon preached to the Continental Society.

Lacunza, Manuel (alias Juan Josafat Ben-Ezra). *Venida del Mesias en Gloria y Magestad* [*The Coming of Messiah in Glory and Majesty*]. Translated by Edward Irving. London, 1827.

Macartney, Clarence. "Edward Irving." *Princeton Theological Review* 20 (1922) : 232 ff.

Miller, Edward. *The History and Doctrines of Irvingism . . . .* London, 1878.

Oliphant, Margaret O. W. *The Life of Edward Irving . . . .* London, 1862. Pure Victoriana, but the author quotes freely from primary documents now apparently lost.

Williams, Meade C. "Edward Irving." *Princeton Theological Review* 1 (1903) : 1–22.

6. CRITICS OF BRITISH MILLENARIANISM

Brown, David. *Christ's Second Coming: Will It Be Pre-millennial?* Edinburgh, 1846.

Fairbairn, Patrick. *The Typology of Scripture Viewed in Connection with the Entire Scheme of the Divine Dispensations.* 2 vols. Edinburgh, 1845–47.

[Grant, James]. *The End of All Things; or, the Coming and*

BIBLIOGRAPHY

Kingdom of Christ. 3 vols. 2d ed. London, 1866–67. An intriguing book with vast amounts of personal information about the career of the millenarian party in England during the mid-nineteenth century.

Waldegrave, Samuel. *New Testament Millenarianism.* London, 1855. The 1854 Bampton Lectures at Oxford University. The book attracted much attention among millenarians.

7. Secondary Works Related to British Millenarianism

Best, Geoffrey F. A. "The Evangelicals and the Established Church in the Early Nineteenth Century." *Journal of Theological Studies* 10 (1959) : 63 ff.
———. "The Protestant Constitution and Its Supporters, 1800–1829." *Trans. of the Royal Historical Society,* 5th series, 8 (1958) : 105–27.

Cowherd, R. G. *The Politics of English Dissent, 1815–1848.* London, 1959.

Hardman, B. E. "The Evangelical Party in the Church of England, 1855–65." Ph.D. thesis, Cambridge University, 1964.

Inglis, K. S. *The Churches and the Working Classes in Victorian England.* Toronto, 1963.

MacClatchey, Diana. *Oxfordshire Clergy, 1777–1869.* Oxford, 1960.

Machin, G. I. T. *The Catholic Question in English Politics, 1820–30.* Oxford, 1964.

Reynolds, J. S. *The Evangelicals at Oxford 1735–1871: A Record of an Unchronicled Movement.* Oxford, 1953.

Thompson, Edward P. *The Making of the English Working Class.* London, 1963.

8. American Millenarianism, 1800–1870

PERIODICALS

American Millenarian and Prophetic Review (New York). Edited by Isaac P. Labagh. 2 vols., 1842–44.

Literalist (Philadelphia). 5 vols., 1840–42.

Prophetic Times (Philadelphia). Edited principally by Joseph Seiss, assisted by George Duffield and Richard Newton. 12 vols., 1863–74. The *Prophetic Times and Watchtower* continued the work of Seiss's periodical. Edited by John G. Wilson, it was published in 7 vols., 1875–81.

Theological and Literary Journal (New York). Edited by David N. Lord. 12 vols., 1848–61. A millenarian journal with style and

Bibliography

content comparable to the British *Quarterly Journal of Prophecy*.

Waymarks in the Wilderness (New York). Edited by James Inglis. 10 vols., 1864–72. An earlier version of the periodical appeared briefly during 1854–57, published in Detroit and Saint Louis.

MILLENARIAN AND MILLENNIALIST BOOKS

Bryant, Alfred. *Millenarian Views*. New York, 1852.

Demarest, John T., and Gordon, William Robert. *Christocracy; or Essays on the Coming and Kingdom of Christ*. New York, 1867. This book resulted from and in large part duplicates the material presented in the Dutch Reformed denominational periodical the *Christian Intelligencer* during the 1860s.

Duffield, George. *Dissertations on the Prophecies Relative to the Second Coming of Jesus Christ*. New York, 1842.

———. *Millenarianism Defended: A Reply to Prof. Stuart's Strictures*. New York, 1843.

Emerson, Joseph. *Lectures on the Millennium*. Boston, 1830.

Hellmuth, J. *The Divine Dispensations and Their Gradual Development*. London, 1866. Hellmuth was principal and professor of divinity at Huron College in London, Ontario. This diocese was particularly open to millenarianism during the nineteenth century.

Henshaw, John P. K. *An Inquiry into the Meaning of the Prophecies Relating to the Second Advent of our Lord Jesus Christ*. Baltimore, 1842. Henshaw was the Episcopal bishop of Rhode Island, 1843–52.

Janeway, Jacob Jones. *Hope for the Jews; or, the Jews Will Be Converted to the Christian Faith and Settled . . . in Palestine*. New Brunswick, 1853. Janeway was a professor of theology at Western Seminary.

Jones, Joel. *Jesus and the Coming Glory: Notes on Scripture*. Philadelphia, 1865. These notes first appeared serially in Lord's *Theological and Literary Journal*.

Kirkwood, Robert. *Lectures on the Millennium*. New York, 1856.

Labagh, Isaac P. *A Sermon on the Necessity of the Personal Return and Reign of Christ on the Earth*. New York, 1842.

———. *Twelve Lectures on the Great Events of Unfulfilled Prophecy*. New York, 1859.

Lillie, John. *The Perpetuity of the Earth*. New York, 1842.

Lord, David Nevins. *The Coming and Reign of Christ*. New York, 1858.

———. *An Exposition of the Apocalypse.* New York, 1847.

Lord, Joseph L. *Briefs on Prophetic Themes.* Boston, 1864. Lord acknowledges the influence of B. W. Newton and S. P. Tregelles.

McCorkle, Samuel M. *Thoughts on the Millennium.* Nashville, 1830.

Noyes, John Humphrey. *The Berean: A Manual for the Help of Those Who Seek the Faith of the Primitive Church.* Putney, Vt., 1847. Noyes was not a millenarian but his views on the second coming of Christ played a large part in his theology and illustrate another facet of the general early nineteenth-century millennial interest.

Priest, Josiah. *A View of the Expected Christian Millennium . . . Embellished with a Chart of the Dispensations from Abraham to the End of Time.* 7th ed. Albany, 1831. Priest was not a millenarian but puts forward some striking opinions illustrated with a particularly elaborate chart.

Ramsey, William. *Messiah's Reign: The Future Blessedness of the Church and the World.* Philadelphia, 1857.

———. *The Millennium and the New Jerusalem Contrasted.* New York, 1844.

———. *The Second Coming of Our Lord . . . before the Millennium.* Philadelphia, 1841.

Read, Hollis. *The Coming Crisis of the World.* Columbus, Ohio, 1861.

Seiss, Joseph A. *The Apocalypse . . . Lectures.* Philadelphia, 1865.

———. *Empire of Evil.* Baltimore, 1856.

———. *The Gospel in the Stars.* Philadelphia, 1882.

———. *Israel and the Coming Antichrist.* Philadelphia, 1879.

———. *The Last Times and the Great Consummation.* Philadelphia, 1863.

———. *The Lord at Hand.* Philadelphia, 1864.

———. *A Miracle in Stone; or, the Great Pyramid of Egypt.* Philadelphia, 1877.

Shimeall, Richard Cunningham. *Christ's Second Coming: Is It Pre-millennial or Post-millennial? (The Great Question of the Day).* New York, 1865.

Spalding, Joshua. *Sentiments, concerning the Coming and Kingdom of Christ.* Salem, Mass., 1796. This early millenarian work was rediscovered by the Millerites and republished by Joshua V. Himes in 1841.

Bibliography

"The Time of the End": . . . *Illustrated by the History of Prophetic Interpretation.* Boston, 1856.

Waller, J. C. *The Second Coming of Christ: The Restitution of All Things.* Louisville, Ky., 1863.

Wellcome, Isaac C. *History of the Second Advent Message and Mission, Doctrine and People.* Boston, 1874. A good discussion of Millerite tradition by an advocate and believer.

Winthrop, Edward. *Lectures on the Second Advent.* Cincinnati, 1843.

————. *Letters on the Prophetic Scriptures.* New York, 1850.

CRITICS OF AMERICAN MILLENARIANISM

Arthur, William. *The Tongue of Fire.* New York, 1880.

Berg, Joseph F. *The Second Advent of Jesus Christ, Not Premillennial.* Philadelphia, 1859. Probably the most influential and noteworthy American attack upon the millenarian position.

Briggs, Charles A. "The Origin and History of Premillenarianism." *Lutheran Quarterly* 9 (1879) : 207–45.

Brown, J. A. "The Second Advent and the Creeds of Christendom." *Bibliotheca Sacra* 24 (1867) : 629–51.

"The Fulfillment of Prophecy." *Princeton Review* 23 (Jan. 1861). Reprinted by the *British and Foreign Evangelical Review* 10 (1861) : 430–460.

"Millennial Traditions." *Methodist Quarterly Review* 25 (1843) : 421–46.

"The Millennium of Rev. XX." *Methodist Quarterly Review* 25 (1843) : 83–110.

Patterson, R. M. "Pre-millenarianism." *Princeton Review,* series 4, 2 (1879) : 415–34.

Seyffarth, Gust. "Chiliasm Critically Examined. . . ." *Evangelical Quarterly Review* 12 (1860–61) : 341–401.

[Wallace, Benjamin J.] "The Apocalypse." *Presbyterian Quarterly Review* 1 (1853) : 529–48.

————. "Millenarianism." *Presbyterian Quarterly Review* 2 (1853) : 19–40.

SECONDARY WORKS

Andrews, Edward Deming. *The People Called Shakers.* New York, 1953.

Billington, Louis. "The Millerite Adventists in Great Britain, 1840–1850." *Journal of American Studies* 1 (1967) : 191–212.

Cross, Whitney R. *The Burned-over District, The Social and In-*

tellectual History of Enthusiastic Religion in Western New York, 1800–1850. 2d ed. New York, 1965.

Goen, C. C. "Jonathan Edwards, A Departure in Eschatology." *Church History* 28 (1959) : 25–40.

Hansen, Klaus J. *Quest for Empire: The Political Kingdom of God and the Council of Fifty in Mormon History.* Lansing, 1967. Chap. 1 is helpful in connection with the relationship of Mormonism to millennialism, but Hansen's attempt to discuss that tradition in general is not entirely competent.

Nichol, Francis D. *The Midnight Cry.* Washington, D.C., 1944. A good study of William Miller.

Tyler, Alice Felt. *Freedom's Ferment.* Minneapolis, 1944.

9. BIBLICAL LITERALISM AND THE PRINCETON THEOLOGY

PRIMARY WORKS

Alexander, Archibald. *Evidences of the Authenticity, Inspiration and Canonical Authority* . . . . Philadelphia, n.d.

Alexander, James W. *Life of Archibald Alexander.* New York, 1857.

Carson, Alexander. *The Inspiration of the Scriptures: A Review of the Theories of the Rev. Daniel Wilson, Rev. Dr. Pye Smith, and the Rev. Dr. Dick, and Other Treatises.* London, 1830.

Dwight, Timothy. *Theology Explained and Defended in a Series of Sermons, with a Memoir of the Life of the Author, to which Is Prefixed an Essay on the Inspiration of the Scriptures.* Glasgow, 1850.

Farrar, Frederic W. *History of Interpretation.* London, 1886.

Gaussen, Louis. *Theopneustia: the Plenary Inspiration of the Holy Scriptures.* Translated from the French. London, 1841.

Haldane, Robert. *The Books of the Old and New Testaments Proved to Be Canonical, and Their Verbal Inspiration Maintained and Established: With an Account of the Introduction and Character of the Apocrypha.* London, 1830.

Hodge, Archibald A. *Outlines of Theology.* 1st ed. New York, 1860. 2d ed. New York, 1879.

Hodge, Archibald A., and Warfield, B. B. "Inspiration." *Presbyterian Review* 2 (1881) : 225–60.

Hodge, Charles. *Systematic Theology.* New York, 1874.

Kelly, James. *Inspiration.* London, 1862.

Lowe, Josiah B. *Inspiration a Reality.* London, 1856.

Pearce, A. E. *Inspiration: What Is It?* London, 1857.

Bibliography

Warfield, Benjamin B. *The Inspiration and Authority of the Bible*. Philadelphia, 1948.

————. "The Present Problem of Inspiration." *Homiletic Review* 21 (1891) : 410–16.

SECONDARY WORKS

Beardslee, John W. "Theological Development at Geneva under Francis and Jean-Alphonse Turretin, 1648–1737." Ph.D. dissertation, Yale University, 1956.

Foster, Frank H. *A Genetic History of the New England Theology*. Chicago, 1907.

Glover, Willis B. *Evangelical Nonconformists and Higher Criticism in the Nineteenth Century*. London, 1954.

Lindsay, Thomas M. "The Doctrine of Scripture: the Reformers and the Princeton School." *Expositor*, fifth series, 1 (1895) : 278–93.

Livingstone, William D. "The Princeton Apologetic as Exemplified by the Work of Benjamin B. Warfield, and J. Gresham Machen." Ph.D. dissertation, Yale University, 1948.

Loetscher, Lefferts A. *The Broadening Church*. Philadelphia, 1957. An excellent history of northern Presbyterianism since 1869.

Maring, Norman H. "Baptists and Changing Views of the Bible, 1865–1918." *Foundations* 1 (July and Oct. 1958) : 52–75, 30–61.

Nelson, John O. "The Rise of the Princeton Theology." Ph.D. dissertation, Yale University, 1935.

Nichols, Robert Hastings. "Fundamentalism in the Presbyterian Church." *Journal of Religion* 5 (Jan. 1925) : 14–36.

Preus, Robert. *The Inspiration of Scripture*. Edinburgh, 1955. A study of the seventeenth-century Lutheran understanding of inspiration.

Relton, Frederic, and Overton, John H. *The English Church from the Accession of George I to the End of the Eighteenth Century*. London, 1906.

Rogers, Jack Bartlett. *Scripture in the Westminster Confession: A Problem of Historical Interpretation for American Presbyterianism*. Kampen, Netherlands, 1966.

10. American Millenarianism, 1870–1900

PERIODICALS

Truth or Testimony for Christ (St. Louis). Edited by James H. Brookes. 23 vols., 1874–97.

Bibliography

Watchword (Boston). Edited by Adoniram J. Gordon until 1895. 19 vols., 1878–97.

BOOKS

Blackstone, William E. *Jesus Is Coming.* 2d ed. New York, 1886. Probably the most widely distributed and influential American millenarian tract of the nineteenth century.

Brookes, James H. *Bible Reading on the Second Coming of Christ.* Springfield, Ill., 1877. Contains the substance of several Bible readings given at one of the earliest Niagara group meetings, held in Swampscott, Mass., July 1876.

———. *God Spake All These Words.* St. Louis, n.d. [ca. 1894]. An argument for the supernatural origin and inerrant inspiration of Scripture.

———. *Maranatha.* St. Louis, 1870. An exposition of the "any-moment" theory of Christ's return.

Cameron, Robert. *The Doctrine of the Ages.* New York, 1896.

Daniels, W. H., ed. *Moody: His Words, Work, and Workers.* New York, 1877.

Dixon, Amzi C., ed. *The Holy Spirit in Life and Service.* No extant copies of this book have been found, but it was advertised as the proceedings of a conference on the ministry of the Holy Spirit held in Brooklyn in Oct. 1894.

3M. *The Person and Ministry of the Holy Spirit.* London, 1891. Proceedings of a Baltimore conference, held 29 Oct. ff. 1890.

Erdman, William J. *The Niagara Conference.* Privately printed, n.d.

Gordon, Adoniram J. *Ecce Venit.* New York, 1889.

———. *How Christ Came to Church: A Spiritual Autobiography.* Philadelphia, 1895.

Graves, James R. *The Work of Christ in the Covenant of Redemption: Developed in Seven Dispensations.* Memphis, 1883.

Kellogg, Samuel H. "Is the Advent Pre-Millennial?" *Presbyterian Review* 3 (1882) : 475–502.

———. "Premillennialism: Its Relation to Doctrine and Practice." *Bibliotheca Sacra* 45 (1888) :234–74.

Miller, William S., and Kyle, Joseph, eds. *Addresses on the Second Coming of the Lord.* Pittsburgh, 1896. The report of the proceedings of the third American Bible and Prophetic Conference held in Allegheny, Penn., 3–6 Dec. 1895.

Munhall, Leander W., ed. *Anti-Higher Criticism; or, Testimony to the Infallibility of the Bible.* New York, 1894. The report of the proceedings of Seaside Bible Conference held at Asbury Park, N.J., 11–21 Aug. 1893.

Needham, George C. *Life and Labors of Charles H. Spurgeon.* Boston, 1882. Contains a letter by James H. Brookes of significance for Brookes's biography.

———. *Preach the Word.* New York, 1892.

———. *The Spiritual Life.* Philadelphia, 1895. Contains a discussion of the origin of Bible conferences.

———, ed. *Primitive Paths in Prophecy.* Chicago, 1891. Report of the first conference of the Baptist Society for Bible Study — a millenarian group — which was held in Centennial Baptist Church, Brooklyn, 18–21 Nov. 1890.

———, ed. *Prophetic Studies of the International Prophetic Conference.* Chicago, 1886. Report of the proceedings of the second in the series of Bible and Prophetic conferences held 16–21 Nov. 1886 in Farwell Hall, Chicago.

Nicholson, William Rufus. *Reasons Why I Became a Reformed Episcopalian.* Philadelphia, 1875.

Peters, George N. H. *Theocratic Kingdom of Our Lord Jesus.* 3 vols. New York, 1884.

Pierson, Arthur T. *Forward Movements of the Last Half Century.* New York, 1900.

———. "The Story of the Northfield Conferences." *Northfield Echoes* 1 (June 1894) : 1–13. This article summarized the first eleven conferences. From this point on the *Northfield Echoes* reported on the conferences as they occurred.

———, ed. *The Inspired Word.* New York, 1888. Report of the proceedings of the Bible Inspiration Conference held in Philadelphia, 15–18 Nov. 1887.

"The Second Coming of Our Lord": Being Papers Read at a Conference Held at Niagara, Ontario, July 14–17, 1885. Toronto, n.d.

Simpson, Albert B. *The Apostolic Church.* Nyack, N.Y., n.d.

Thompson, Albert Edward. *A Century of Jewish Missions.* Introduction by W. E. Blackstone. Chicago, 1902.

Tyng, Stephen H., Jr. *He Will Come.* New York, 1877.

West, Nathaniel, ed. *Premillennial Essays.* Chicago, 1879. The report of the proceedings of the first American Bible and Prophetic Conference, held in New York City, 30 Oct.–1 Nov. 1878.

BIBLIOGRAPHY

SECONDARY WORKS

Ashby, L. *Keswick and Its Message.* London, 1933.

Behney, John Bruce. "Conservatism and Liberalism in the Theology of Late 19th Century American Protestantism: A Comparative Study of A. J. Gordon and Wm. N. Clarke." Ph.D. dissertation, Yale University, 1941. Not very discerning a study with regard to Gordon.

Carter, Paul A. "The Reformed Episcopal Schism of 1873: An Ecumenical Perspective." *Historical Magazine of the Protestant Episcopal Church* 33 (Sept. 1964) : 225–38.

Dollar, George W. "The Reverend F. L. Chapell." *Bibliotheca Sacra* 120 (1963) : 126–36.

Erdman, Charles R. "William Whiting Borden: An Ideal Missionary Volunteer." *Missionary Review of the World* 36 (Aug. 1913) : 567–77.

Figgis, John B. *Keswick from Within.* London, 1914. Not a scholarly work but quite detailed and helpful, especially on the origins.

Findlay, James F., Jr. *Dwight L. Moody: American Evangelist, 1837–1899.* Chicago, 1969. The best biography of Moody.

———. "Preparation for Flight: D. L. Moody in Illinois and the Midwest, 1865–1873." *Journal of Presbyterian History* 41 (June 1963) : 103–16.

Gordon, Ernest B. *Adoniram Judson Gordon.* New York, 1896.

Hague, Dyson. *Bishop Baldwin.* Toronto, 1927. Maurice S. Baldwin was Bishop of Huron, 1883–1904.

Headley, Phineas Camp. *George F. Pentecost: Life, Labors and Bible Studies.* Boston, 1880.

McLoughlin, William G. *Modern Revivalism.* New York, 1959.

Mullins, Isla May. *Edgar Young Mullins.* Nashville, 1929.

Patterson, T. A. "The Theology of J. R. Graves." Th.D. thesis, Southwestern Baptist Theological Seminary, Fort Worth, 1944.

Pierson, Arthur T. *Keswick Movement in Precept and Practice.* New York, 1903.

Pierson, Delavan Leonard. *Arthur T. Pierson.* New York, 1912.

Pollock, John C. *Moody.* New York, 1963.

Rudnick, Milton L. *Fundamentalism and the Missouri Synod.* St. Louis, 1966.

Sloan, Walter B. *These Sixty Years: The Story of the Keswick Convention.* London, 1935.

Smith, Timothy L. *Called unto Holiness.* Kansas City, 1963. A good history of the Nazarene denomination.

Bibliography

Taylor, Dr. and Mrs. Howard. *By Faith: Henry W. Frost and the China and Inland Mission.* Philadelphia, 1938.

Thompson, A. E. *The Life of A. B. Simpson.* Brooklyn, 1920.

Tyng, Charles Rockland. *Record of the Life and Work of the Rev. Stephen Higginson Tyng, D.D. and History of St. George's Church, New York, to the Close of his Rectorship.* New York, 1890.

Warfield, Benjamin B. *Perfectionism.* New York, 1931. In vol. 2 there is an excellent discussion of Keswick and the Victorious Life Movement.

Williams, David R. *James H. Brookes: A Memoir.* St. Louis, 1897.

11. AMERICAN MILLENARIANISM AND FUNDAMENTALISM, 1900–1930

PERIODICALS

Our Hope (New York). Edited by Arno C. Gaebelein until his death in 1945. 64 vols., 1894–1957.

Watchword and Truth (Boston). Edited by Robert Cameron. 23 vols., 1898–1921.

BOOKS

Addresses of the International Prophetic Conference Held December 10–15, 1901, in the Clarendon Street Baptist Church, Boston, Mass. Boston, n.d.

Baptist Fundamentals: Being Addresses Delivered at the Pre-Convention Conference at Buffalo, June 21 and 22, 1920. Philadelphia, 1920.

Blanchard, Charles A. *Light on the Last Days.* Chicago, 1913.

———. *President Blanchard's Autobiography.* Boone, Iowa, 1915.

Blanchard, Frances Carothers. *The Life of Charles Albert Blanchard.* New York, 1922.

Cameron, Robert. *Scriptural Truth about the Lord's Return.* New York, 1922.

Carver, William O. *Out of His Treasure.* Nashville, 1956. An autobiography.

Case, Shirley Jackson. *The Millennial Hope.* Chicago, 1918. An attack upon millenarian positions.

———. "The Premillennial Menace." *Biblical World* 52 (July 1918) : 16–23.

Coming and Kingdom of Christ. Chicago, n.d. Report of the proceedings of another in the series of Bible and Prophetic conferences, this one held 24–27 Feb. 1914 at Moody Bible Institute, Chicago.

"Dispensationalism and the Scofield Reference Bible: Are They Heresies?" *Sunday School Times* (20 Feb. 1937), pp. 130, 132, 133.

Dixon, Amzi C., ed. *Back to the Bible: The Triumphs of Faith.* London, [1912]. An English republication of material that had already appeared in *The Fundamentals.*

Dixon, Amzi C., Meyer, Louis, and Torrey, Reuben A., eds. *The Fundamentals: A Testimony to the Truth.* 12 vols. Chicago and Los Angeles, 1910–15.

Erdman, William J. *A Theory Reviewed.* Privately printed, n.d. Erdman explains why he has found it necessary to reject the "any-moment" theory of Christ's second coming.

Frost, Henry W. *The Second Coming of Christ.* Grand Rapids, 1934.

Gaebelein, Arno C. *Half a Century.* New York, 1930. An autobiography.

———. "The Story of the Scofield Reference Bible." *Moody Monthly* 43 (Oct. 1942): 65–66, 97, and serially through March 1943.

———, ed. *Christ and Glory, Addresses Delivered at the New York Prophetic Conference, Carnegie Hall, November 25–28, 1918.* New York, 1919.

Garrard, Mary N. *Mrs. Penn-Lewis: A Memoir.* London [1930?].

God Hath Spoken: Twenty-Five Addresses Delivered at the World Conference on Christian Fundamentals, May 25–June 1, 1919. Philadelphia, [1919?].

Haldeman, Isaac M. *The Kingdom of God: What Is It? — When Is It? — Where Is It?* New York, 1931.

Heagle, David. *That Blessed Hope.* Philadelphia, 1907. Not a millenarian work.

Hutchinson, Paul. "The Conservative Reaction in China." *Journal of Religion* 2 (1922): 337–61. A fair-minded analysis and description of the Fundamentalist controversy among missionaries in China.

Light on Prophecy: Proceedings and Addresses at the Philadelphia Prophetic Conference, May 28–30, 1918. New York, 1918.

Machen, J. Gresham. *Christianity and Liberalism.* New York, 1924.

———. "Fundamentalism, False and True." *British Weekly,*

Bibliography

11 Sept. 1924. This especially interesting article was part of a series which ran in the *British Weekly* during the summer of 1924.

McNicol, John. "Fundamental but Not Dispensational." *Toronto Bible College Recorder* 52 (March 1946):1–11.

Mauro, Philip. *The Gospel of the Kingdom*. Boston, 1928. A former dispensationalist's attack upon dispensationalism.

Parker, T. Valentine. "Premillenarianism: An Interpretation and an Evaluation." *Biblical World* 53 (1919): 37–40.

Rall, Harris Franklin. "Premillennialism." *Biblical World* 53 (1919): 339–47, 459–69, 617–27.

Scriptural Inspiration versus Scientific Imagination: Messages Delivered at the Great Christian Fundamentals Conference at Los Angeles, California. Los Angeles, n.d. The conference was held 25 June–2 July 1922.

Snowden, James H. "Summary of Objections to Premillenarianism." *Biblical World* 53 (1919): 165–73.

"The Stewarts as Christian Stewards: The Story of Milton and Lyman Stewart." *Missionary Review of the World* 47 (1924): 595–602.

Trumbull, Charles G. *Prophecy's Light on Today*. New York, 1937. A defense of the author's dispensationalism.

The Victorious Christ: Messages from Conferences Held by the Victorious Life Testimony in 1922. Philadelphia, 1923.

The Victorious Life: Messages from the Summer Conferences at Whittier, Calif., June; Princeton, N.J., July; Cedar Lake, Ind., Aug. 1917. Philadelphia, n.d.

Victory in Christ: A Report of Princeton Conference, 1916. Philadelphia, 1916. The Victorious Life Movement was related to the English Keswick holiness movement.

West, Nathaniel. *The Apostle Paul and the "Any Moment" Theory*. Philadelphia, 1893.

Woelfkin, Cornelius. "The Religious Appeal of Premillennialism." *Journal of Religion* 1 (1921): 255–63.

SECONDARY WORKS

Ashworth, Robert A. "The Fundamentalist Movement among the Baptists." *Journal of Religion* 4 (1924): 611–31. A summary of the 1920–24 Northern Baptist conventions; fair and helpful.

Bradbury, John W. "Curtis Lee Laws and the Fundamentalist Movement." *Foundations* 5 (Jan. 1962): 52–58.

Delnay, Robert G. "A History of the Baptist Bible Union." Th.D. dissertation, Dallas Theological Seminary, 1963.

Bibliography

Dixon, Helen C. A. *A. C. Dixon.* New York, 1931.

Gaebelein, Frank E. *Christian Education in a Democracy.* New York, 1951. Helpful on the Bible institute movement.

Gatewood, Willard B., Jr. *Preachers, Pedagogues and Politicians: The Evolution Controversy in North Carolina, 1920–1927.* Chapel Hill, 1966.

Hull, Lloyd B. "A Rhetorical Study of the Preaching of William Bell Riley." Ph.D. dissertation, Wayne State University, 1960.

McBirnie, Robert Sheldon. "Basic Issues in the Fundamentalism of William Bell Riley." Ph.D. dissertation, State University of Iowa, 1952.

Ottman, Ford C. *J. Wilbur Chapman: A Biography.* New York, 1920.

Roark, Dallas M. "J. Gresham Machen: The Doctrinally True Presbyterian Church." *Journal of Presbyterian History* 43 (1965) : 124–38, 174–81.

Runyan, William M. *Dr. Gray at Moody Bible Institute.* New York, 1935.

Smith, Wilbur M. *Arno C. Gaebelein: A Memoir.* New York, 1945.

Stonehouse, Ned B. *J. Gresham Machen.* Grand Rapids, 1955.

Stowell, Joseph M. *Background and History of the General Association of Regular Baptist Churches.* Hayward, Calif., 1949.

Trumbull, Charles G. *Life Story of C. I. Scofield.* New York, 1920.

 Index

Index

Index

Index

Index